SpringerWienNewYork

edition: 'ʌngewʌndtə
Book Series of the University of Applied Arts Vienna
Edited by Gerald Bast, Rector

VISUAL CATALOG: GREG LYNN'S STUDIO AT THE UNIVERSITY OF APPLIED ARTS VIENNA

Edited by Kristy Balliet and Brennan Buck
with an Introduction by Greg Lynn

SpringerWienNewYork

VISUAL CATALOG: GREG LYNN'S STUDIO
AT THE UNIVERSITY OF APPLIED ARTS VIENNA

Head of the Institute of Architecture: Wolf D. Prix
Editors: Kristy Balliet, Brennan Buck
Design: Paulus M. Dreibholz, Emma Williams
Atelier for Typography and Graphic Design
Prepress: Nicolas Berthelot
Printing: Holzhausen Druck GmbH

SpringerWienNewYork is a part of Springer Science + Business Media
springer.at

Printed on acid-free and chlorine-free bleached paper

SPIN: 12594849

Library of Congress Control Number: 2009929414

ISSN 1866-248X
ISBN 978-3-211-99192-3 SpringerWienNewYork

SpringerWienNewYork

IOA INSTITUTE OF ARCHITECTURE

CONTENTS

INTRODUCTION

GREG LYNN

The Angewandte is a unique university for three key reasons; its legacy as an incubator for creativity and criticality in design culture; the combination of international teachers and students in a variety of design disciplines; and finally its commitment to depth as shown by the structure of the school where students study with the same design professor for their entire academic career. The *Visual Catalog* reflects the general character of the University more than it does any of the preoccupations and topics that I have assigned over the years. One thing all students from the Angewandte have in common is that they understand the strength of design and creativity and they diligently and critically employ design technique not just for its own sake but as a historical mode of critical thinking. The most poignant characteristic of all of the Angewandte students, whether in architecture, design, media or fashion, is the respect for a tradition of radical change. The reverence for tradition at the Angewandte is for creative pursuit and innovation rather than the imitation of history. The *Visual Catalog* is not a pattern book of forms nor is it a pragmatic manual. It is an attempt to ask the next important design questions for future architects.

We begin each semester with an architectural question rather than a set of solutions, but this does not preclude instrumental solutions to cultural problems. For example, instead of beginning a design studio with the problem: "how do I solve the problem of designing a lobby for a music hall on the Ringstrasse when the site has two important faces?" we define the problem as: "in the past, facades were thought of as vertical planes where the volumes of the interior of the building were projected at a ninety degree angle onto the city; now that we are using complex curved surfaces for design how do you project interior volumes onto a sculptural surface?". By defining the architectural problem first, the extra-architectural functional, urban, cultural and civic problems get redefined based on emerging creative solutions. In the studio we understand that culture and urban life is constantly evolving and mutating and by redefining the architectural design problems in concert with these new types of urban and cultural life a more robust design culture is fostered among our students. Combined with the many disciplines of design represented at the Angewandte it provides a fertile culture for our students' growth and critical acumen.

Sometimes the design tasks that we pose to the students have a specific focus on structure, building systems, building envelope design, site planning, vertical circulation or some other discrete architectural problem and sometimes the questions are broadly defined. The *Visual Catalog* is a collection of the design questions we have given the students during the last five years and their work defining and elaborating these questions through creative design thinking. This is why it is a "visual" catalog and not a style manual or pattern book. This pedagogical approach is only possible at a university where the students have continuity of instruction, because we can for example afford to tell a student to focus on the design of the ground plane, stairs, ramps and handrails for an entire semester, as we know that the next semester this same student can then focus on the design of a building's structure. The students are able to go into more depth and focus on specific topics because we are not under the pressure to schematically design a building in 12 weeks over and over and over again for 5 years with different studio instructors. The ability to focus on specific and sometimes myopic issues is unique in the world to the Angewandte and this is what makes this university so special.

In contrast to most other universities our students are surrounded by world class professors and their students from a much broader range of fields than only architecture, landscape architecture or urban planning. They are housed in a building with media, fashion, industrial, and every other kind of design student that can be defined. This puts a pressure on and opens up the opportunity for the students to get into dialogue with contemporary design in the broadest sense. The *Visual Catalog* is grounded in the traditions of architectural education while remaining in dialogue with contemporary design culture. We are often inspired to ask certain questions from the perspective of our neighboring colleagues: how does a fashion design student think about folding and draping, for example, and what would a media design student do for lighting in the building?

At the Angewandte the penultimate moment in every student's career is their diploma. As arrogant as a statement like this is, we educate our students with the expectation that they will all become great architects. We are not a technical university despite the fact that we give our students a technical education. We aspire to be educating leaders in design who will have a profound impact on culture and society through design. Because of this ambition to educate innovators and leaders in design, the students graduate when they are prepared to make a statement of their ambitions. We call this statement of ambitions the diploma project. It is at the diploma that the students are tasked with coherently forming and presenting their own question, a question they are expected to work on for the rest of their careers. The diploma is also a test of vocational capabilities and technical knowledge, but at the Angewandte there is a higher level expectation: that the student has developed significantly enough as an individual designer to be able to state a design question worth investigating. The diploma is a statement of a paradigm. In order to prepare the students to develop their own critical and creative capacities to be able to define their future professional project, we spend four and one half years in studio looking at specific design problems where we define the question and ask the students for their responses. Through this process, the students gain enough experience to define their own problems for their diploma projects.

Finally a word on analysis. Twenty five years ago when I was a student we were taught design through the analysis of architectural masterpieces. We would analyze a work by Corbusier, Wright, Mies, Hoffman, Loos, Lutyens, Ledoux, Palladio, Bernini, Borromini or others for volume, mass, structure, fenestration (windows and openings), landscape, vertical circulation or façade. All over the world, for some inexplicable reason, most likely the use of the computer by amateurs, universities began to teach design through the analysis of data. For the last two decades students have been taught to analyze transportation, financial markets, library catalog systems, or other extra-architectural statistics and turn that into a form and then interpret that form as architecture. By architects of older generations, this is often skillfully interpreted through the transformed language of Corbusier, Mies or others, but for students who have never been taught design skills through the analysis of great works of architecture, the results are less meritorious and certainly less interesting. The *Visual Catalog* is highly dependent on digital tools and media, but it is not a collection of data analysis by CAD jockeys. The student work is guided by analysis of architectural design methods and often it launches from the analysis of one or more building precedents by great architects. Again, this is a reflection of the Angewandte's commitment to rethinking tradition from within a tradition of architecture as much as it is of our own peculiar studio's interests and objectives.

INNOVATION CYCLE

KRISTY BALLIET

An architectural education, analogous to an architectural career, is a collection of parts that comprise a whole. These parts include historical and contemporary precedents, academic environments, mentor influences, individual motivation, peer interaction, and exhaustive levels of research and analysis. This complex array of input requires tools to evaluate and acknowledge dynamic shifts in design culture that often occur fluidly. In this book we have emphasized the cycle of innovation, distinguishing between the iterative process that advances ideas and abrupt newness. It highlights various techniques that were essential for the development of design, assessing the smooth transitions, which emerged within Studio Greg Lynn.

Our studio is uniquely positioned to assess these innovation shifts as it resides within an environment that supports a sustained critical approach to design. In most architecture schools, a student selects a different design studio each semester, allowing a different group of students to work together under a different professor. In contrast, the unique Meisterklasse system specifies that students pursue the majority of their design education within a single studio. The Meisterklasse structure is unique within the realm of contemporary architectural education, posing a rare opportunity to peer into the depth of work and utilize the accumulated research to discover core issues that are emerging. The inherent energy that is generated lacks the traditional release valve or remix button that is standard in the alternating studio structure. The categorization of work in this catalog takes advantage of this anomaly and introverts the focus by highlighting the collection of references emerging from the cumulative study trips, lectures, and research undertaken by our studio. These experiences result in a dilated view that provides a platform for discussion and critique.

The difference between generating something "new" and something "innovative" is that the innovative evaluates the current spectrum of a problem by looking within and beyond its own discipline to calculate ways to develop the next step or evolution. It is necessary to evaluate and understand the past in order to contribute and develop something innovative. The studio is constantly looking to historical precedents for inspiration and inserting past developments into a new context. These acts of reappropriation are common to the realm of art and culture. The extent to which artists, designers and architects borrow from one another, previous genres and nature is boundless. In the seminal book *Learning from Las Vegas*, Robert Venturi and his co-authors associate the word "evolutionary" with the use of historical precedents in his comparison of the Guild House and Crawford Manor. They argue that the evolutionary is contrary to the revolutionary (or anti-traditional) attitude that does not lead to a deeper architecture but one that is 'empty and boring'. In the same text, Venturi is critical of '...the modern architect's tendency to glorify originality through copying it.' While he does not condone this action, he suggests that, '...the replication would have been done better if it had been accepted philosophically and used wittingly...' These observations are still relevant today as every design whim is proliferated instantly through rampant blogging, saturating the field with "new" ideas. We are again in a moment when we need to acknowledge the tools and techniques of our time and work to advance their position. While there are differences between Greg Lynn's design tools and those of Robert Venturi, the pedagogic interests are akin to one another. In reviewing a recent studio project, that was accompanied by the explanation, 'it is new', Greg Lynn responded, 'We are not interested in producing something new but in advancing ideas.'

I am drawing a fine line between what is new and what is innovative, however it is a warranted discussion within a design studio. Advancing design concepts is paramount to the contemporary architectural education which must constantly evolve, incorporating new tools and methods of instruction. As illustrated in this catalog, architectural knowledge can be gleaned from a multitude of adjacent and far reaching fields. Critical evaluation of work within and around the discipline of architecture is an essential component of a design education. Our catalog indexes a selection of visual references and their consequent transformation and manifested language in the architectural projects of the studio. These projects sit at an important point of reflection and observation, serving to evaluate the collective efforts of many students and instructors over five years. It is not meant as a "best of" or as a comprehensive collection but instead isolates innovation in a categorical and critical way useful for appraising the work of the studio and charting future trajectories.

In architecture it is profoundly difficult and tremendously rewarding to oscillate between and negotiate the multiple facets of the architectural discourse through practice, academia and research. In order to make an impact, architects must limit their area of innovative focus, while remaining receptive to relevant agendas and strategies. A goal within the studio is to develop a student's interest in a technique that can pose questions and challenges that will propel them deep into their careers. It is critical to understand that architects do not blindly design something new within a bubble but rather seek innovation within an elaborate history.

Productive themes of the studio lie at the intersection of form and fabrication, where we are consistently seeking innovative forms through digital investigation and perfect and refine them through large scale, digitally fabricated physical models. The potential for reinvention comes from the unexpected discoveries made in these two-dimensional to three-dimensional processes that push both the form and material to profound new limits. Theoretical and formal exuberance lead to architectural invention. In the studio we intentionally move from far reaching topics like space tourism to typologically grounded projects like a performance hall on the ring located directly across from the Vienna Opera House. It is important for students to both consider fresh ideas (like space tourism) alongside the age old problems of section, sequential movement, and facade. The shifts are often abrupt and intentional in order to agitate and avoid reflex.

Our studio is a collective exploration. It encompasses the curiosities of many students, each diligently working to develop their own design language in dialogue with each other, architecture and other disciplines. The oscillation between these two considerations, the part and the whole, creates a system that is in constant evolution. In a recent lecture at the CCA, Greg Lynn referenced his flatware design for Alessi, describing that, 'it really works like a family, i love everyone equally, but no one is better than any of the others, they are like my kids'. This analogy points to a process of fertile generation, visualizing a relationship between the individual and the collective.

This book serves to frame a moment in time of a constantly evolving studio, discipline and discourse. It was conceived as a means of internal evaluation, but we hope that the result inspires others to evaluate, catalog and question the current directions of their own work. All work is derived from somewhere and/or something prior, innovation is not only about creating something new but also understanding and acknowledging what preceded the current iteration.

THE CONTEMPORARY APPRENTICE

BRENNAN BUCK

The Meisterklasse, the studio structure maintained at the Angewandte nearly since it was formalized in the 19th century, is a reinvention of the medieval relationship between master and apprentice. One professor designs and runs the curriculum for every semester of a student's five years in the school. Greg Lynn accepted an Angewandte professorship in 2002, and with it began formulating a 21st century form of this very traditional structure. This book maps the hybrid form that developed, consolidating the students' collective research over the last five years into a taxonomy of design devices—configurations of technique and sensibility that evolved within the studio.

The studio Lynn inherited from Hans Hollein when he arrived in Vienna was largely defined by two characteristics: consistency (students remained in the class for five years, and tutors normally were there for much longer) and collectivity (vertical integration insured that first through fifth-year students worked on the same design task every semester). The evolving studio ecology that has unfolded since balances individual and collective study, allowing students to engage in a consistent, collective exploration of a wide range of aesthetic and technological cultures from outside the discipline while asking each one to define an individual disciplinary 'project'. That ecology inhabits a middle ground between two potential excesses of the Meisterklasse: stylistic replication, where a single aesthetic based on the professor's work becomes dominant, subsuming a wider range of competing techniques and sensibilities, and at the other pole, the autonomous, intuitive exploration that can develop from the singularity of the master-apprentice relationship as students look inward to develop a personal approach in opposition to that of the professor.

Our attempt to formulate a contemporary Meisterklasse and to re-present it here is centered on a set of design devices that synthesize modes of production and expression. The thirteen devices we describe are essentially relationships between contemporary production techniques—fabrication, manufacturing and construction—and contemporary sensibilities—effects of light, color and surface. Although they are largely culled from design cultures beyond the boundaries of architecture, they have re-emerged in architectural form in the studio work over time. They are assembled as a loosely structured collection, a visual catalog that makes the relationships within and between devices explicit. As a taxonomy, this book is also intended to give consistency and identity to an eclectic collection of work, potentially making it useful and relevant beyond the bounds of Studio Lynn.

As way to understand and find consistency in architectural practice, the taxonomy has been reconstituted in a number of ways since 2000, most notably by Alejandro Zaera-Polo and Farshid Moussavi in their monograph *Phylogenesis*. In the book's introductory essay they write that consistency is necessary for a body of work to become operative, to produce resonance between individual projects and a broader set of effects. The set of patterns or techniques that emerge is more likely to have an effect on the broader discourse and practice of architecture than any single project in isolation. Traditionally, architects have relied on two types of consistency— one forced on them by geographic or typological limitations (many offices work in a limited geographical area or specialize in a particular building type) and the other generated by auteur architects who bring an identifiable personal style to every project. For architects engaged in globalized practice and testing disciplinary boundaries that call into question traditional modes of authorship (through a range of projects too broad to benefit from a singular style) new sorts of consistency are called for. For Moussavi and Zaera-Polo, the taxonomy of their work presented in *Phylogenesis* maps out a consistent territory and identity from a diverse population of projects. The emergent signature that results is not made up of a priori types to be replicated but mutating strains that reveal both evolving trends and under-explored niches.

Excluding *Phylogenesis*, recent architectural taxonomies might be themselves largely classified as either technique- or effect-based. Lisa Iwamoto's collection *Digital Fabrications* or Ben Aranda and Chris Lasch's book *Tooling* categorize varied small-scale construction projects as morphological techniques such as folding, forming, weaving and tiling. Recent effect-based architectural taxonomies include *The Function of Ornament*, Moussavi's well-discussed attempt to name a series of affects produced by building envelopes. The Pics database, a 'synchronous sensuous platform' created by the Japanese magazine *Ten Plus One* invites users to categorize buildings as dense, protean, voluptuous, or keen.

Studio Lynn is neither purely technique nor affect-driven; it seeks to develop an understanding of both technological processes and the sensibilities central to design culture. The class proceeds on an understanding that technique and sensibility are inherently bound up and interdependent. Techniques suggest a set of formal qualities or configurations. Liquid plastic *injection-molding* essentially produces objects of cured paint, very often with a brightly colored, candy-coated appearance. *Die cutting* creates sharply outlined figures from standard sheets of material or amorphous three-dimensional volumes. *Superflat layering* produces highly graphical but non-hierarchical, densely patterned surfaces. In the same way, the proliferation of computational techniques which facilitate repetition and variation rely on and reinforce an aesthetic tendency toward pattern, proliferating parts, and serial detail. This relationship flows in both directions; the Visual Catalog also presents visual effects that suggest organizational strategies; *albedo*, *creasing*, *figuration*, and *flatness* are all used to produce spatial configurations.

Both technological processes and aesthetic effects have political implications. Repetition and variation, porosity and figure all potentially produce physical boundaries and expressive content. They keep people out (or in), orchestrating social striations or collections. They also portray these social structures to the outside world. The thirteen devices presented here create resonance between strains of discourse, technology and aesthetic culture.

Like an apparatus or a contraption, a device is designed for a specific purpose, often to produce an affect. A rhetorical device consolidates a complex idea into a shared concept that is more accessible and therefore more convincing. An electronic or mechanical device, like any tool, is designed primarily with an effect in mind. At the same time, a device may have an aesthetic presence itself. The physicality of a Rube Goldberg contraption is more elaborate and important than the result it produces. The personal devices that became popular during the Renaissance had symbolic content, acting as a form of heraldry and symbolizing a specific individual. So a device, and the work in the book, allows us to think about technique and sensibility not as separate means and ends, but as a single performative and aesthetic package. It incorporates both a strategy and a final configuration.

The *Visual Catalog* presents the shared territory of research produced over five years by over 90 students. And while it is a partial document of that work, it is also intended to be a diagram of possibilities for other students and practitioners. It is a set of overlapping territories or trajectories which can be fleshed out to greater degree or used to define new territories in between. The thirteen devices are organized according to whether they produce surface or volume and whether they initially reference formal techniques or visual effects. But regardless of its initial reference point, each chapter of the book is primarily a visual argument for the link between architectural sensibilities and architectural performance.

SURFACE: FORM

TOPO-PANELIZATION

The discrete subdivision of a surface into separate parts, based on rigorous limitations of surface geometry, material characteristics and constructive dimensions.

Topo-panelization is the development of a language of surface based on architectural concerns of assembly rather than a sculptural interest in the monolithic. It invests smooth surfaces with varied articulation, potential systems of aperture and an integral relationship to structure. It can also infuse them with associations: studying the panelization of robots, life-size, toy and animated, has given some recent projects in the studio a sterile futuristic roboticism and others a hint of mechanical dynamism.

1 **Marloes Ten Bhömer**
Hunt Shoe, collection 2001–03
image courtesy of
Marloes Ten Bhömer
www.marloestenbhomer.squarespace.com

2 **Chris Cunningham / Björk**
All is full of love, album cover
www.director-file.com/cunningham

3 Ross Lovegrove
Go Chair, 2001
image courtesy of
Ross Lovegrove
www.rosslovegrove.com

4 **David Flores**
Bad and Evil, *Dunny*
image courtesy of David Flores
www.davidfloresart.com

5 **Hussein Chalayan**
Airplane Dress, 2000
image Courtesy of
The Metropolitan Museum of Art / Art Resource / Scala, Firenze

6 **Gundam Weapons / Zeta Weapons**
Hobby Japan, 2006

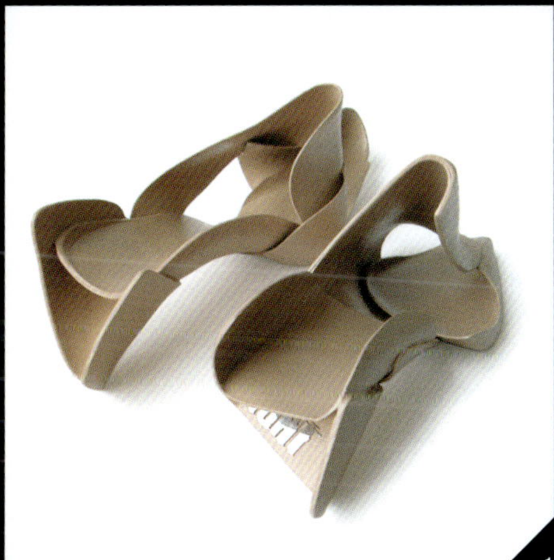
1

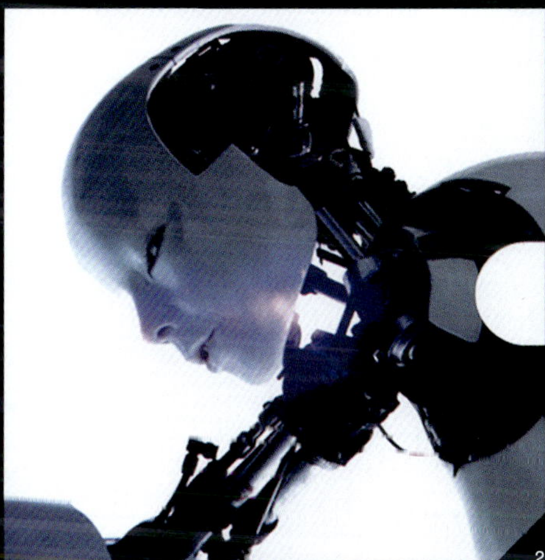
2

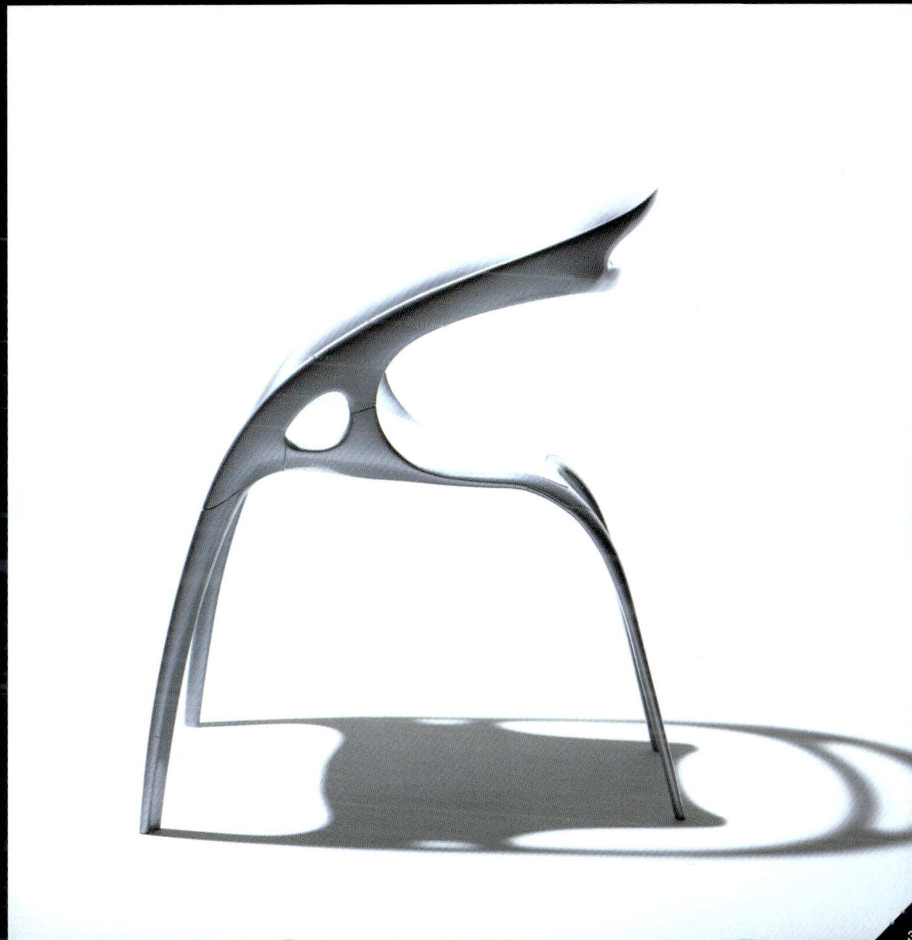
3

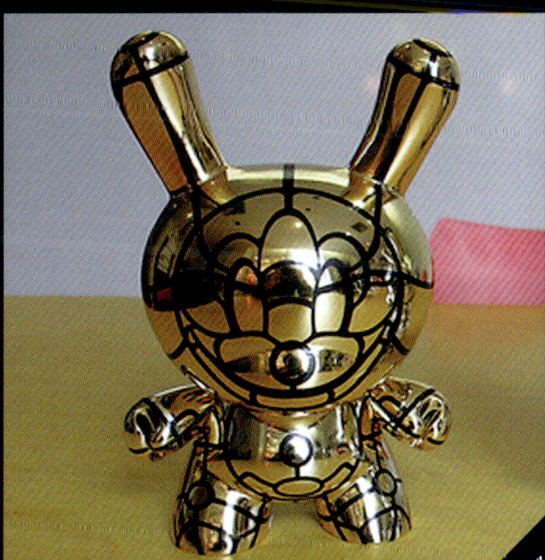
4

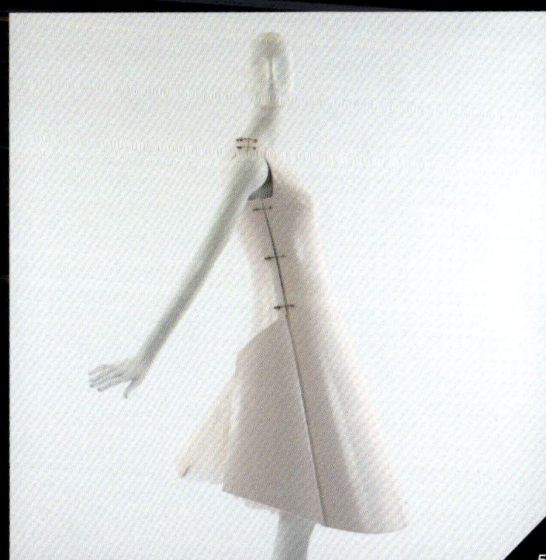
5

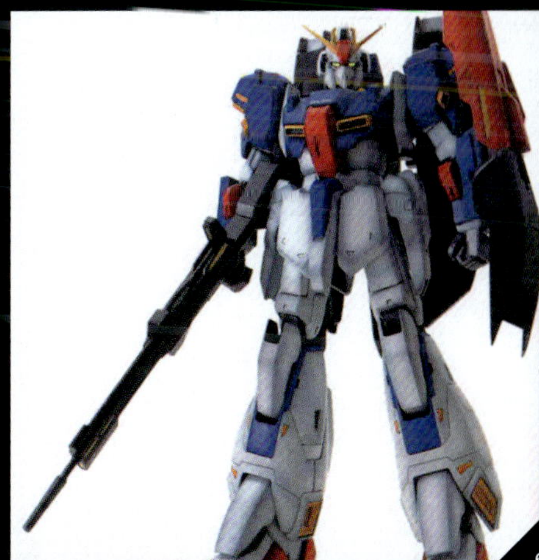
6

Günther Dreger, Andi Krainer and Reini Blaha

Potato Problem

2003

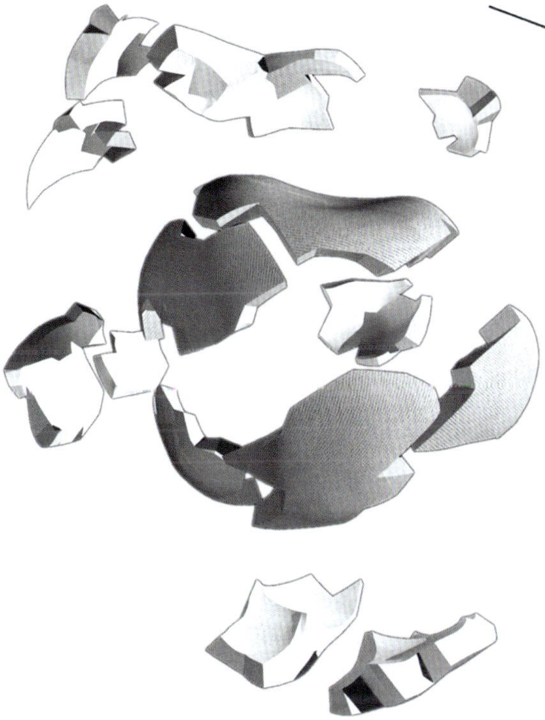

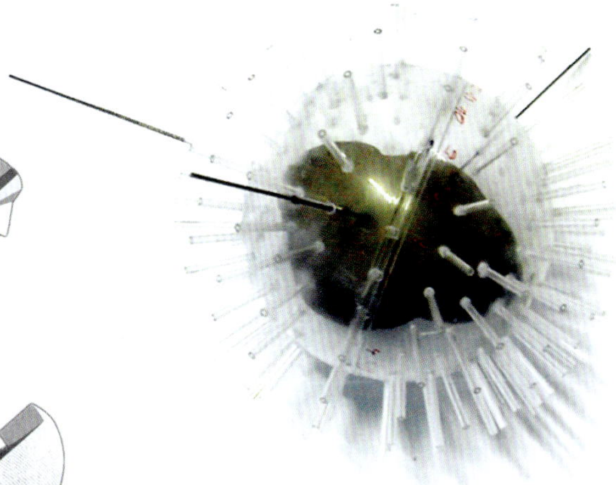

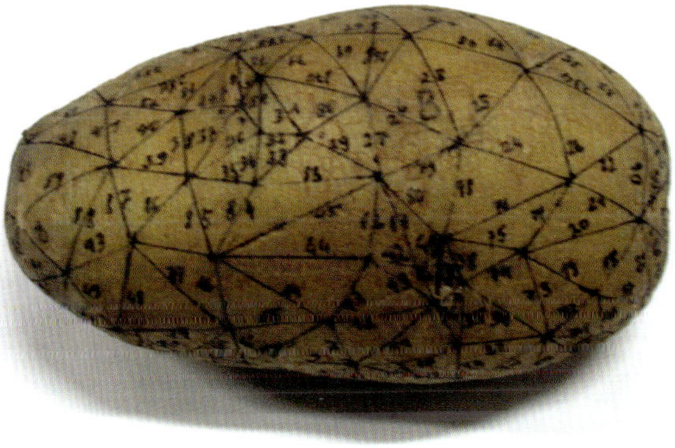

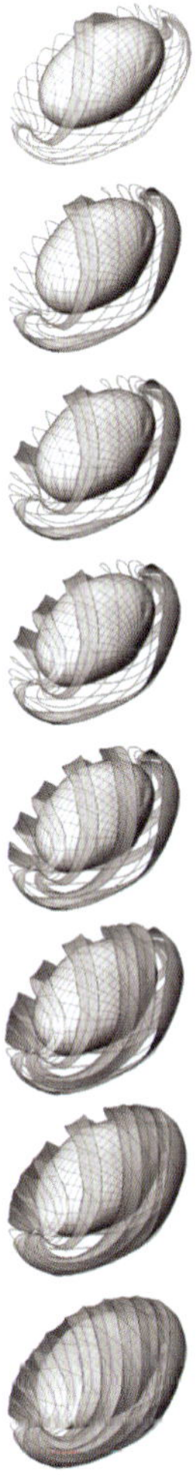

Lisa Sommerhuber
Space Collective
2007

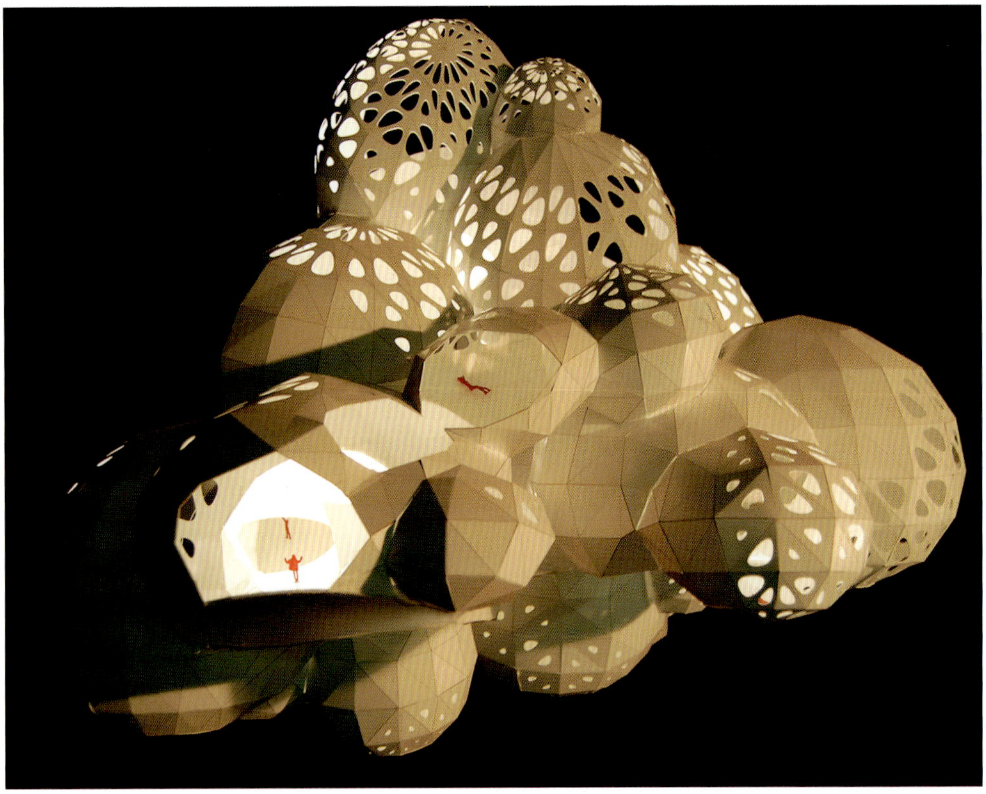

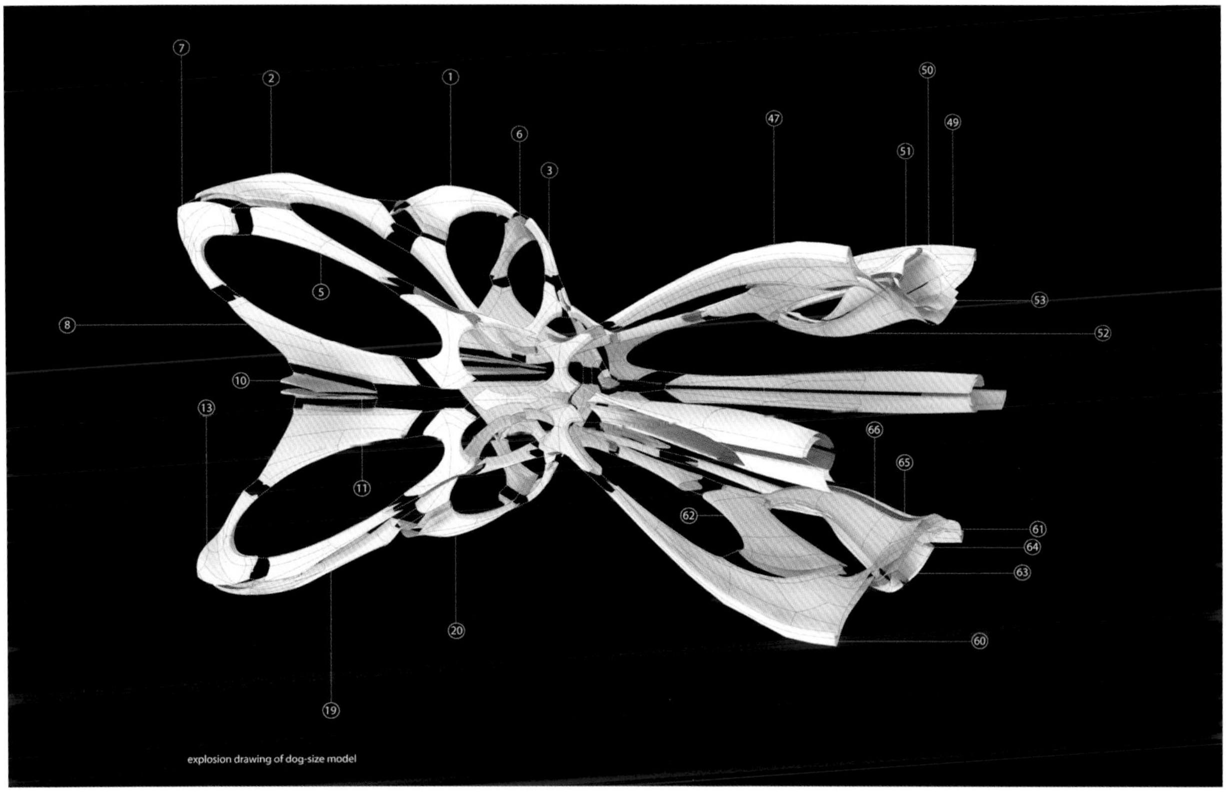

explosion drawing of dog-size model

Adam Vukmanov and Jiri Matura
Car Design Center
2006

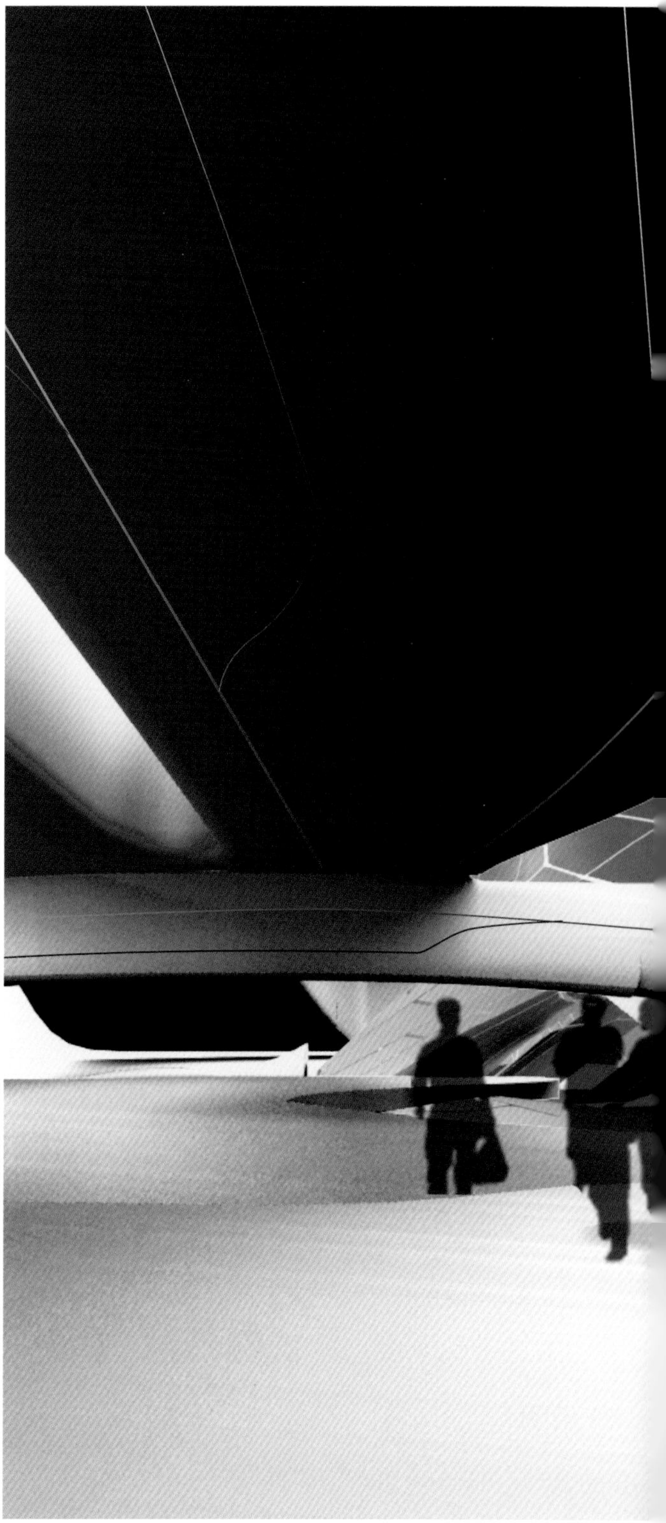

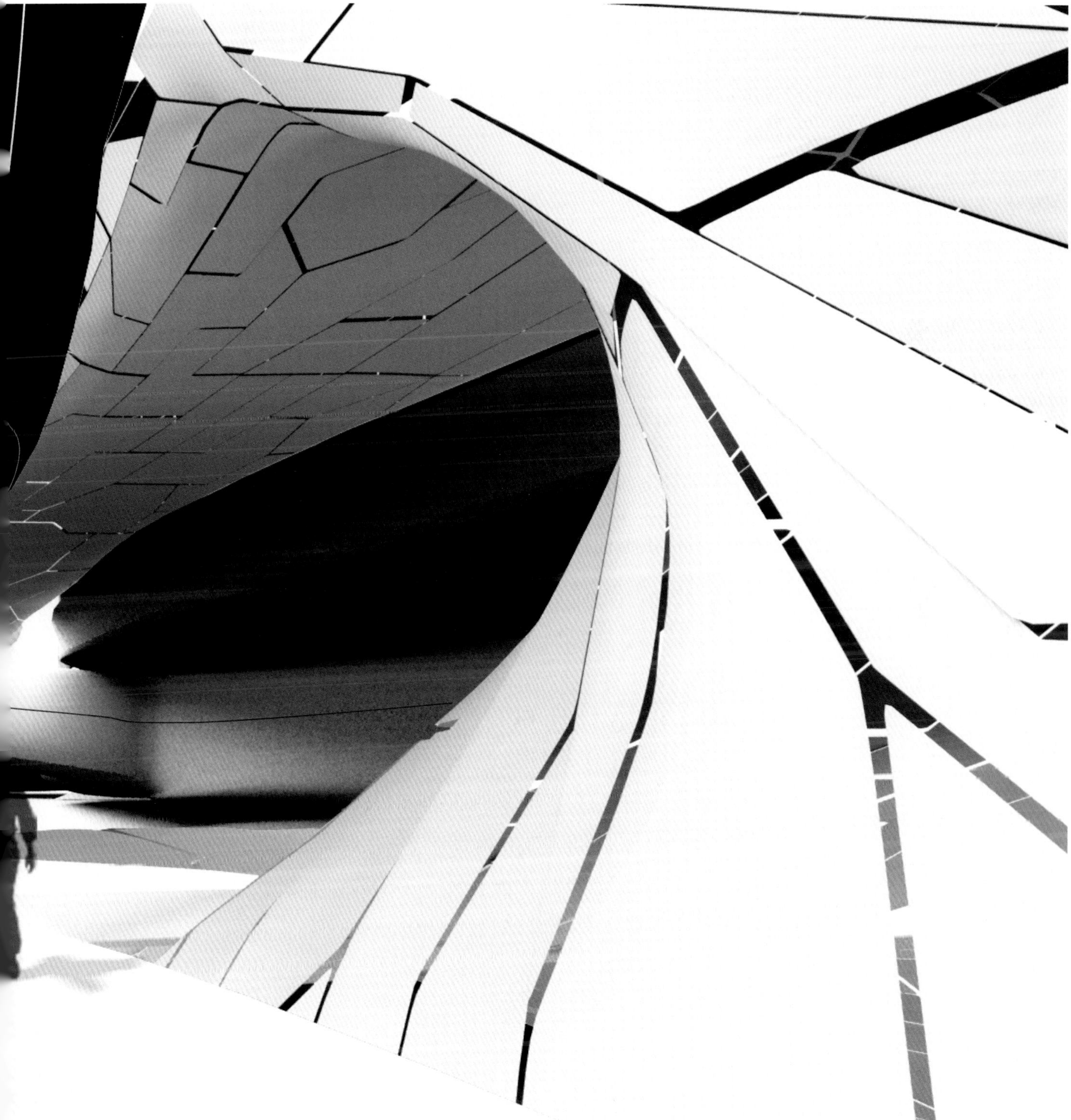

Nora Graw
Space Collective
2007

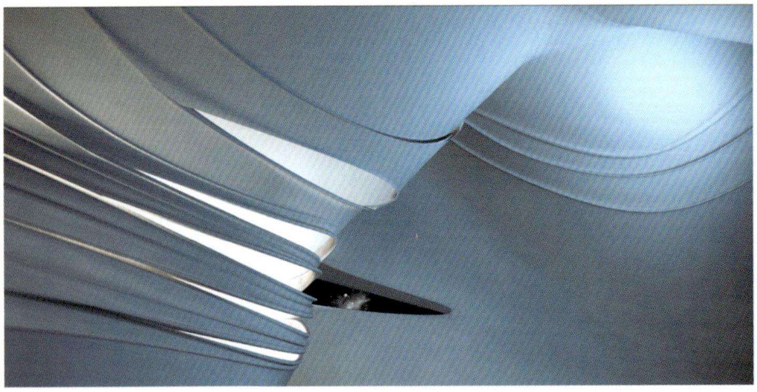

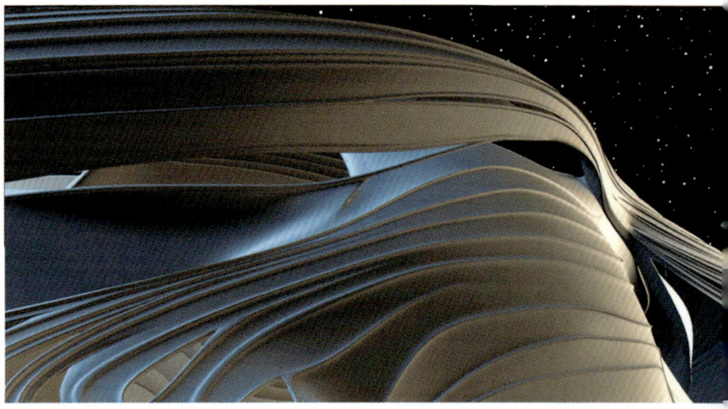

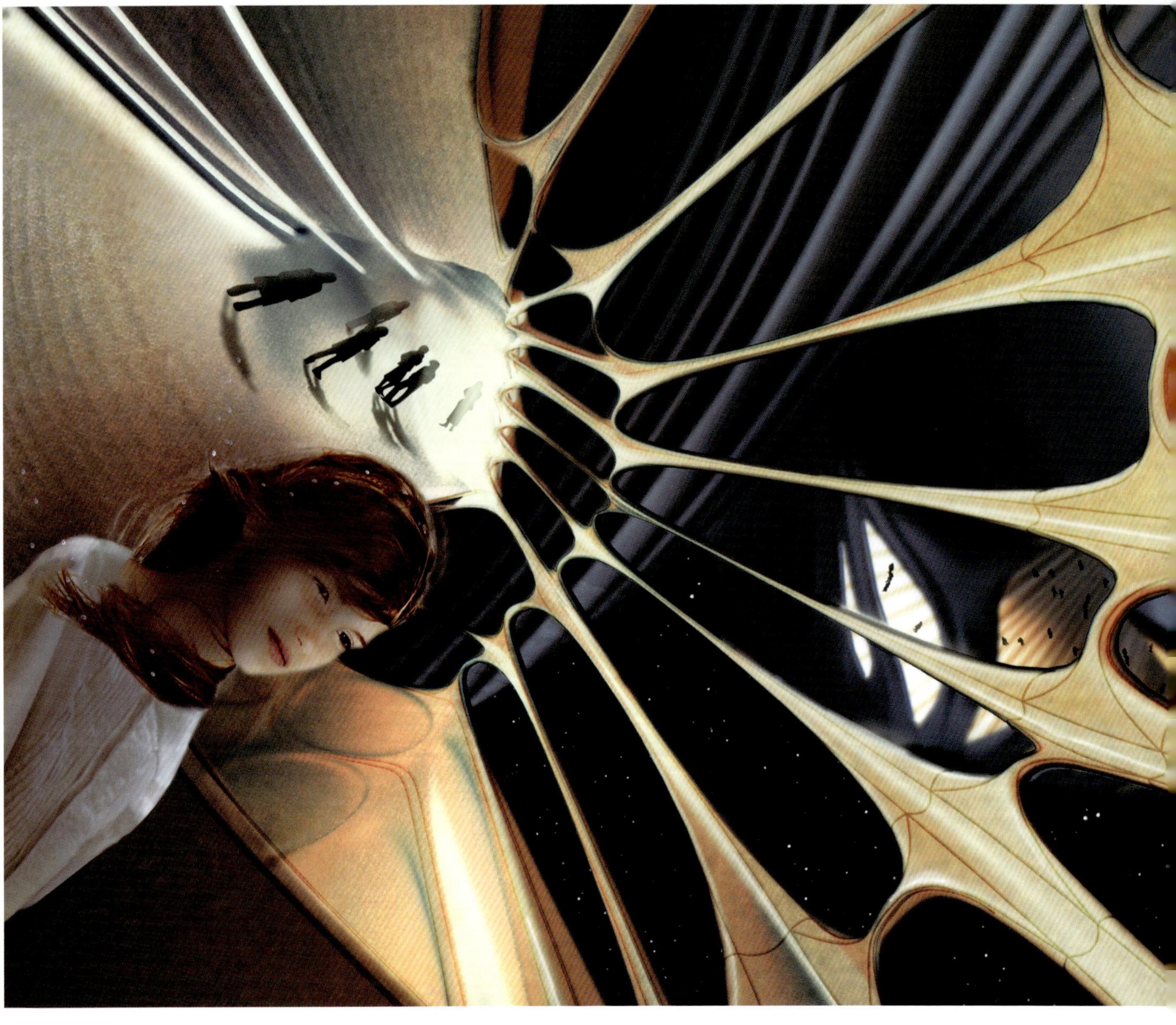

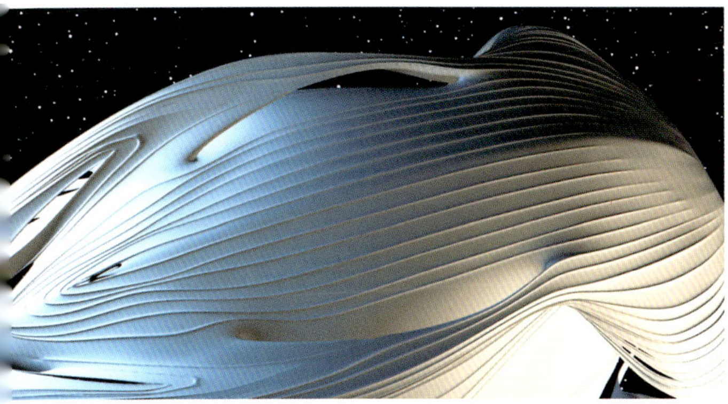

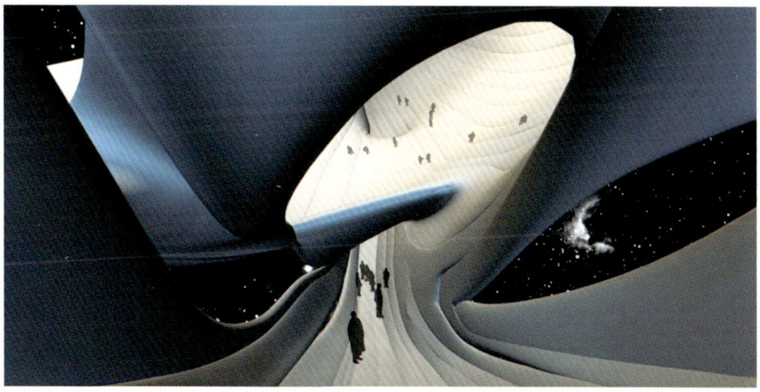

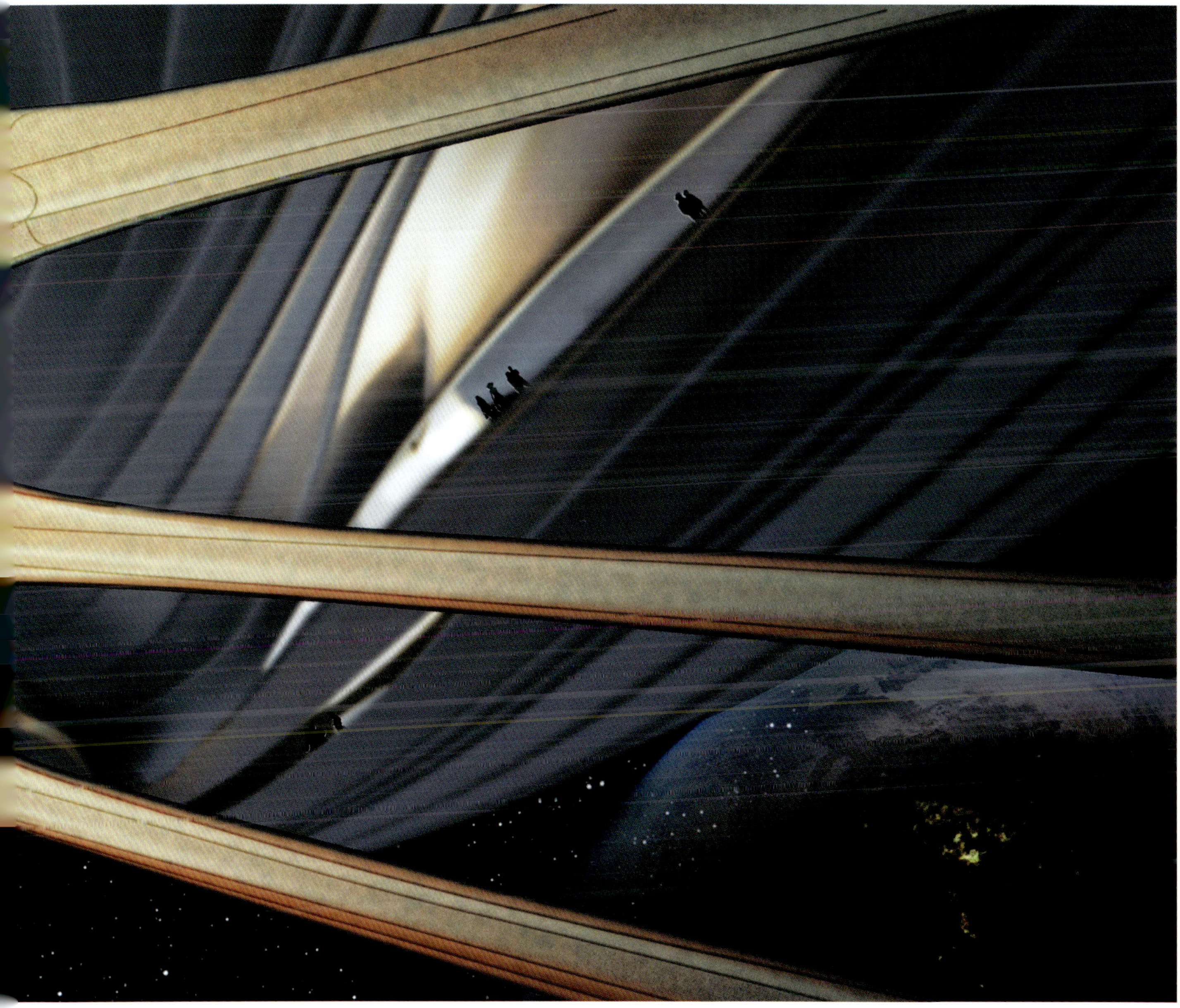

Adam Vukmanov
Giant Robot (video stills)
2006

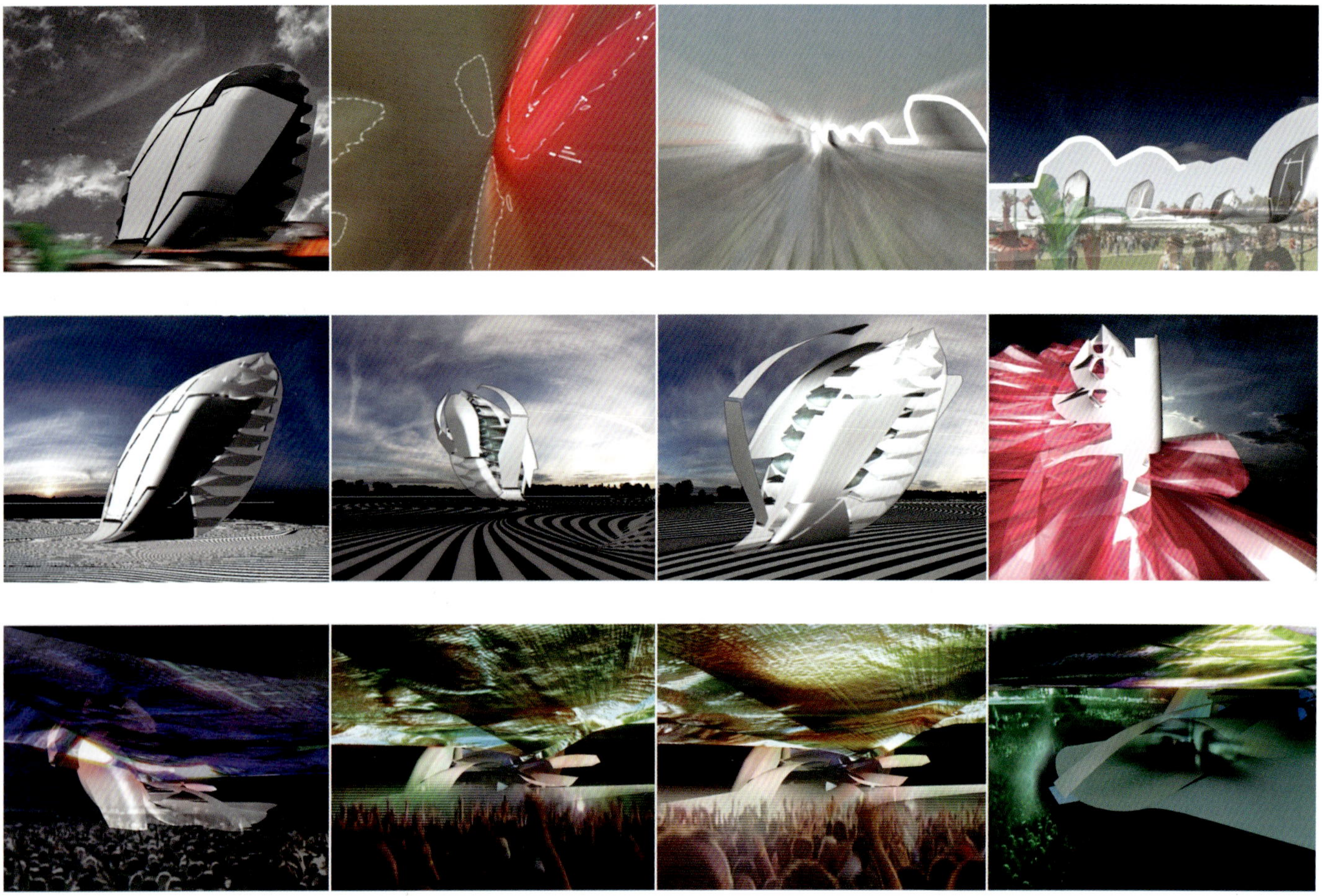

Julia Körner
Giant Robot (video stills)
2006

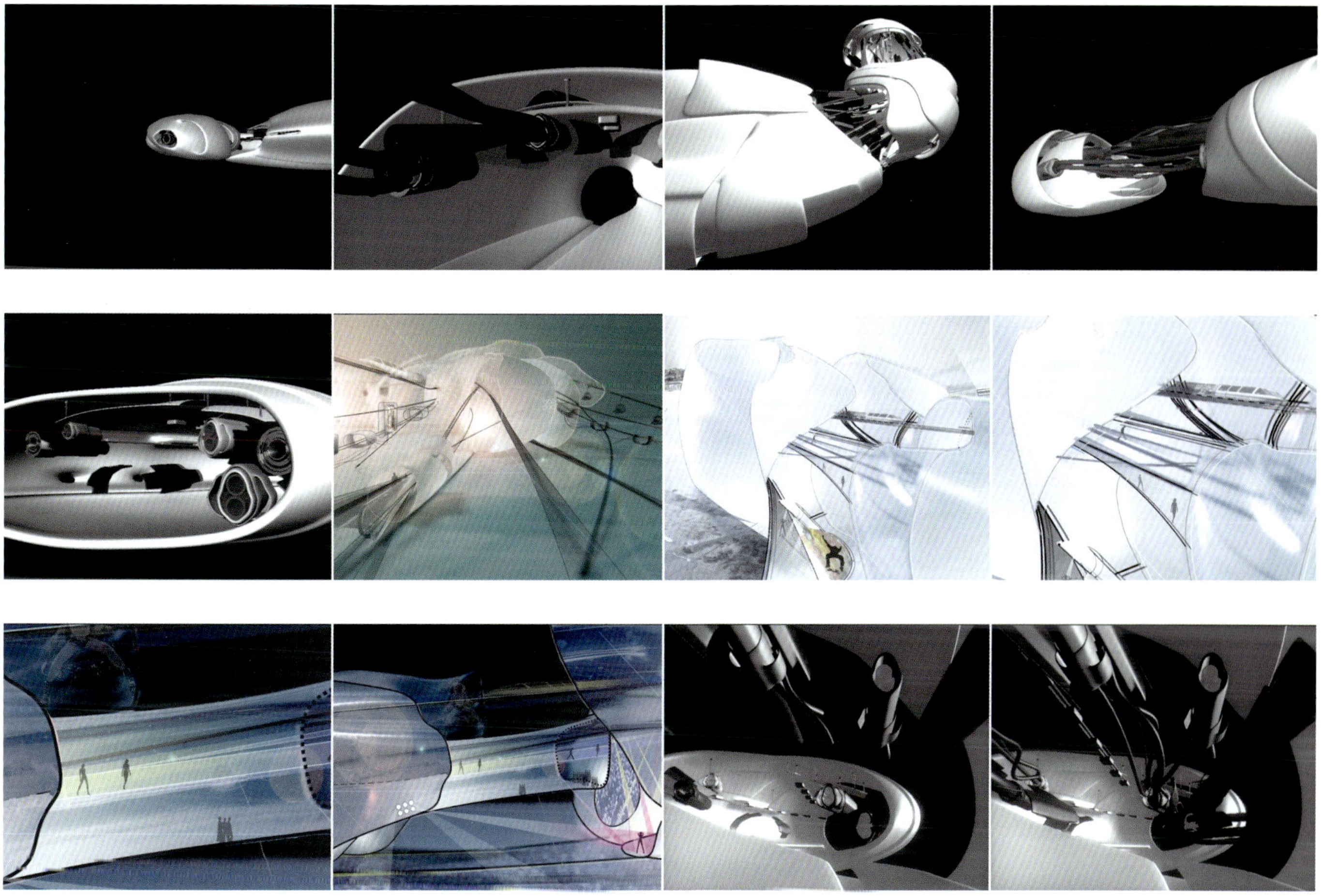

SELECTED EXCERPTS

The Seam
Gottfried Semper
Style in the Technical and Tectonic Arts, trans: Harry Francis Mallgrave and Michael Robinson
Los Angeles: Getty Publications Program, 2004
pp.153–54 and p.158

The unassuming nature of this heading should not cause anyone to underestimate its significance in relation to art and style. The seam is an expedient that was invented to join pieces of a homogeneous nature—namely surfaces—into a whole. Originally used in clothing and coverings, it has through an *ancient association of ideas* and even through *linguistic usage* become the universal analogy and symbol for any *joining of originally discrete surfaces* in a tight connection. A most important and prime axiom for artistic practice is most simply, most originally, and at the same time most cogently expressed in the seam —*the principle of making a virtue out of necessity*. It teaches us that anything that is must be patchwork, because the material and means at our disposal are insufficient and should not be made to appear otherwise. If something is originally separate we should characterize it not as *one* and *undivided* but, by deliberately stressing how the parts are connected and interlaced toward a common end, all the more eloquently as coordinated and unified...

The seam differs from the band discussed above both in structure and in principle. The seam works across the width of its extension; the band, along the length. In the seam there is an interaction from left to right, which can be most simply represented by a zigzag or a double zigzag, an image consistent with the technical means used in sewing. I will pass over here many more developed forms and patterns that in part arise from this simplest of motifs and in part embody the structural—formal concept under discussion...
But one remark about the most general stylistic justification for these ornamental forms is appropriate here, namely, that they should refer directly to the units to be joined. The first impression they make must always be that they form a chain, move back and forth, fasten, tie, tack, or do anything else related to this basic concept. This function also implies that the accessory ornamental element also corresponds to the nature and propensity of the elements tied and stitched together, from which it then follows that the ornament also draws attention to whatever has the stitched cover and thus reveals it as something unified and as the final reference.

Architecture versus Sculpture
Greg Lynn
Barefoot on White-hot Walls
Germany: Hatje Cantz Publishers, 2005
p.157 and p.161

The reception of Peter Eisenman's work polarizes oppositions between intellectualism and sensual experience, between academicism and design, and between architecture and sculpture.

While the relationship between sculptural space and architectural space is significant, defining their differences has become important in an era of disciplinary confusion. Both fields have been problematized by the coincidence of minimalist sculpture and analytic formalist architecture in the 1970s. Hal Foster's comparison between the work of Richard Serra and Frank Gehry is a glaring example of the confusion that arises when there is no distinction made between the disciplinarity and history of architecture and sculpture. Formal and spatial qualities are less important to architecture than they are to sculpture as the relationships between panalization, interiority, volumetric shelter, aperture and the structure are neither thematic nor expressive in sculpture. Although some large-scale sculptures, such as those of Anish Kapoor, Jeff Koons and others, may require structure and panelization, these necessities are not thematic in their field and can therefore be repressed or ignored...

The real issue of the relationship between architecture and sculpture emerges around the question of curved space. When sculptors do situate their work in architecture it is most often without success, as the translation usually ignites the disciplinary history and methods of architecture. Donald Judd's transmigration into architecture caused the banalization of his sculpture, but it also had a reciprocal effect in that it invited a simplification of 1970s analytic formalist architecture into a kind of denuded minimalist modernism now common to contemporary museum spaces and upscale department stores. This is to say that Judd was not concerned with the expression of either structure or interiority coming from the discipline of sculpture. The limitations of his flirtations with architecture were defined by his blindness to its disciplinarity. To transfer sculptural concerns to architecture or architectural concerns into sculpture may be provocations but these transfers rarely yield important results. Curiously, the more relevant exchange between contemporary architecture and sculpture is not with Judd, LeWitt, Serra or Stella but with a sculptor like Tony Cragg who is working on perforated envelopes and interior volume. This work theorizes and innovates interiority through sculptural concerns that also articulate architecture's preoccupation with modulating across envelopes and facades.

SURFACE: FORM

PLEATED SURFACES

A type of surface fold that changes the character of its surface, from infinitely thin to excessively thick, structured and precisely articulated.

Borrowed from the tectonics of fashion, pleating combines the material effects of soft and hard. The most common pleat, the knife pleat, is sharp and crisp, while other gathering techniques emphasize roll and curvature. They can also introduce other sensibilities from fashion design, such as injecting lightweight, airy, voluptuous or wavy qualities. Like other modes of surface articulation, pleats have the potential to generate a sequence of transitions that can vary from smooth and subtle to sharp and abrupt. They maintain a clear affinity for repetition, strong rhythm, continuity and precision. Pleating expands a two-dimensional surface, producing structural depth and mediating the dichotomy between surface

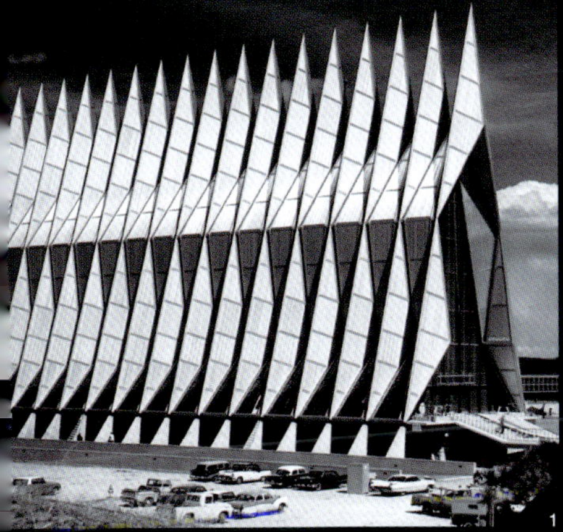
1

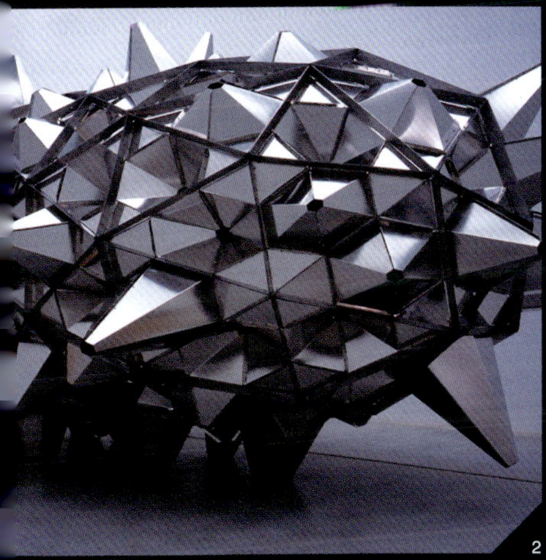
2

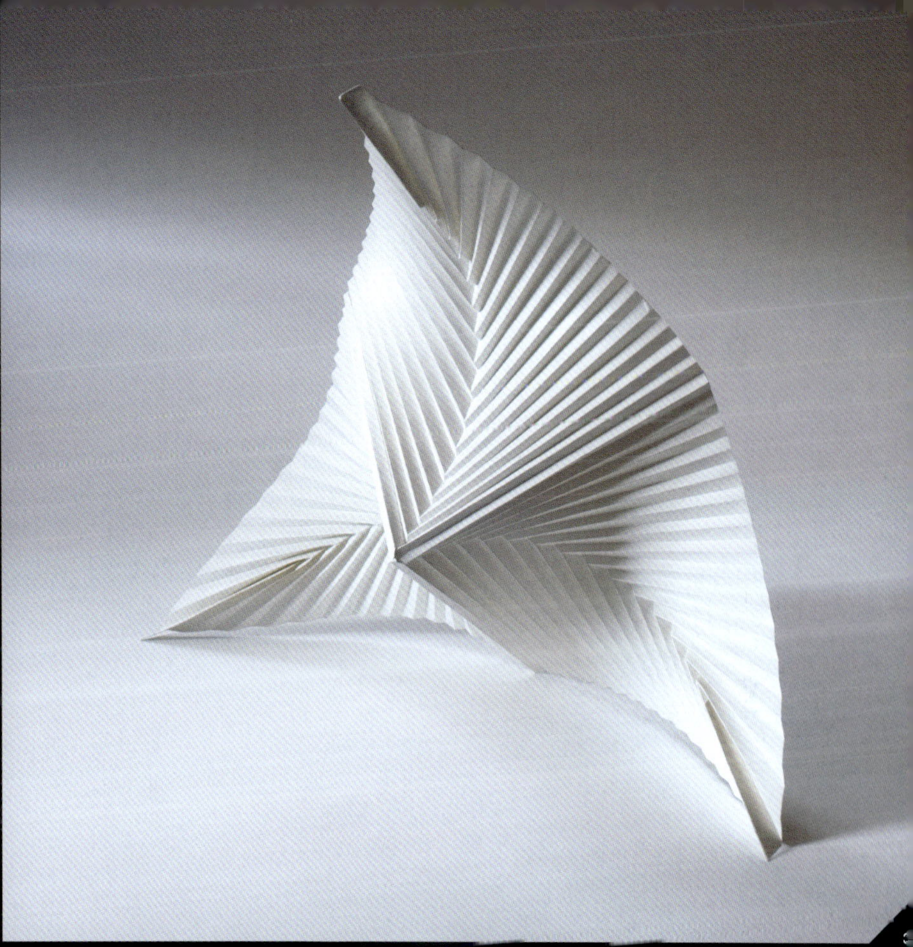
3

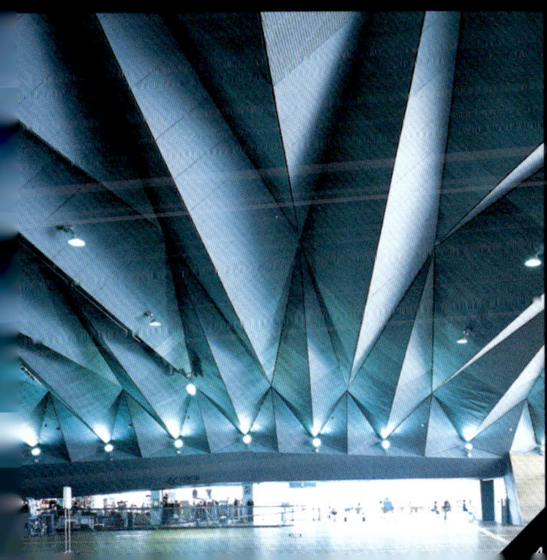
4

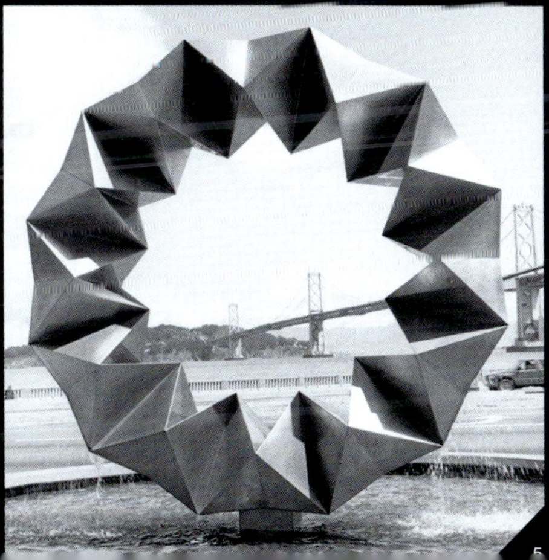
5

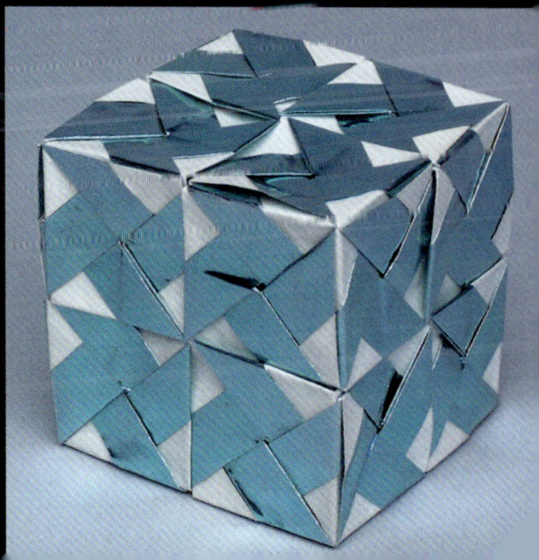

Bengt Stiller
Performance Hall
2007

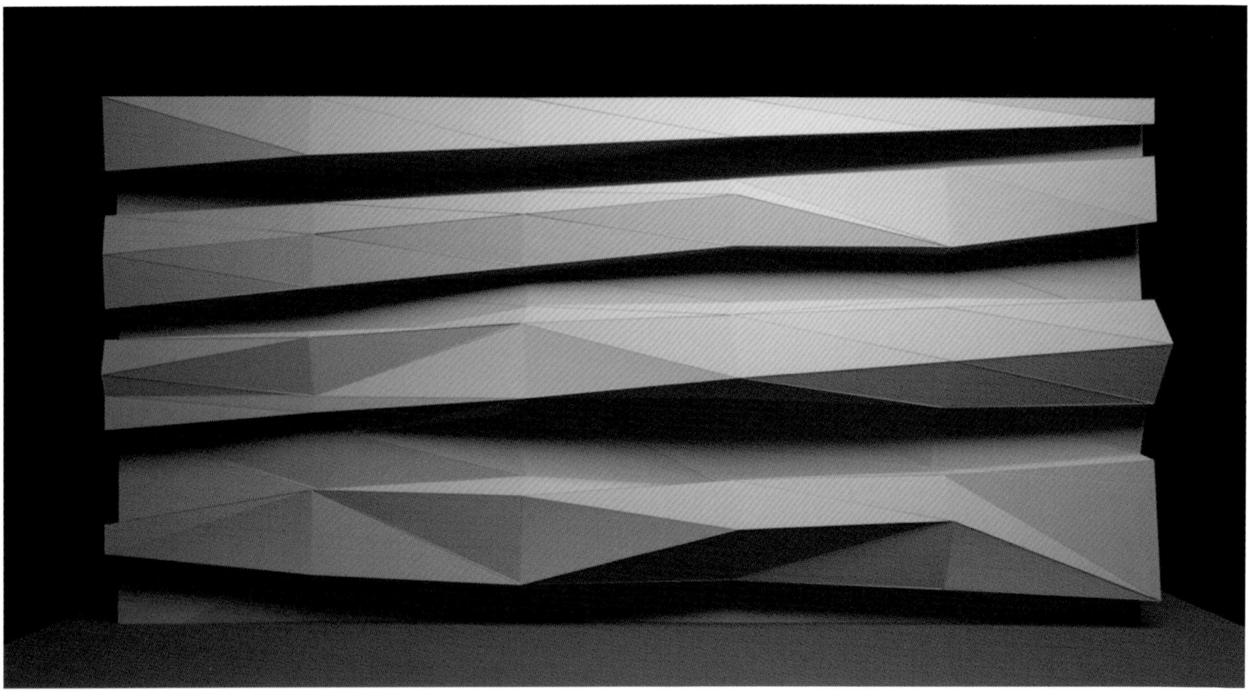

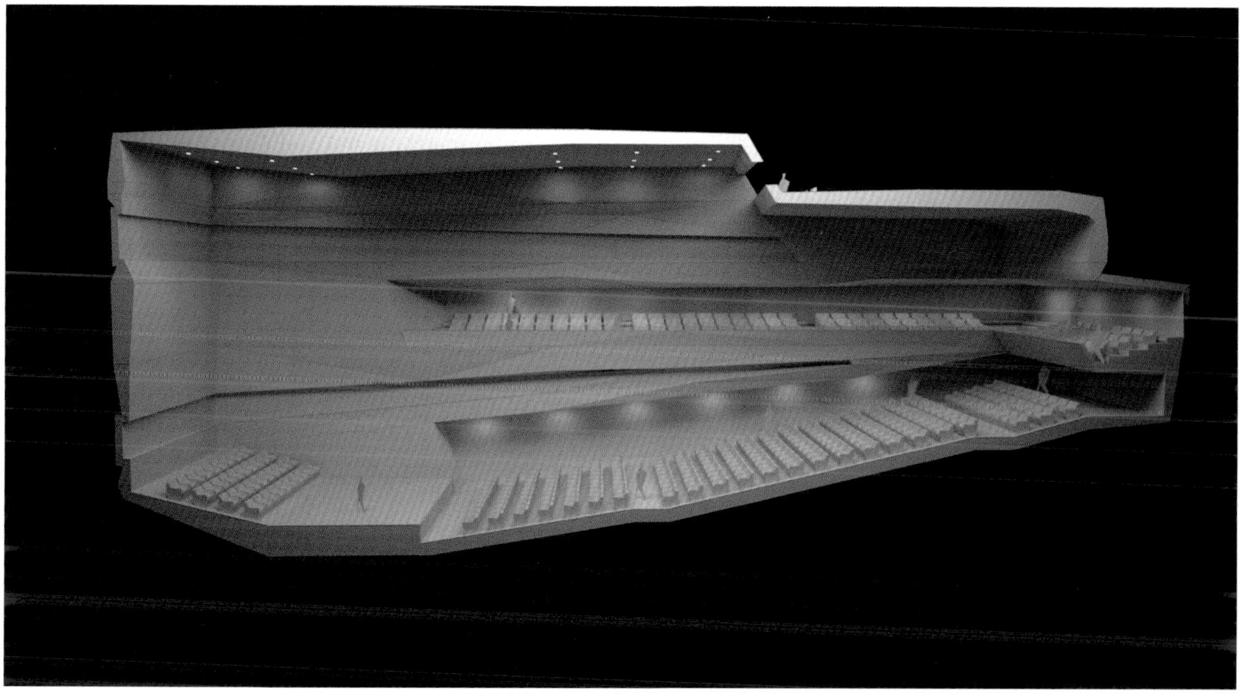

Anna Psenicka
Red Bull Pavilion
2006

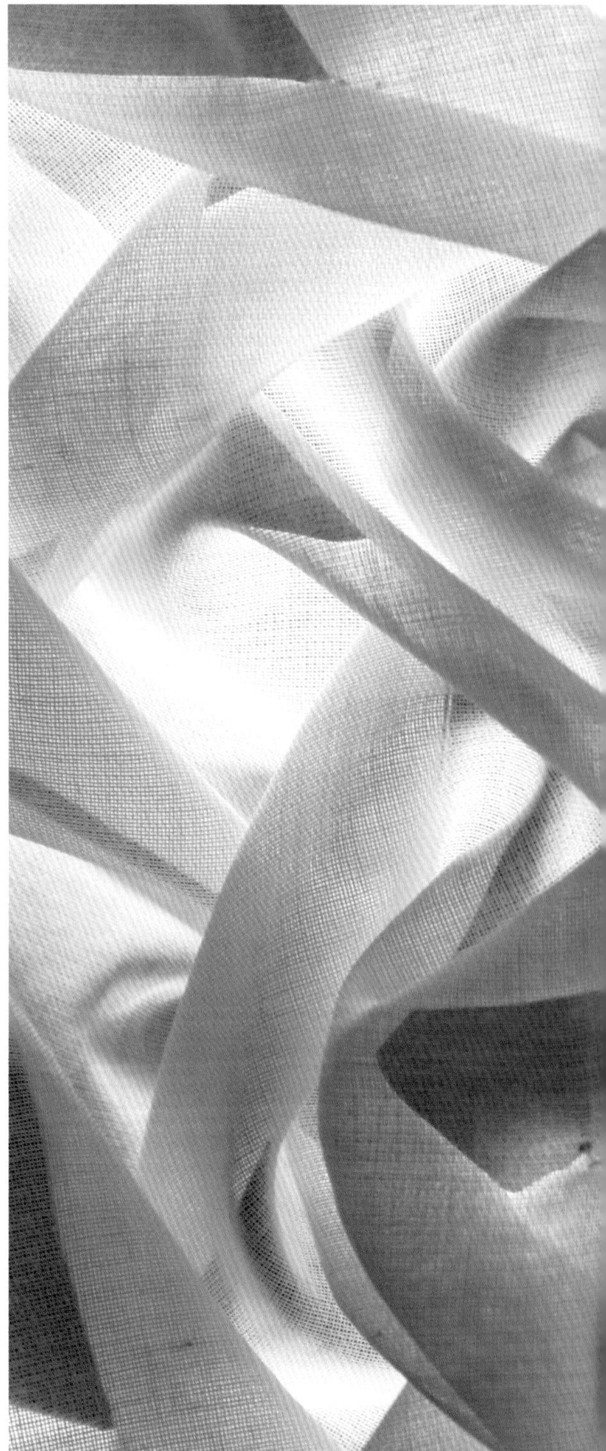

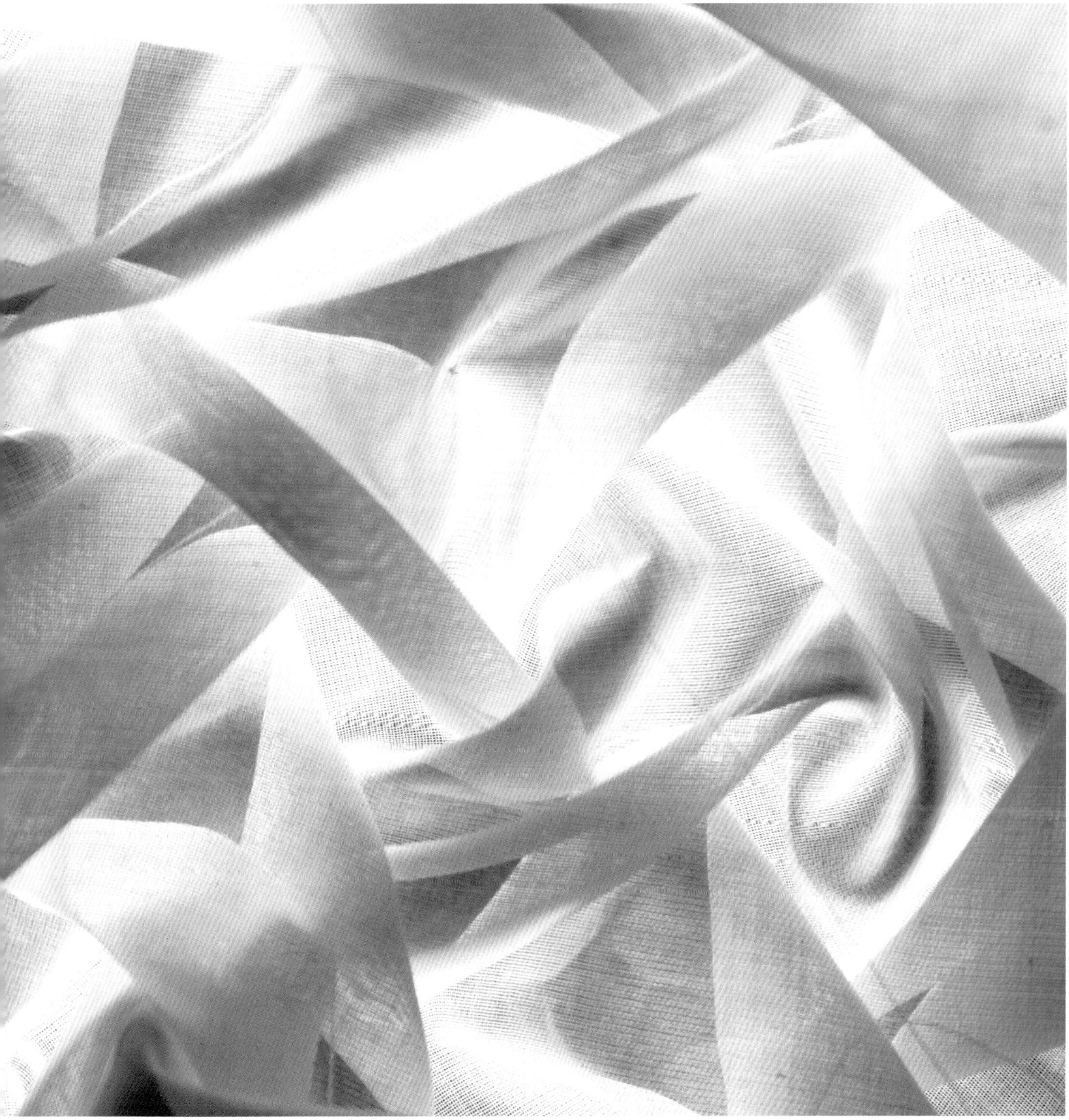

Aurelius Weber
Red Bull Pavilion
2006

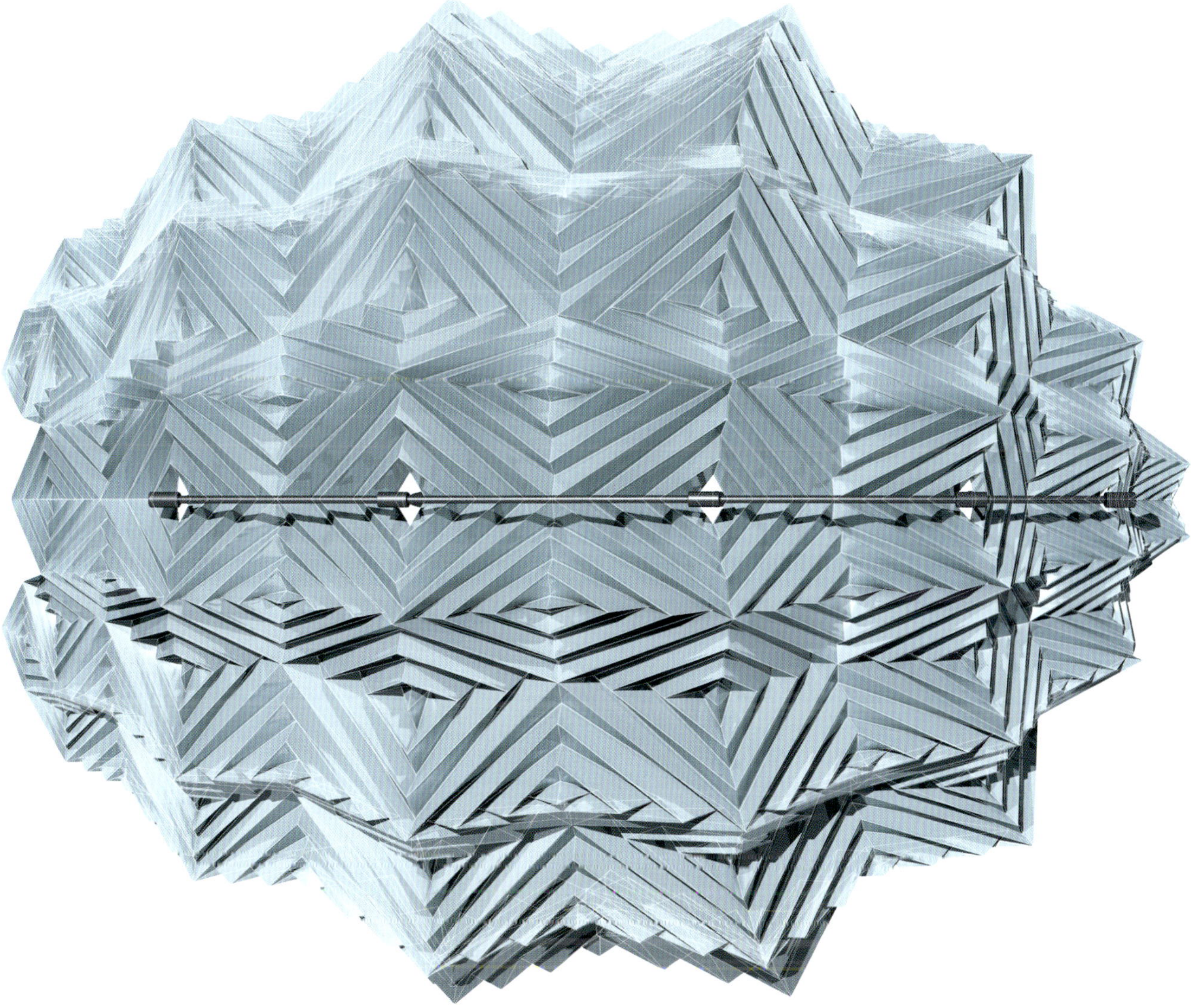

Martin Zangerl
Diploma: Center for Digital Art and Media Technology
2006

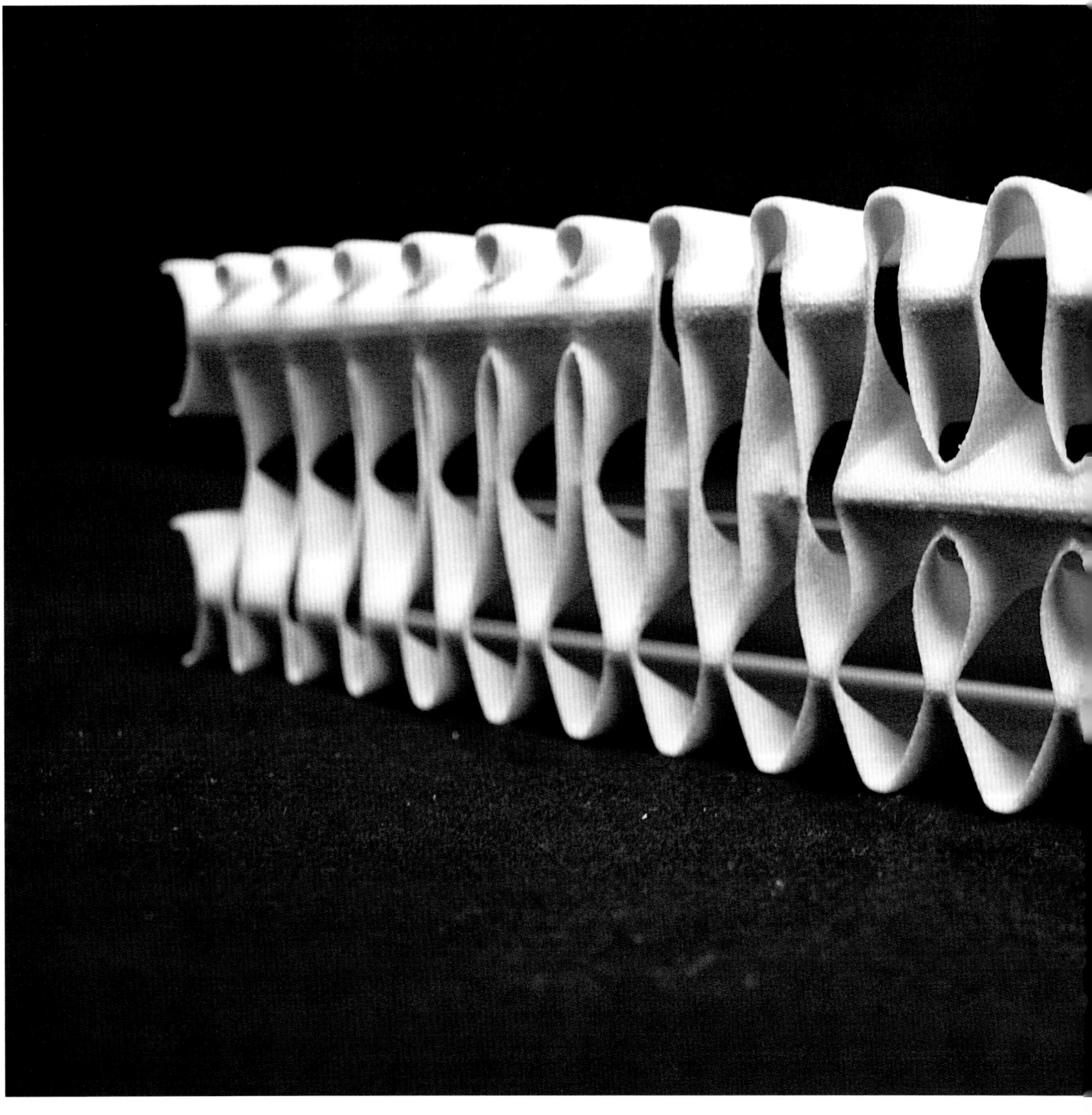

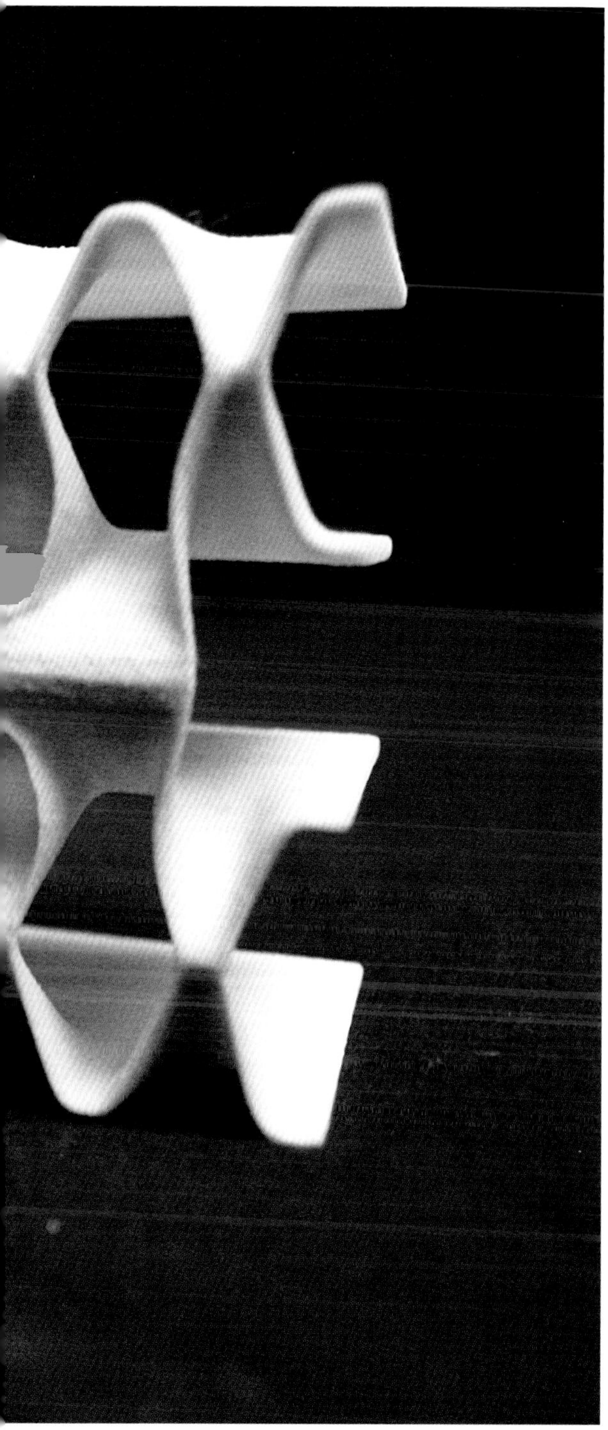

SELECTED EXCERPTS

Skin + Bones: Parallel Practices in Fashion and Architecture
Brook Hodge
New York: Thames & Hudson, 2006
p. 11

That fashion and architecture have a great deal in common may be surprising, given the obvious differences between the two disciplines. Fashion is thought of as ephemeral and superficial, using soft, sometimes fragile, materials, wheras architecture is considered monumental and permanent, using rigid, highly durable materials. Their scales of production, too, are wildly different: fashion designers create garments for the human body, while architects create buildings large enough for many bodies to inhabit simultaneously. Regardless of scale, however, the point of origin for both practices is the body. Both protect and shelter, while providing a means to express identity-whether personal, political, religious, or cultural.

While the fashion designer and architect create objects that differ in size and materials, their creative processes can be strikingly similar. Both begin with a flat two-dimensional medium, transforming it to create complex three-dimensional forms. The same prevailing aesthetic tendencies, ideological and theoretical foundations and technologies innovations have influenced each, resulting in garments and buildings that share stylistic or structural qualities or derive from common creative impulses. And, over time, designers in both fields have drawn from each other for inspiration as well as certain technical strategies. Vocabulary derived from architecture has been applied to garments ("architectonic", "constructed", "sculptural", etc.), and architects have also borrowed and adapted sartorial strategies and vocabulary from the fashion world (draping, wrapping, weaving, folding, printing, pleating surfaces and materials). The significant and manifold parallels manifested in the skin and bones of both garments and buildings are the subject of this exhibition and catalogue.

Pleat of Matter, Folds of the Soul
Giuliana Bruno
Log 1
New York: Anyone Corporation, 2003
pp. 118–119

The Futurist *modificante* understood the sartorial architecture of mood. [Issey] Miyake's pleats take this notion of the modifier of mood from decor and ornament to the very architecture of clothing. Madam-T is itself a *modificante*. It is a complete architecture of mood. As you continue to play with it, its mood keeps on changing, and it always surprises you. Every time it emerges as something subtly different. In its unfolding metamorphosis, Madam-T suits your ever-changing moods. It can be stark, pensive, and melancholic or playful, joyous, and frivolous. It can morph from one shade of mood to the next, or go directly for the opposite affect. It can do this in single takes, in assemblage, or in sequence. The folds can transport you from one affective atmosphere to the next. Their draping motion embodies the motion of an emotion. This is the perfect cloth to suit your soul. It shows its innner folds. It contains the force of spirit exerted on the architecture of your body, molding its inner surfaces. To fold, after all, means to envelop, embrace, and hug. It is the intensity you covet. “Pleats, please.”...

Home of the fold, fashion resides with the reversible continuity that, rather than separating, provides a breathing membrane—a skin—to the world. Fashion is an interior map in reverse, where a trace of emotional address is left on the outer dress in a two-fold projection. First, as a chart in the negative, it is an affect that is projected outward as if onto a screen and, in such a way, written on the skin of the world. Next, in the transport of dress and address, a passage to intimacy takes place. A mapping of this intimacy is liminally designed on the surface of the address/dress. It unfolds on the wall, the skin, and the screen as folds of matter and pleats of the soul.

SURFACE: FORM

INFLECTION POINTS

Variation in a continuous surface or system that allows an entirely new type to develop.

Anomalies such as points of focus in a continuous field or biological orifices on smooth skin develop from within an overarching system but produce dramatic changes in function or typology. They operate at the asymptote of maximum difference, incorporating a maximum level of complexity. In architectural terms, these inflection points can transform pattern (i.e. orthogonal to irregular), structure (truss to space frame) or organization (closed to open).

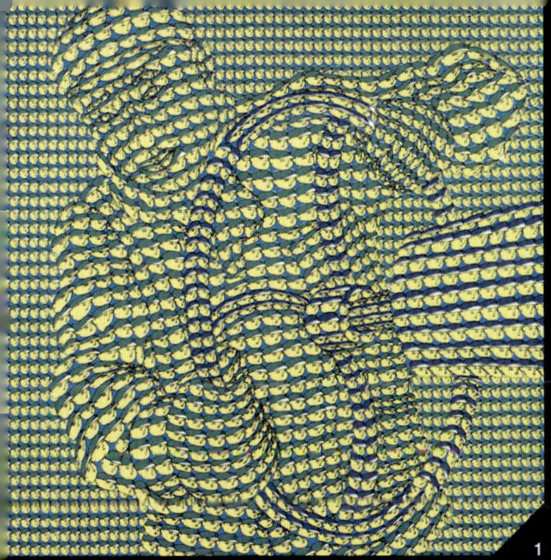

1

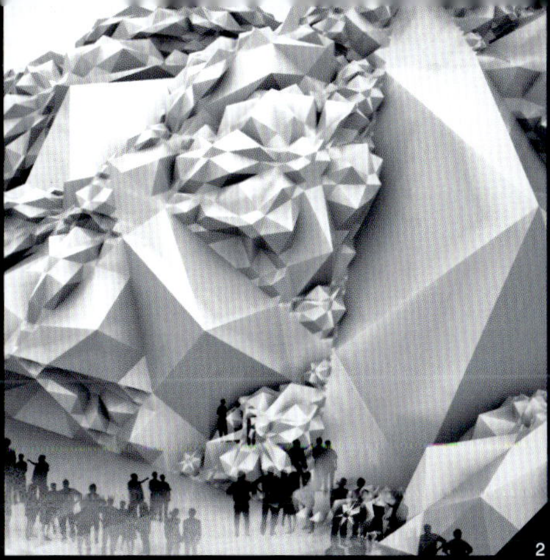

2

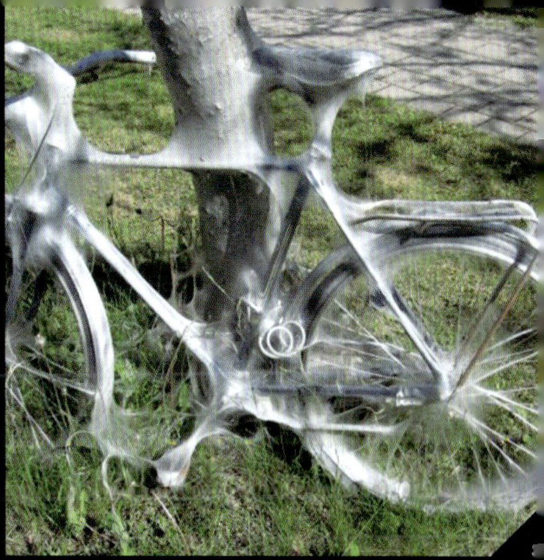

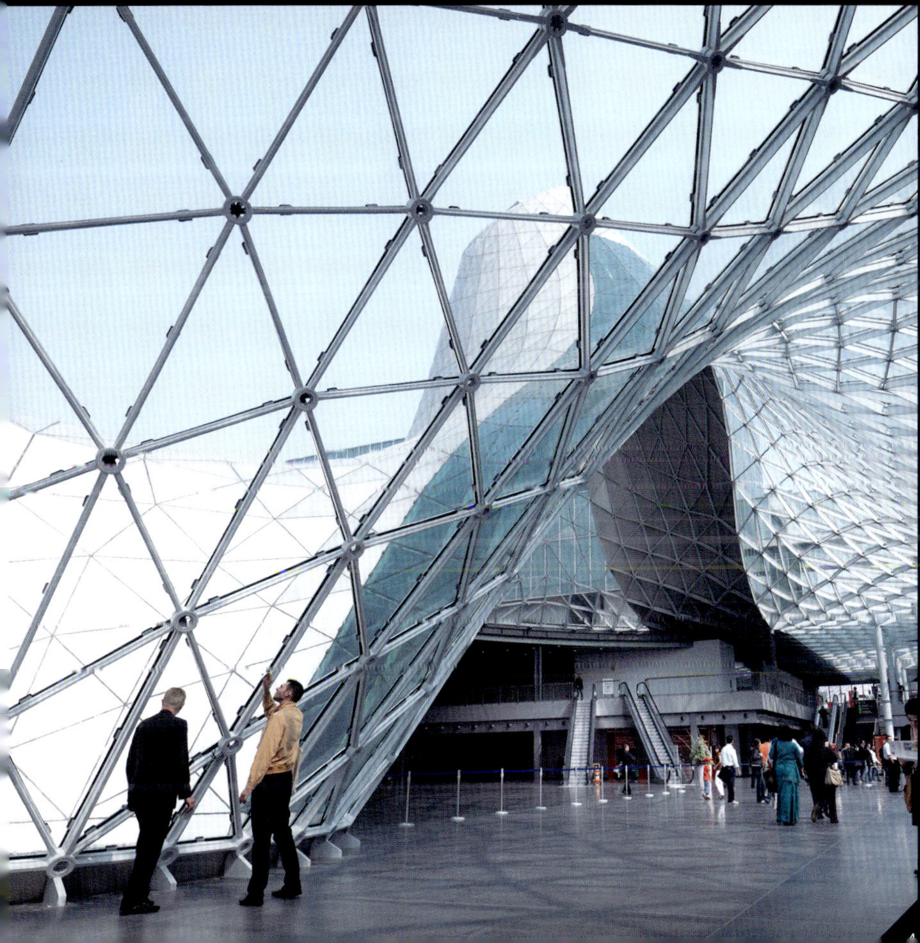

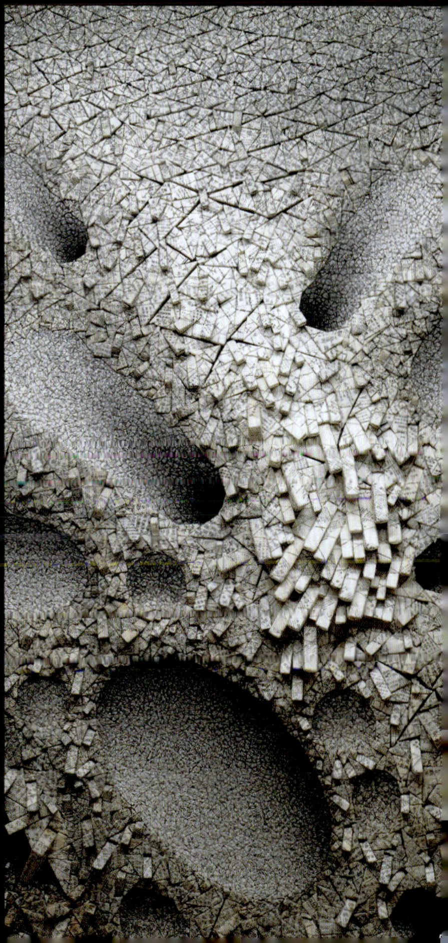

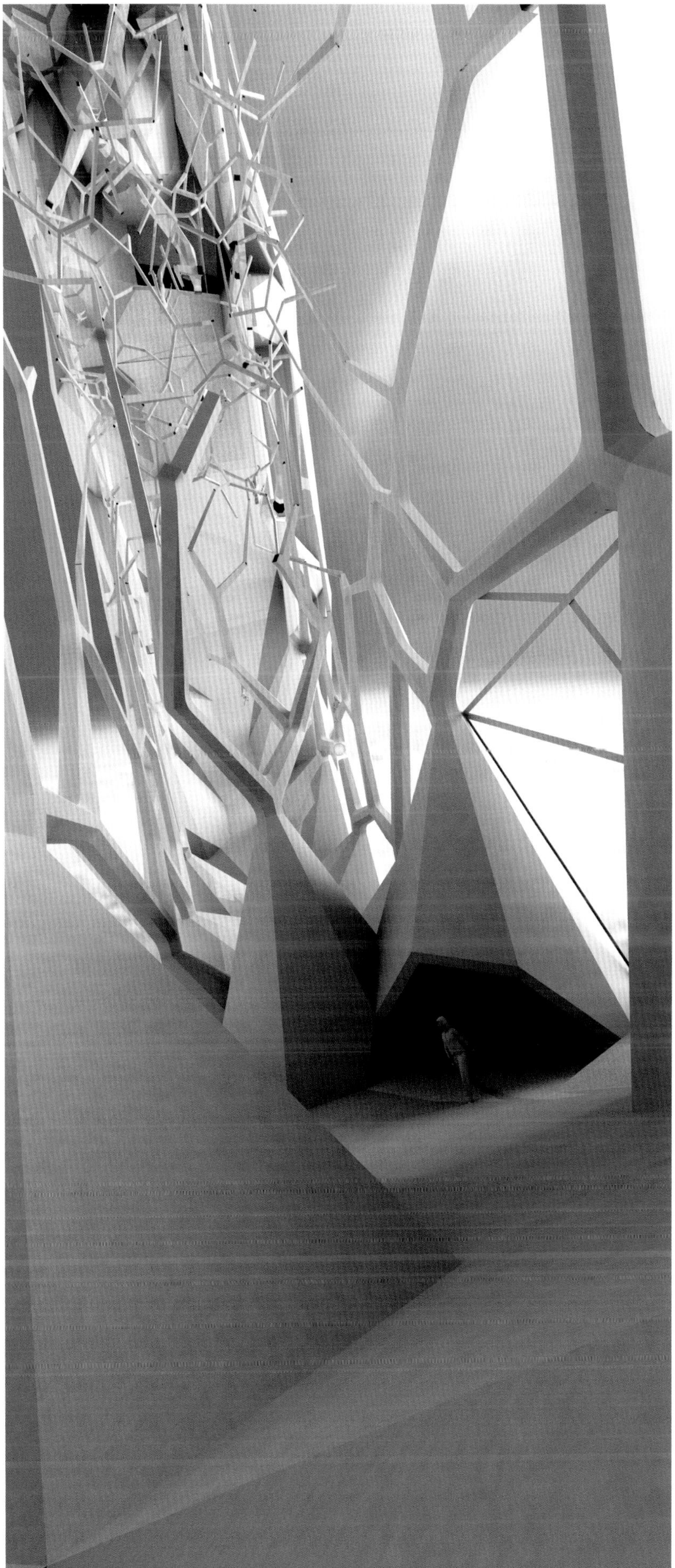

Claudia Cavallar
Diploma: Piscine Jackson Pax
2005

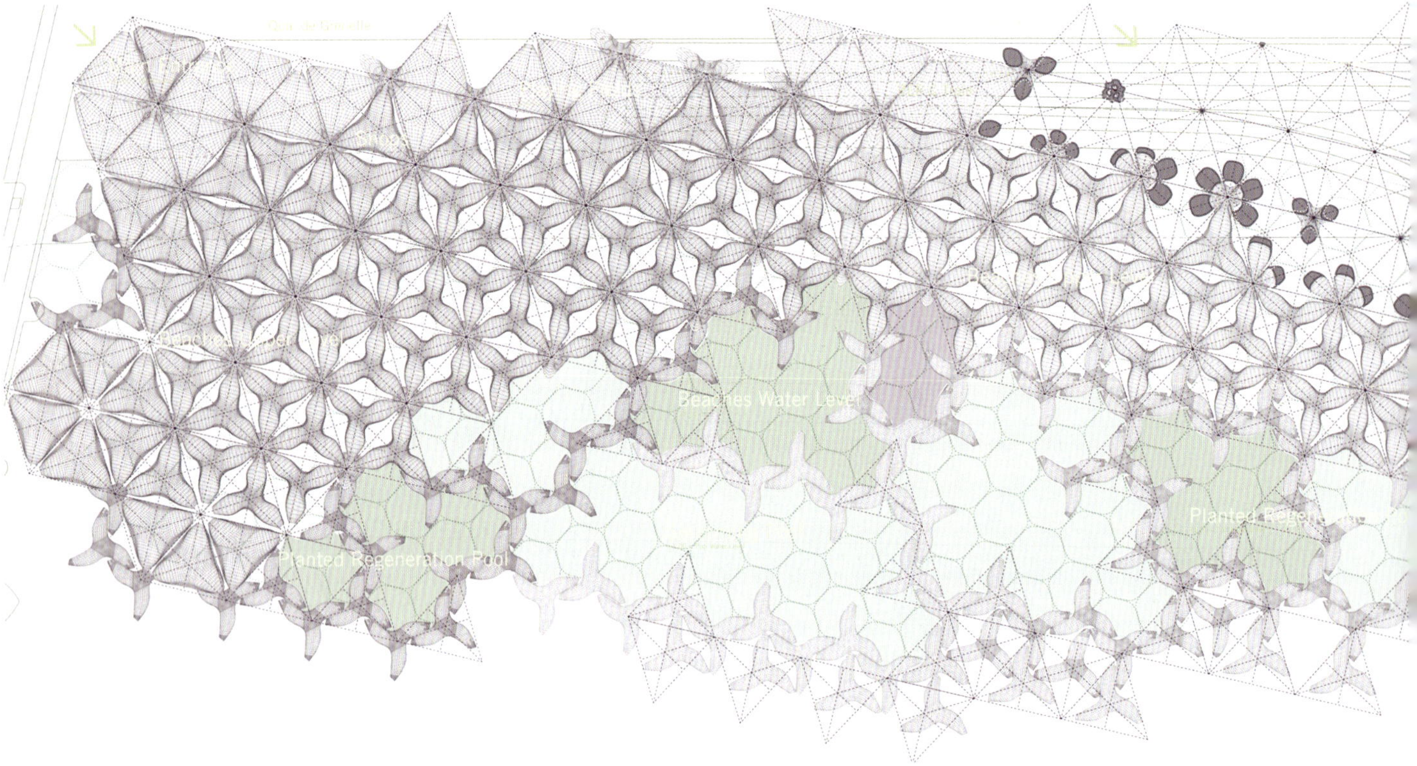

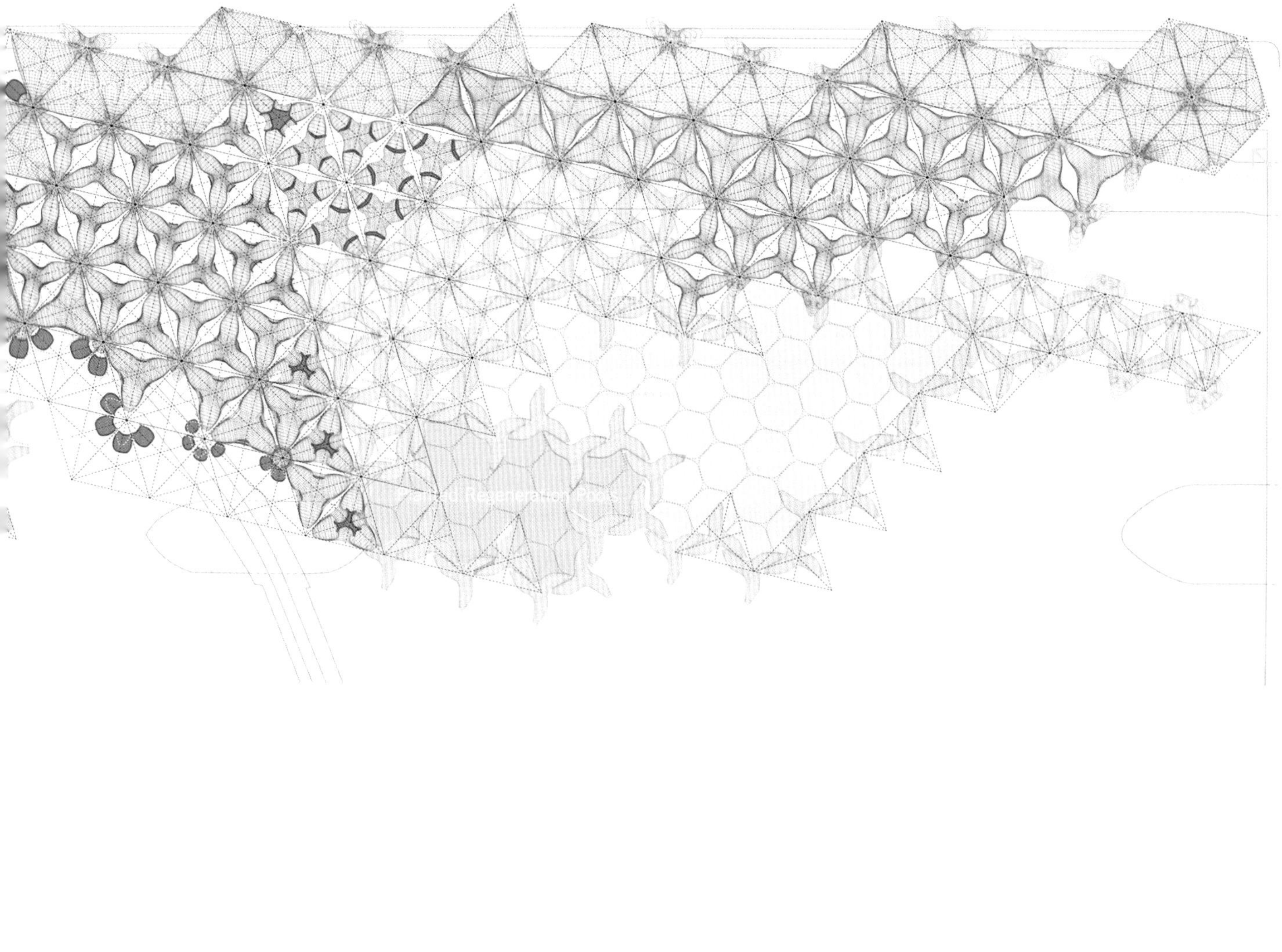
Regeneration Pools

Maja Ozvaldic, Eva Diem and Dumëne Comploi
Interplaying Surfaces
2004

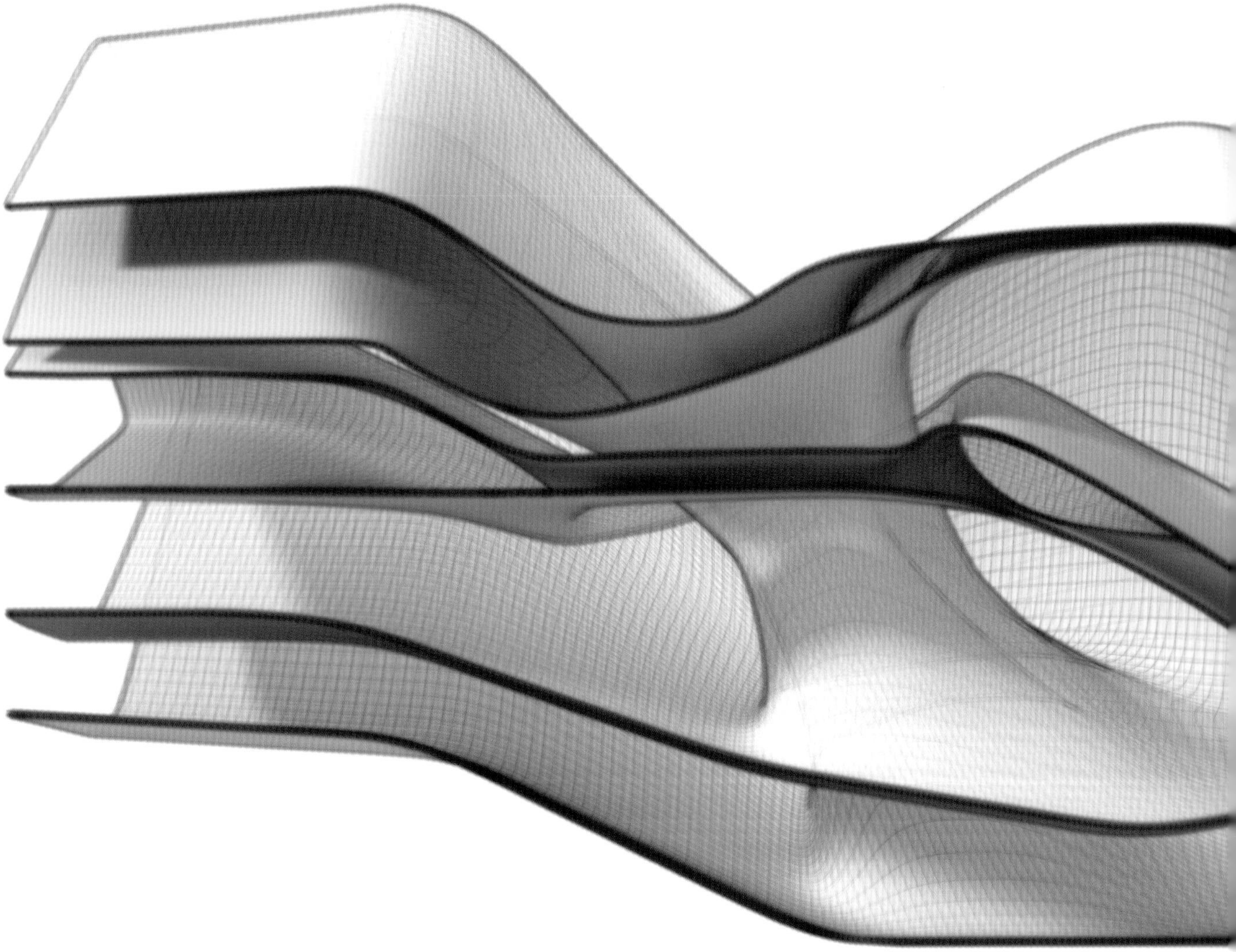

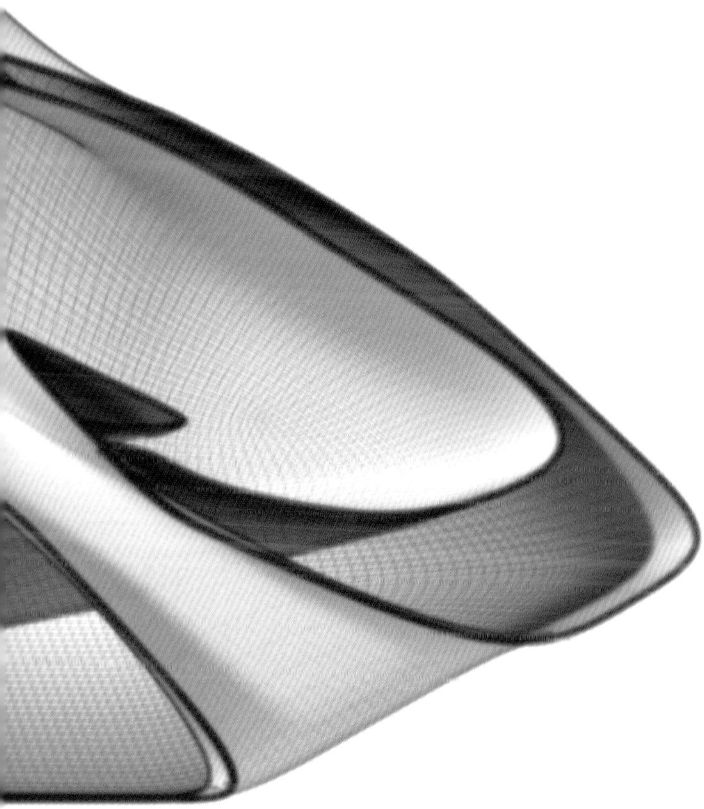

Peter Vikar
Diploma: Woven Source
2007

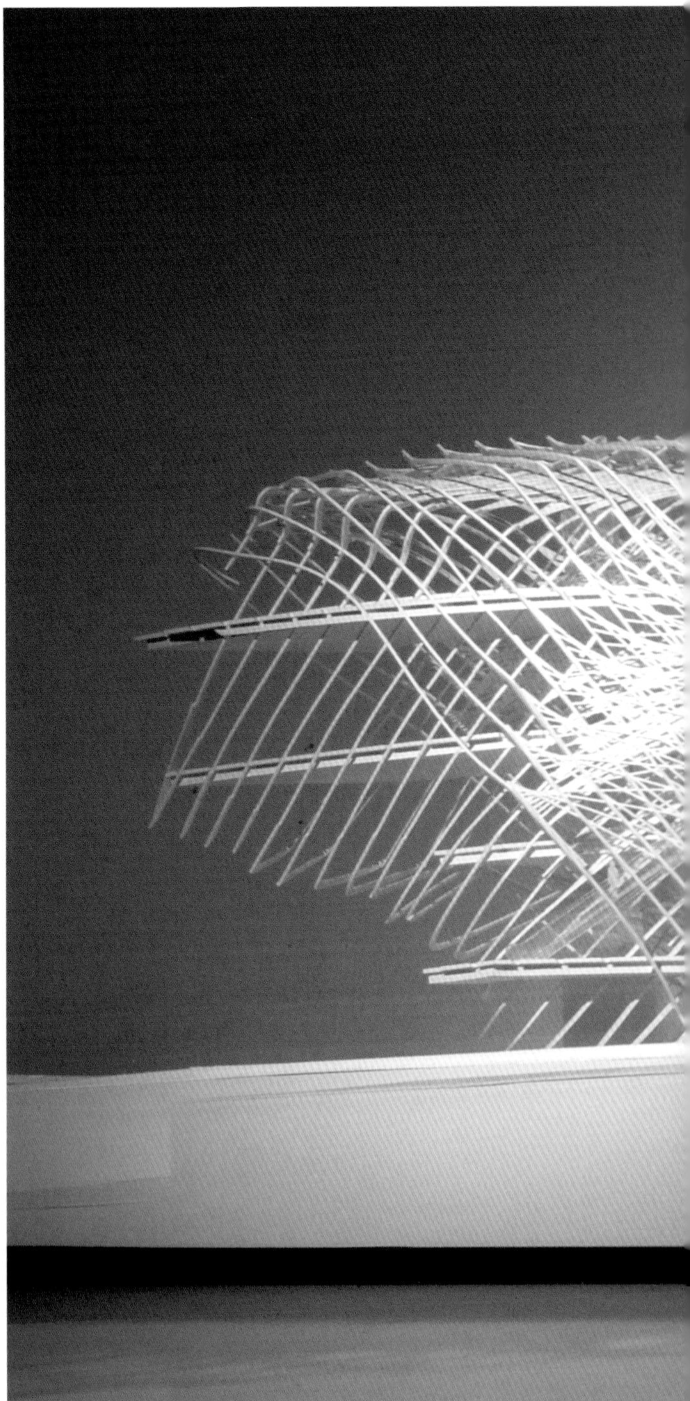

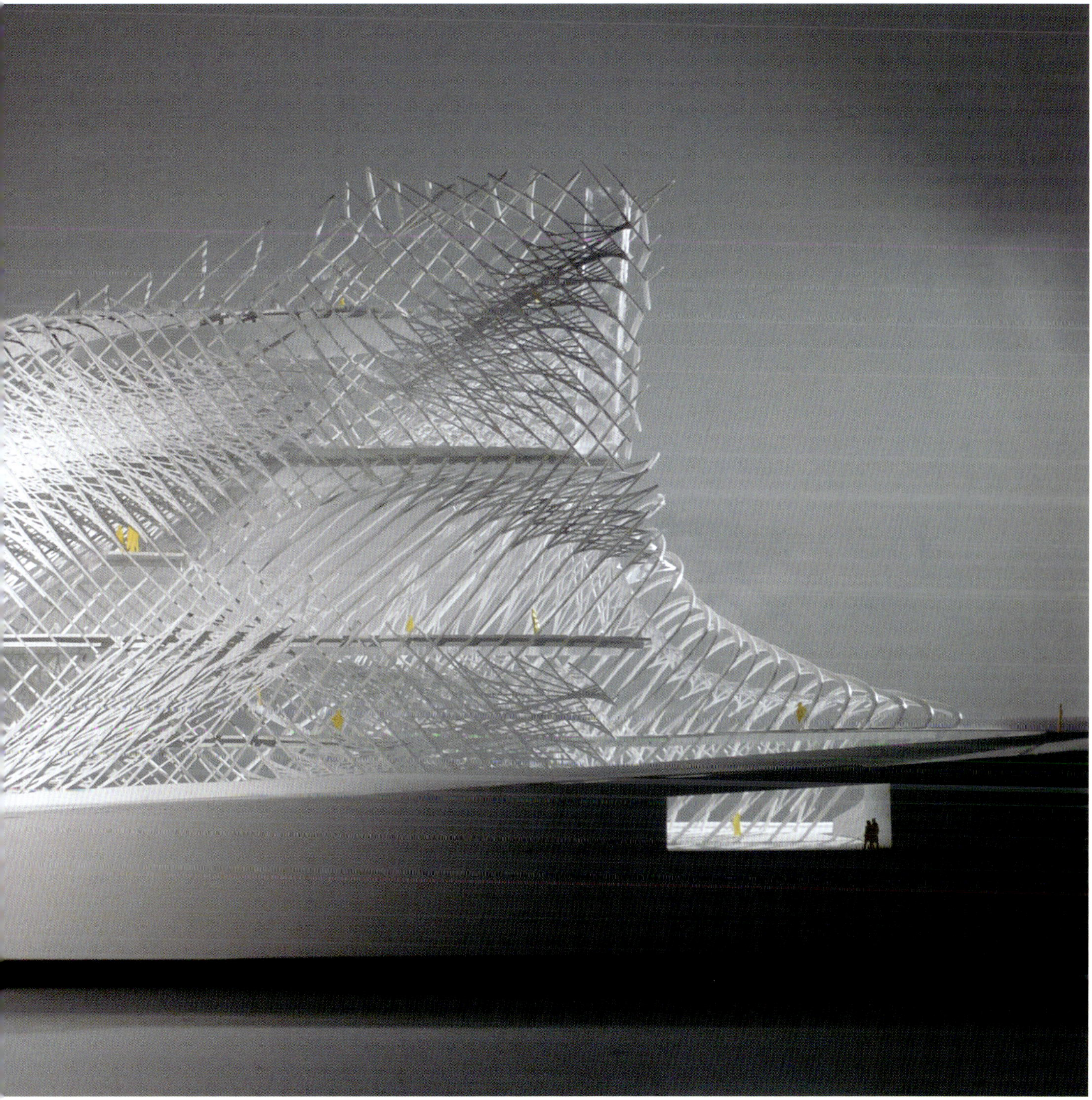

SELECTED EXCERPTS

Territorial Image
Bernard Cache
Earth Moves: The Furnishing of Territories
Cambridge, London: MIT Press, 1995
pp.16–17

In mathematics, what is said to be singular is not a given point, but rather a set of points on a given curve. A point is not singular: it becomes singularized on a continuum. And several types of singularity exist, starting with fractures in curves and other bumps in the road. We will discount them at the outset, for singularities that are marked by discontinuity signal events that are exterior to the curvature and are themselves easily identifiable. In the same way, we will eliminate singularities such as backup points (*points de rebroussement*). For though they are indeed discontinuous, they refer to a vector that is tangential to the curve and thus trace a symmetrical axis that is constitutive of the backup point. Whether it be a reflection of the tangential plane or a rebound with respect to the orthogonal plane, the backup point is thus not a basic singularity. It is rather the result of an operation effectuated on any part of the curve. Here again, the singular would be the sign of too noisy, too memorable an event, while what we want to do is to deal with what is most smooth; ordinary continua, sleek and polished. We will then retain two types of singularity. On one hand there are the extrema, the maximum and minimum on a given curve. And on the other there are those singular points that, in relation to the extrema, figure as in-betweens. These are known as points of inflection. They are different from the extrema in that they are defined only in relation to themselves, whereas the definition of the extrema presupposes the prior choice of an axis or an orientation, that is to say of a vector.

Indeed, a maximum or a minimum is a point where the tangent to the curve is directed perpendicularly to the axis of the ordinates (y-axis). Any new orientation of the coordinate axes repositions the maxima and the minima; they are thus extrinsic singularities. The point of inflection, however, designates a pure event of curvature where the tangent crosses the curve; yet this event does not depend in any way on the orientation of the axes, which is why it can be said that inflection is an intrinsic singularity. On either side of the inflection, we know that there will be a highest point and a lowest point, but we cannot designate them as long as the curve has not been related to the orientation of a vector. Points of inflection are singularities in and of themselves, while they confer an indeterminacy to the rest of the curve. Preceding the vector, inflection makes of each of the points a possible extremum in relation to its inverse: virtual maxima and minima. In this way, inflection represents a totality of possibilities, as well as an openness, a receptiveness, or an anticipation.

A line on a surface that simultaneously articulates that surface into distinct regions and unifies separate parts or zones in to a coherent whole.

Car designers often crease surfaces as they are sculpted, introducing a subtle feeling and virtuosity, but also placing focus on the ultra-thin surface itself and thus on surface effects such as reflection, smoothness, sharpness or speed. Creases often have complex relationships with seams and edges, crossing from one panel to another or merging with a seam to produce ambiguity that ties parts of the car body together. Unlike folds, creases tend to emerge from and die into smooth surfaces. Their visual power is too weak to produce the clear figure of iconography; the supplest of surface effects, creases generate only affect.

1 **Preston Scott Cohen, Inc.**
Torus House, New York, 1998–1999
graphic image directed by Preston Scott Cohen, Inc. and rendered by Chris Hoxie.
Reprinted courtesy of Preston Scott Cohen Inc.
www.pscohen.com

2 **Marloes Ten Bhömer**
Paperfolded Shoe, 2006
www.marloestenbhomer.squarespace.com

4 **Chris Bangle**
BMW Z4 Series, 2002
image courtesy of BMW AG
www.bmwgroup.com

5 **Preston Scott Cohen, Inc.**
Tel Aviv Museum of Art, 2003–2010
graphic image directed by Preston Scott Cohen, Inc. and rendered by Chris Hoxie.
Reprinted courtesy of Preston Scott Cohen Inc.
www.pscohen.com

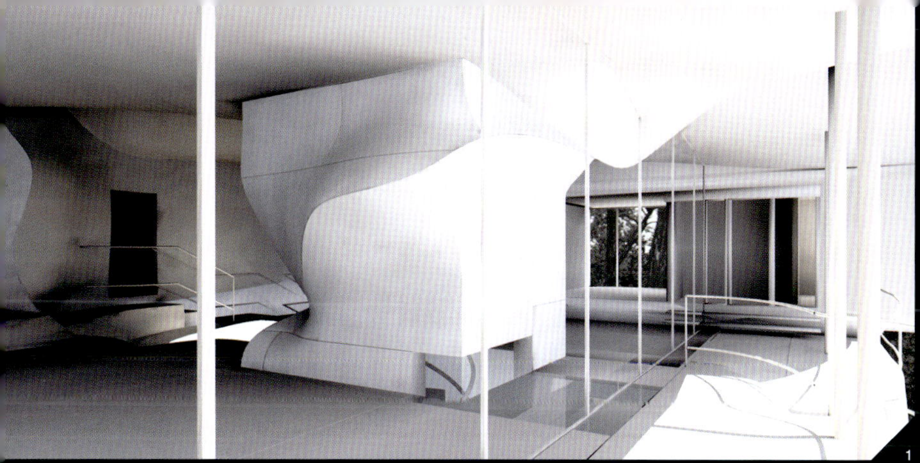
1

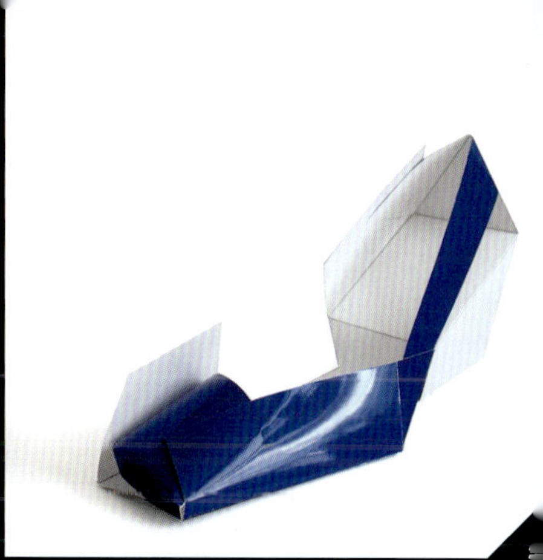

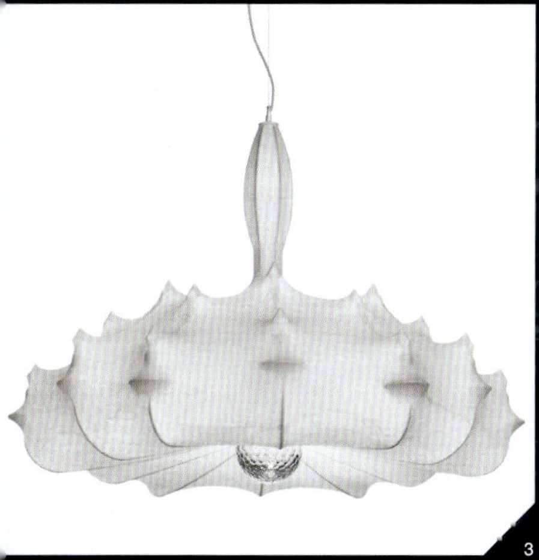
3

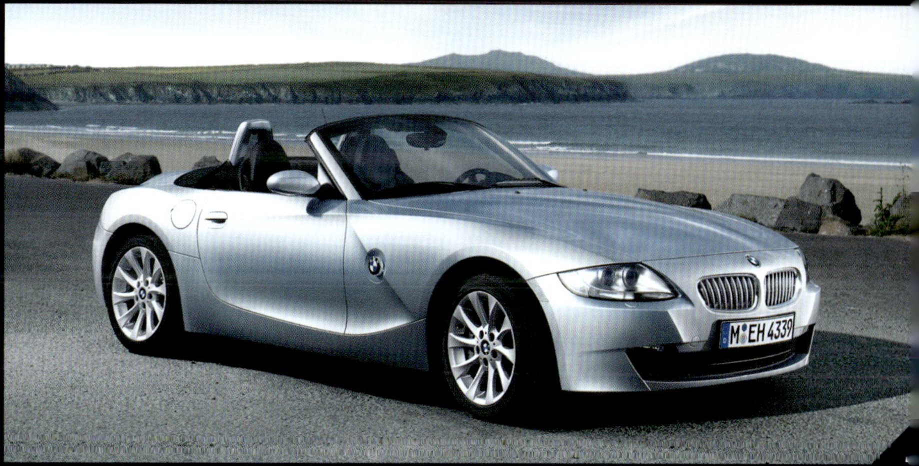

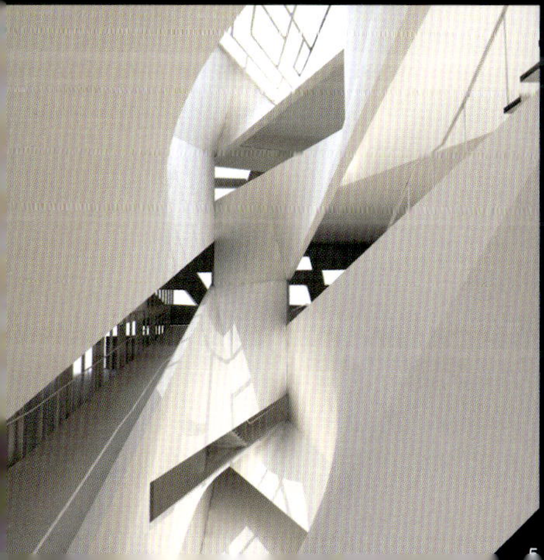
5

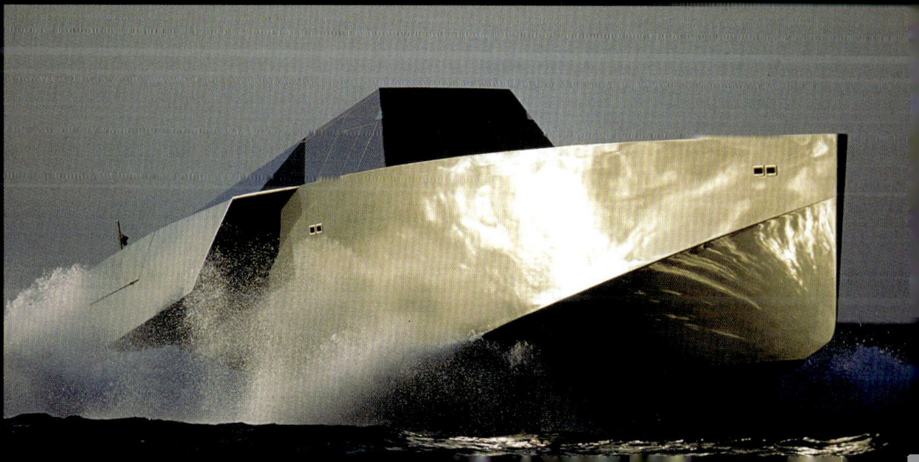

Bence Pap
Multiplex
2005

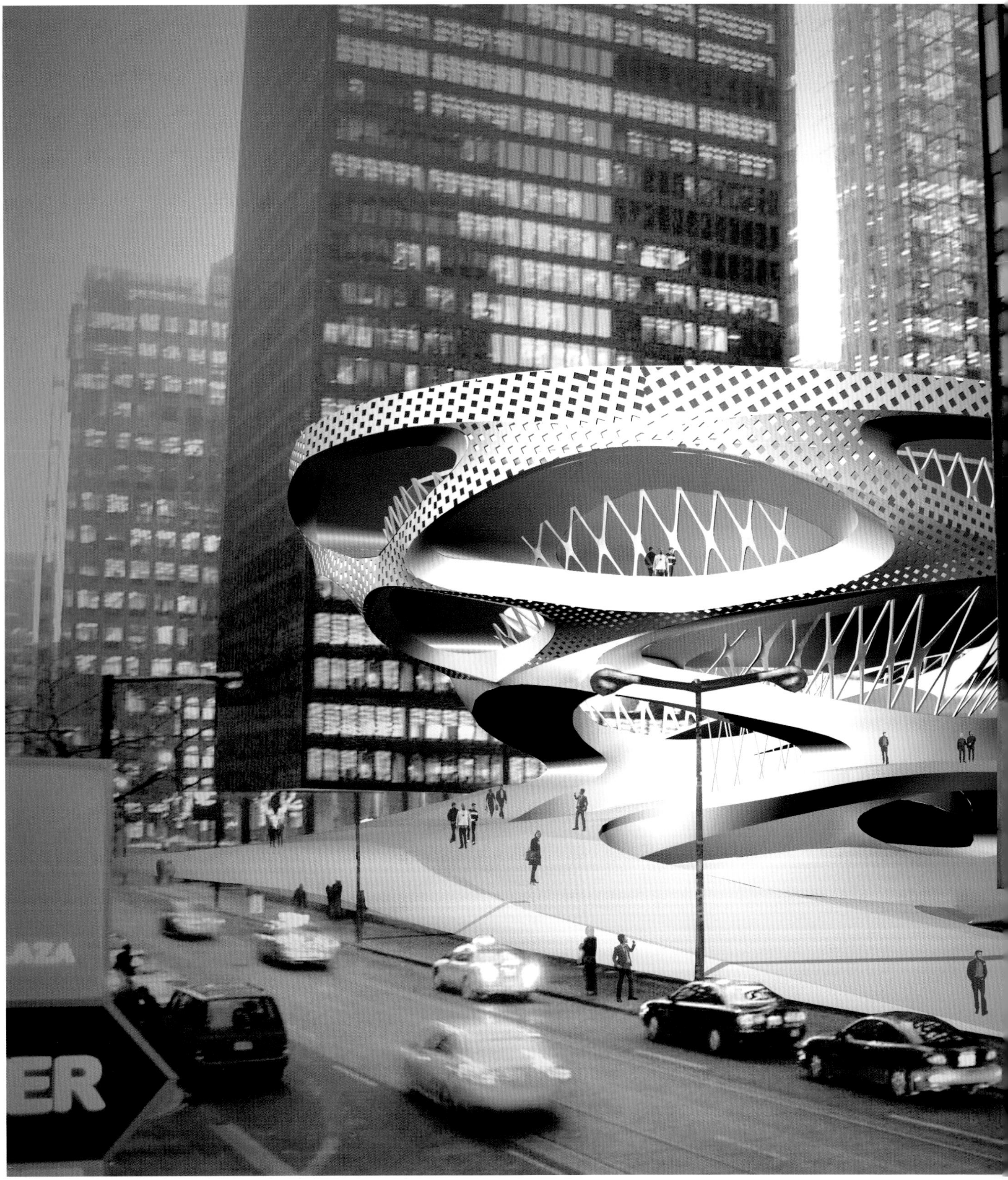

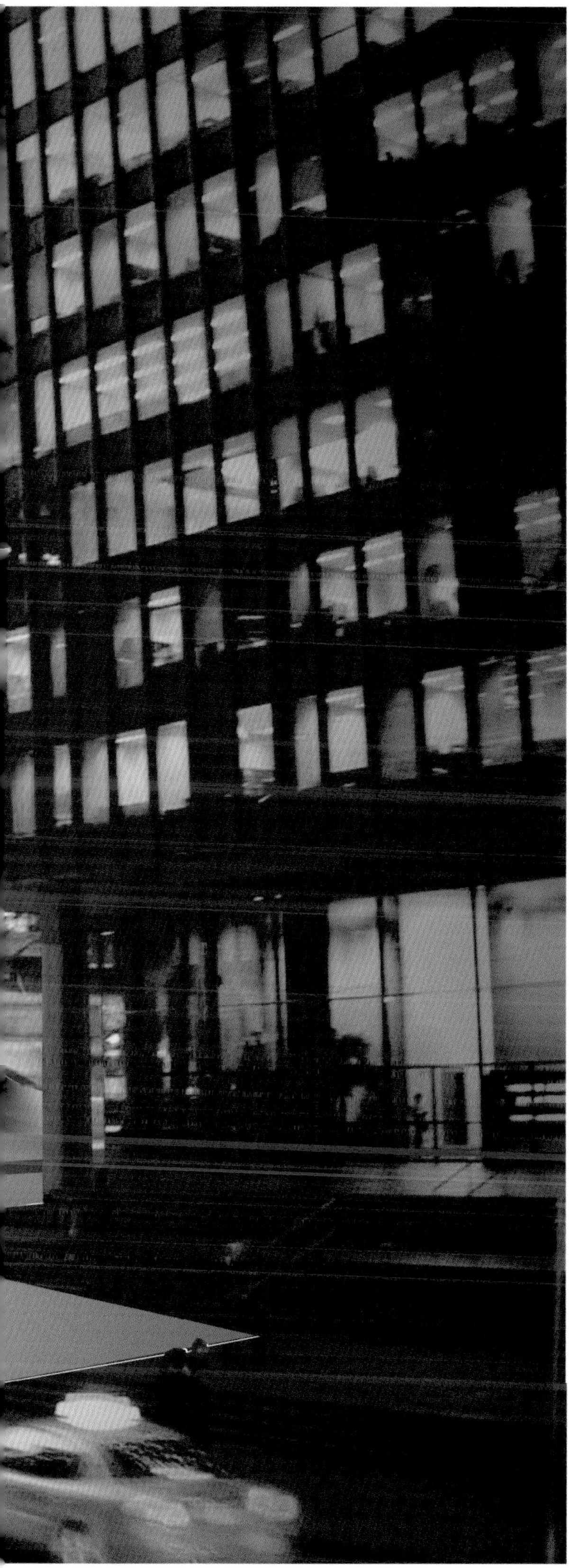

Dumëne Comploi
Diploma: C3D
2008

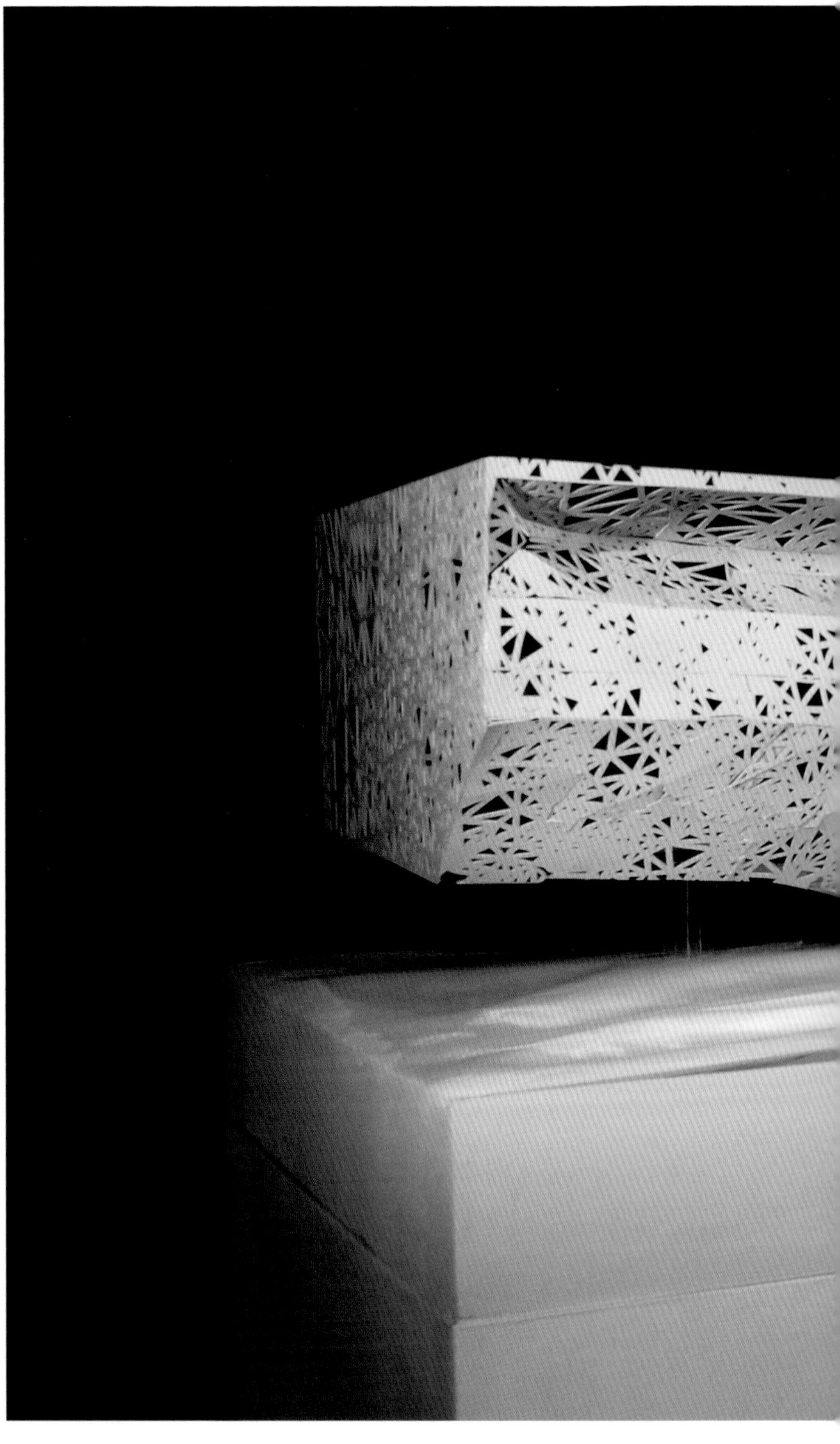

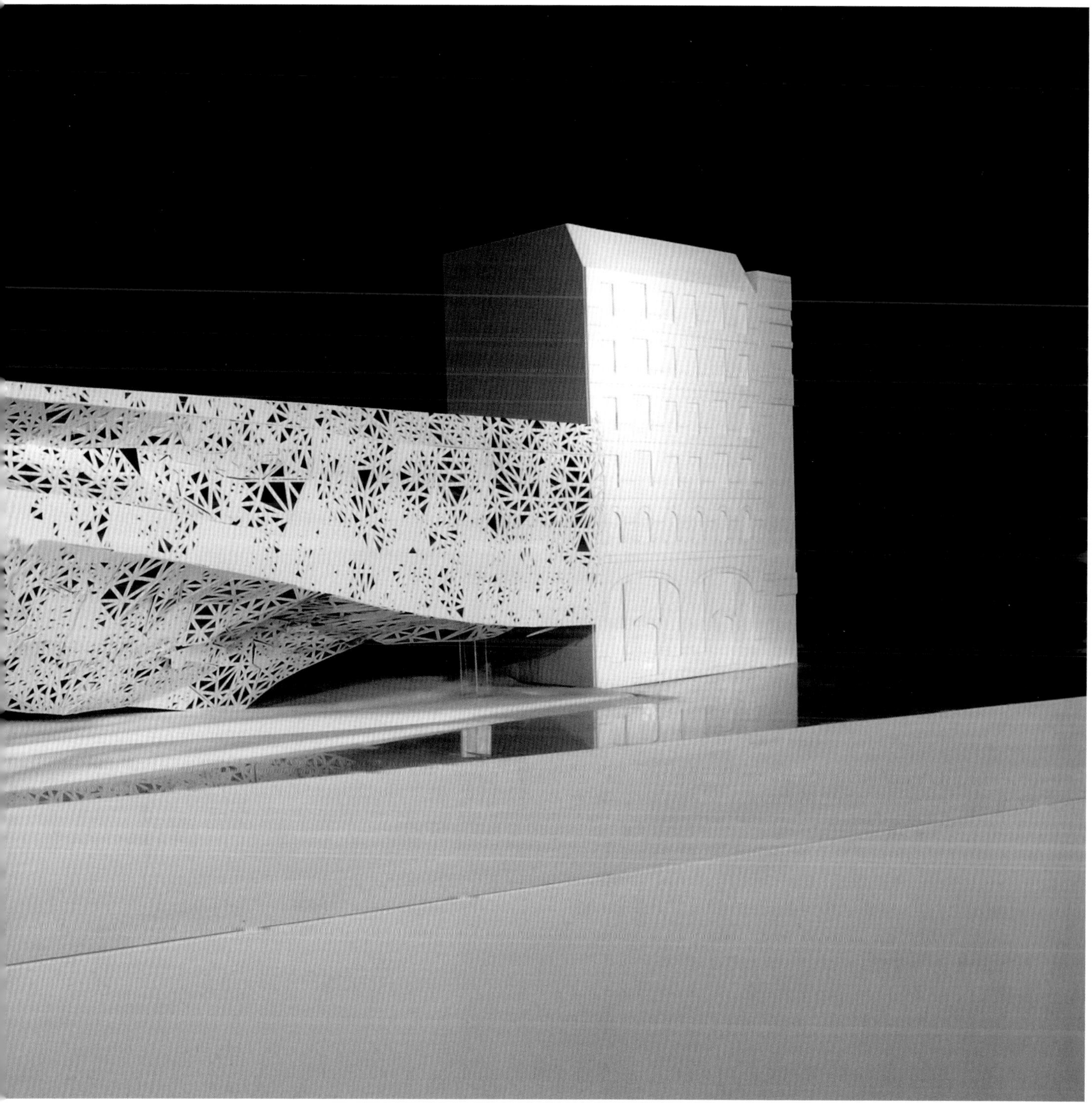

Eva Diem, Mihaela Dumitru, Baptiste Bernard
Factory for Today
2008

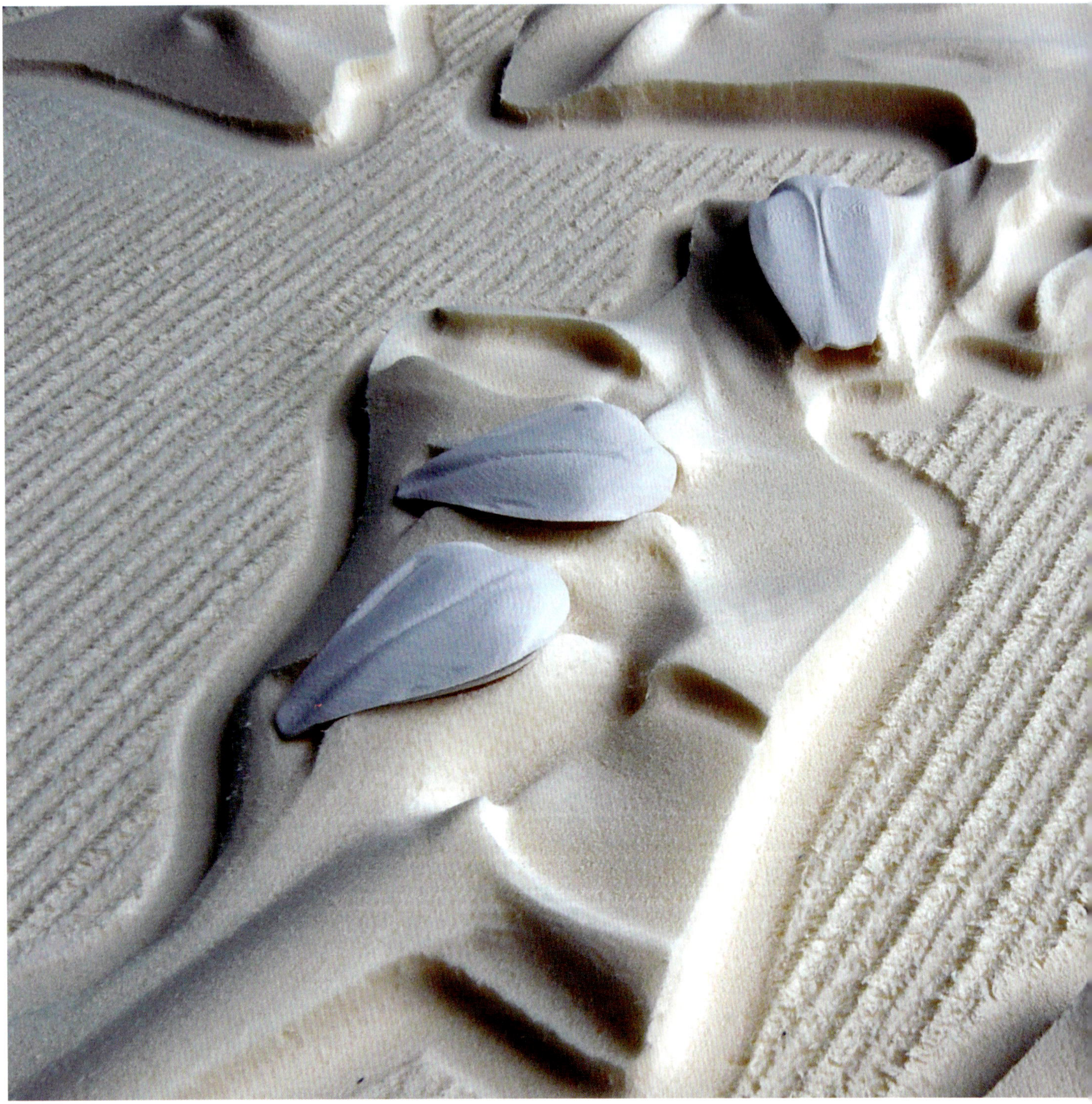

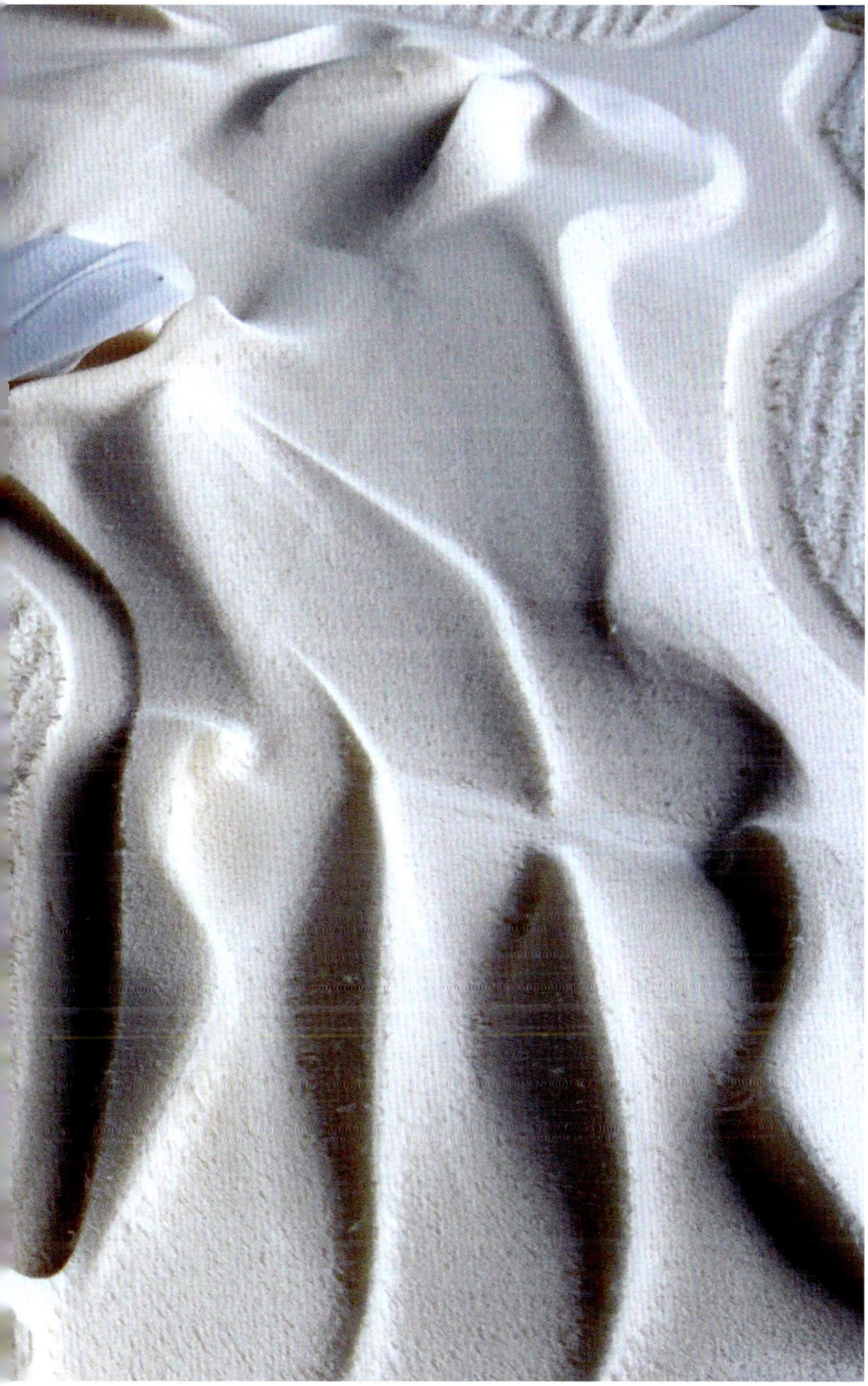

Cornelia Faisst
Diploma: City Centre TV, Vienna
2006

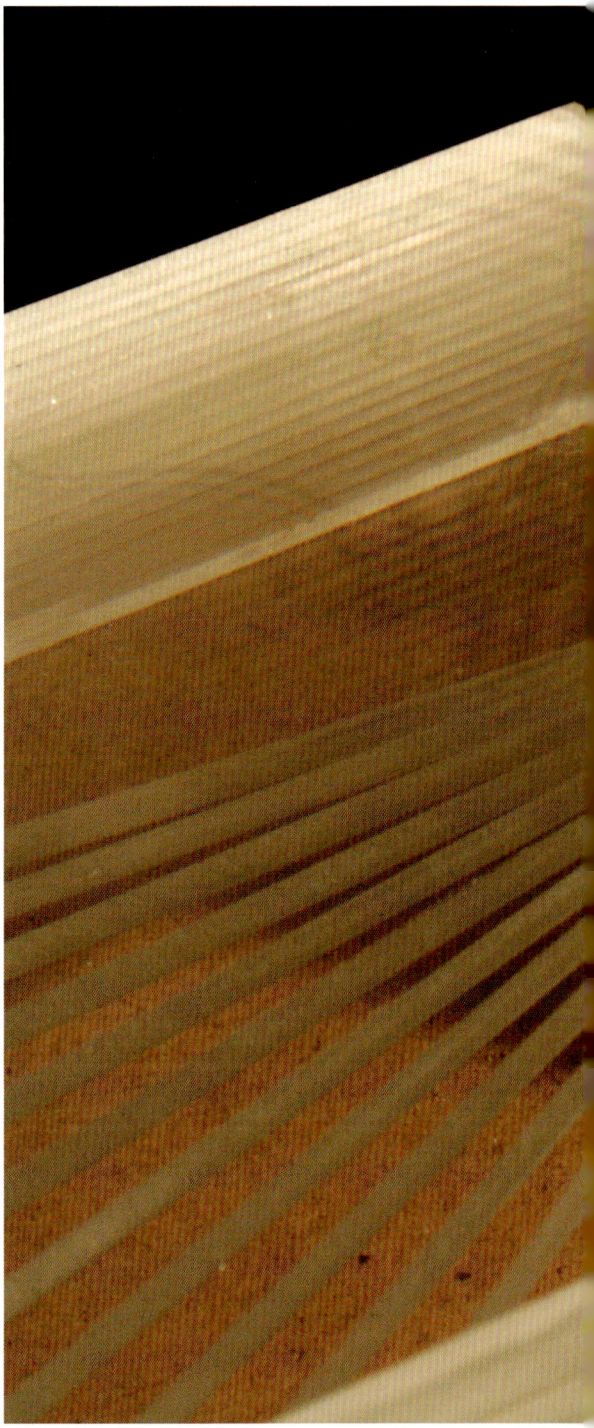

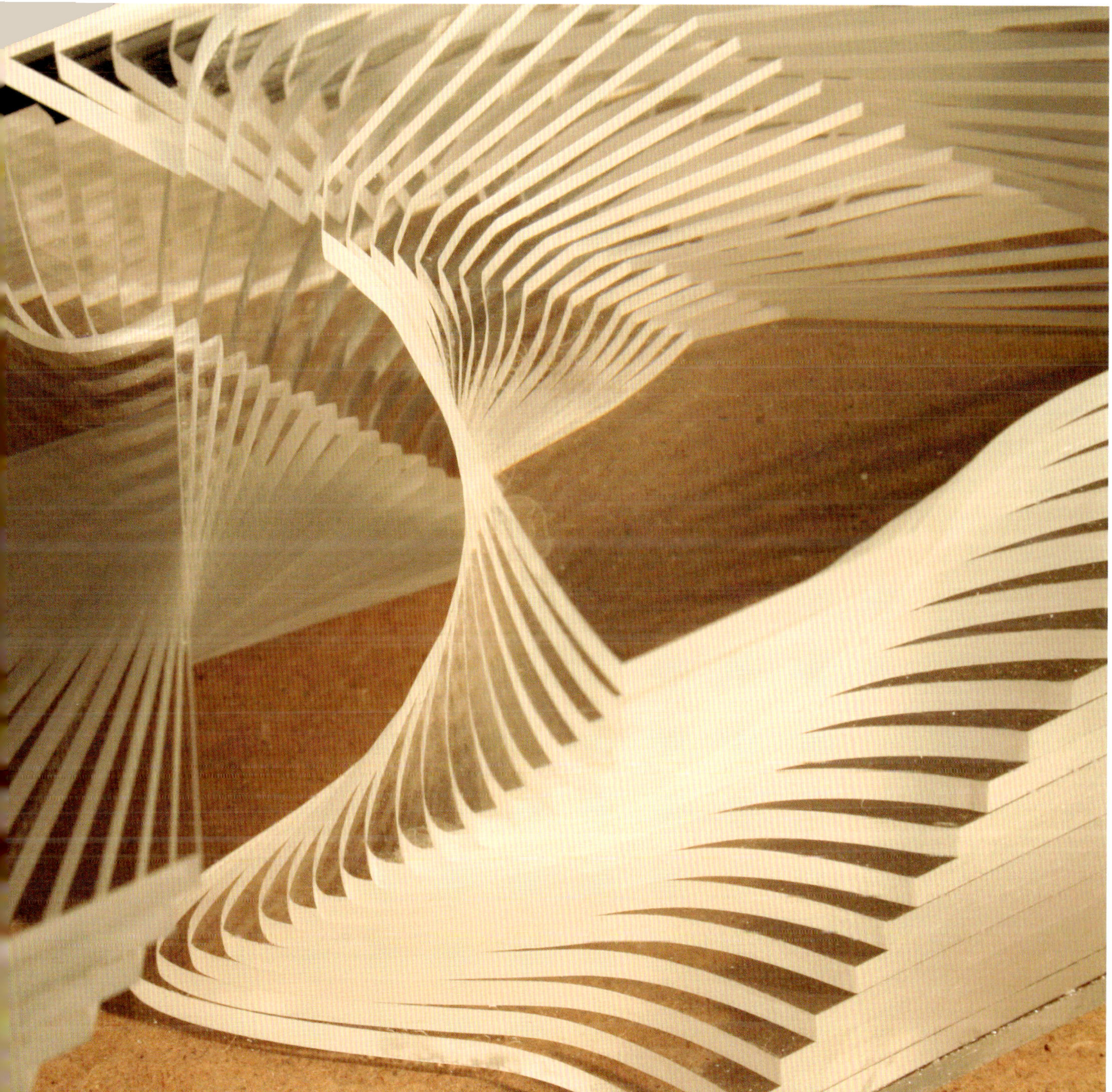

SELECTED EXCERPTS

First Interstate Bank Tower: A Note on the Architectonics of Folding
Henry Cobb
Architectural Design: Folding in Architecture
West Sussex: John Wiley & Sons, 1993
pp. 111–112

Bending is a manipulative strategy of objects. Folding is a manipulative property of surfaces. For example, when we refer to a sheet of paper as being folded we are engaging in an elision. The full statement would be that the sheet of paper is being bent while each of its surfaces is being folded. It is important to understand that the fold in one surface is distinctly separate from the fold in the other. We feel justified, because paper is dimensionally thin, in eliding these distinctions by compressing the statement "the paper is being bent and its two surfaces folded" into "the paper is being folded."

However, when we increase the material thickness from that of paper (+/−1/100") to that of building wall construction (6" minimum) we can no longer afford to elide these distinctions: we must acknowledge explicitly that the wall as a constructed object is being bent, and hence that we will achieve an architectonic manifestation of folding only to the extent that we can locate the visible architecture of the wall on a single plane corresponding to the wall's outer surface...

The primary purpose of this note is not to argue why we would desire the architectural manifestation of folding, but to explicate how it can be achieved through a rigorous architectural treatment of materials and space. In the First Interstate Bank Tower the fold has been developed as an architectural response to the contingencies of commercial development. Here, the fold is considered from within a discipline of materiality and does not begin with an ideology of folding.

1 An architecture of folding is by definition an architecture of surface. Therefore, the first requirement is that the constructional elements that make up the surface to be folded must be assembled in such a way that they are manifested only on that surface. This is more of a challenge than it may seem, as the components of buildings by necessity have varying depths yet the fold can occur at only one surface. So, if a fold is to occur at the scale of a building rather than the scale of a piece of paper, it has to be assembled out of pieces which have depth in themselves and are set into a structure with depth also. When giving architectural form to these methods of construction through a strategy of folding, all constructional elements have to be reduced, in terms of their expressive capacity, to a single surface.

2 Buildings exist at a scale so large that they cannot be monolithic like a single piece of paper which is folded or a single stone that is carved. Buildings must be constructed out of pieces. Inevitably, there are joints between these pieces. A fundamental rule for an architectural manifestation of folding is that the folding must never occur at a joint between the elements which make up the surface to be folded.
A joint is a void between two pieces and cannot be folded. Any fold which coincides with a joint is not a fold but

the manipulation of two separate pieces. A fold does not exist in the interval between elements but describes their shared surface. The pleasure of the fold is that it occurs on a shared surface that has the ability to unite elements through manipulation. The fold both flattens and animates; it folds elements together on a continuous plane while differentiating the same surface.

3 The logic of construction suggests that the building components which make up a surface are typically orthogonal; whether the glass panels that actually constitute the surface or the metal frames that support the glass. If the building components are indeed orthogonal in their organization, one way to dramatize vividly the act of folding is to locate the fold on a diagonal. A diagonal fold (in a direction oblique to the orthogonal grid of construction) is inevitably more eloquent than an orthogonal fold (in a direction parallel to the orthogonal grid of construction) which lacks the unpredictable drama of uniting constructional elements with a system oblique to their own order.

SURFACE: EFFECT

ALBEDO

Loss of detail in a continuous surface or system which results in a locally washed out visual effect.

Albedo is a measure of diffuse reflection used by astronomers to gauge the materiality and texture of distant planets and by car designers as a visual index of subtle changes in surface curvature. In both car design and architecture, the albedo or highlight can

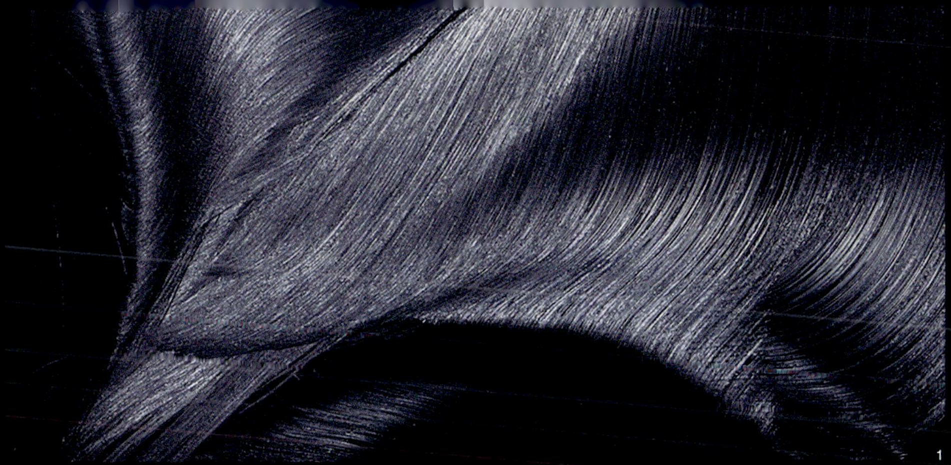

1

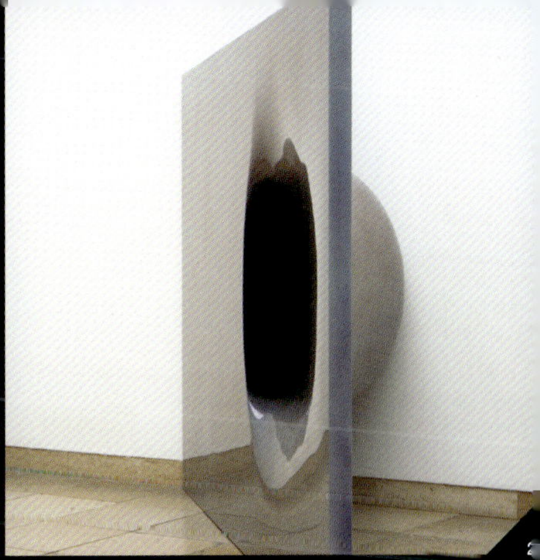

2

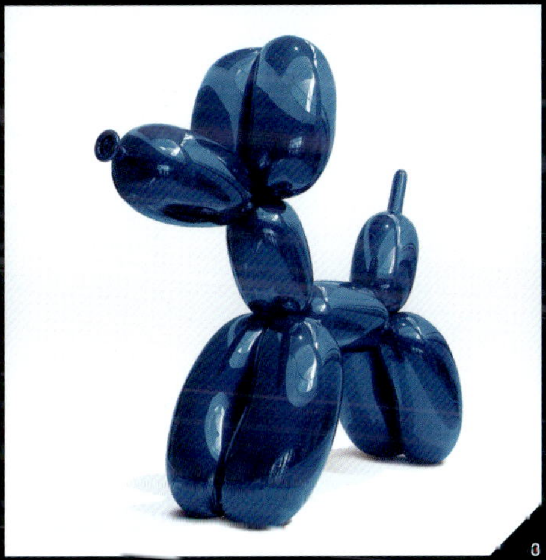

3

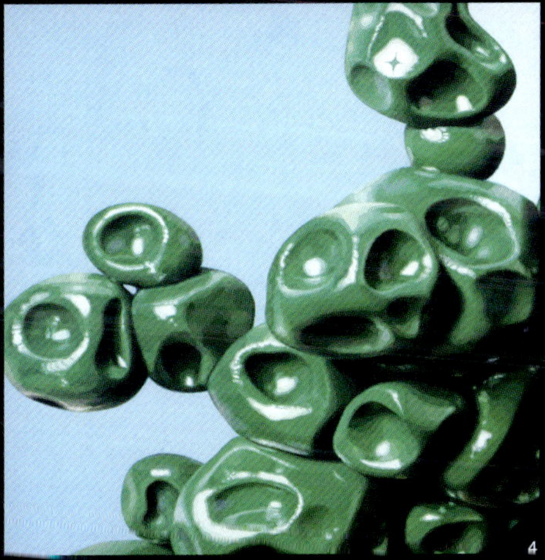

4

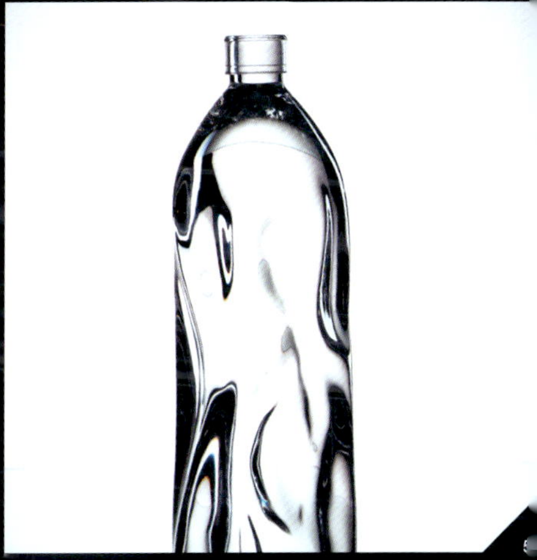

5

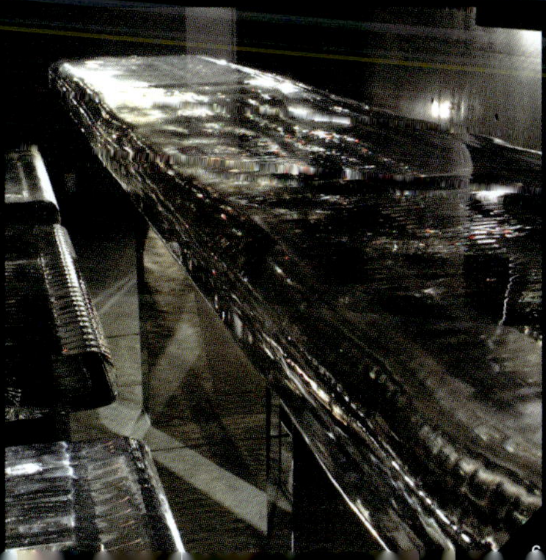

6

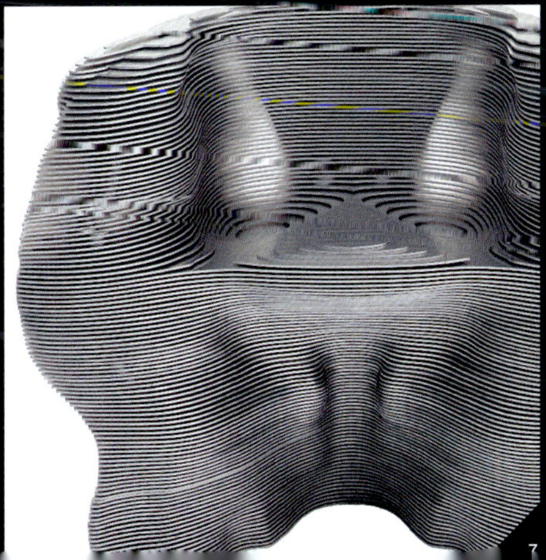

7

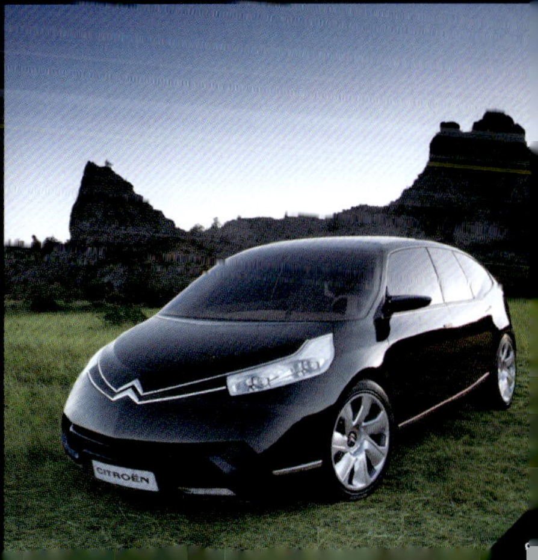

Peter Vikar
Red Bull Pavilion
2006

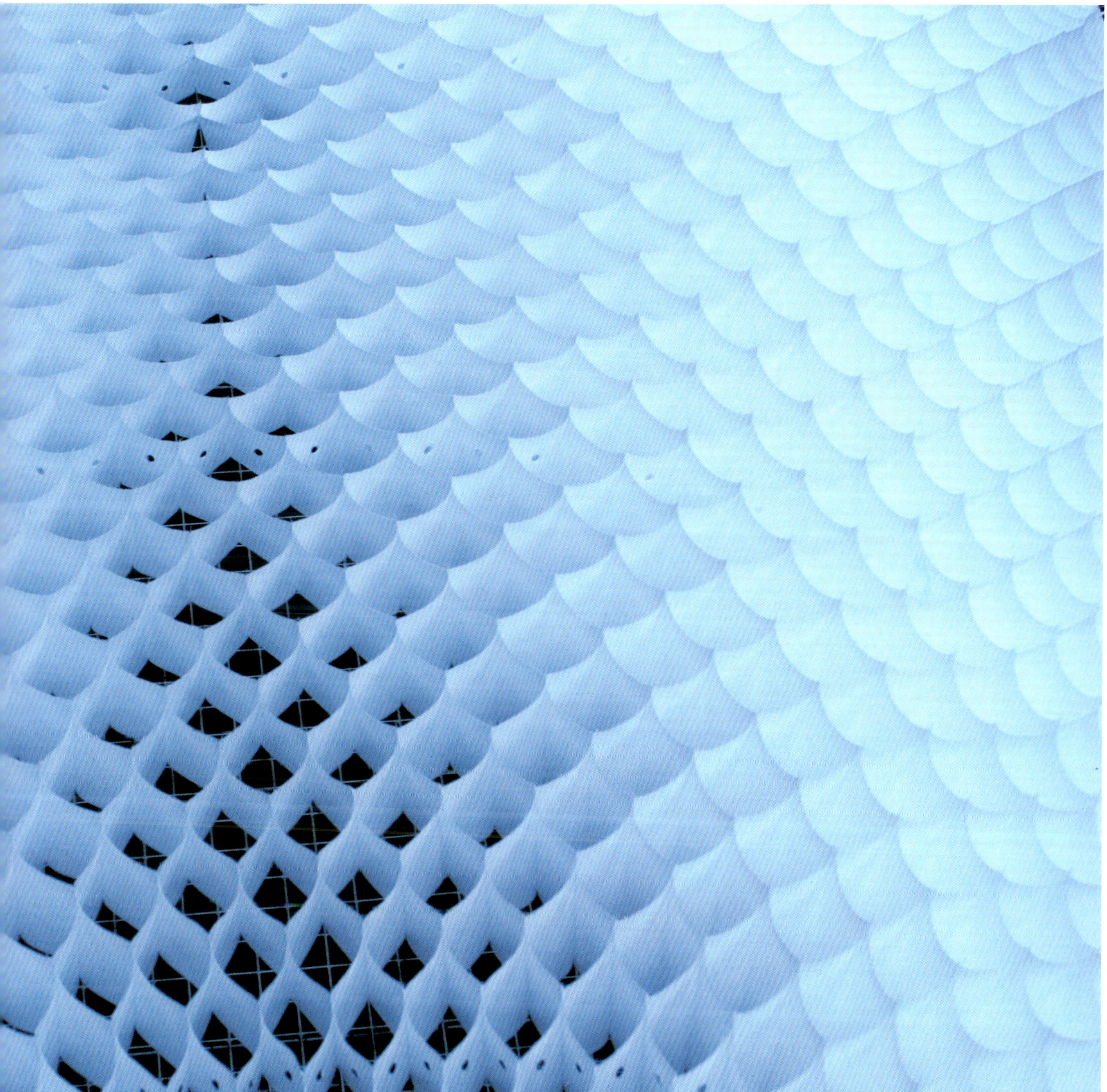

Nora Graw and Julia Körner
Car Design Center
2006

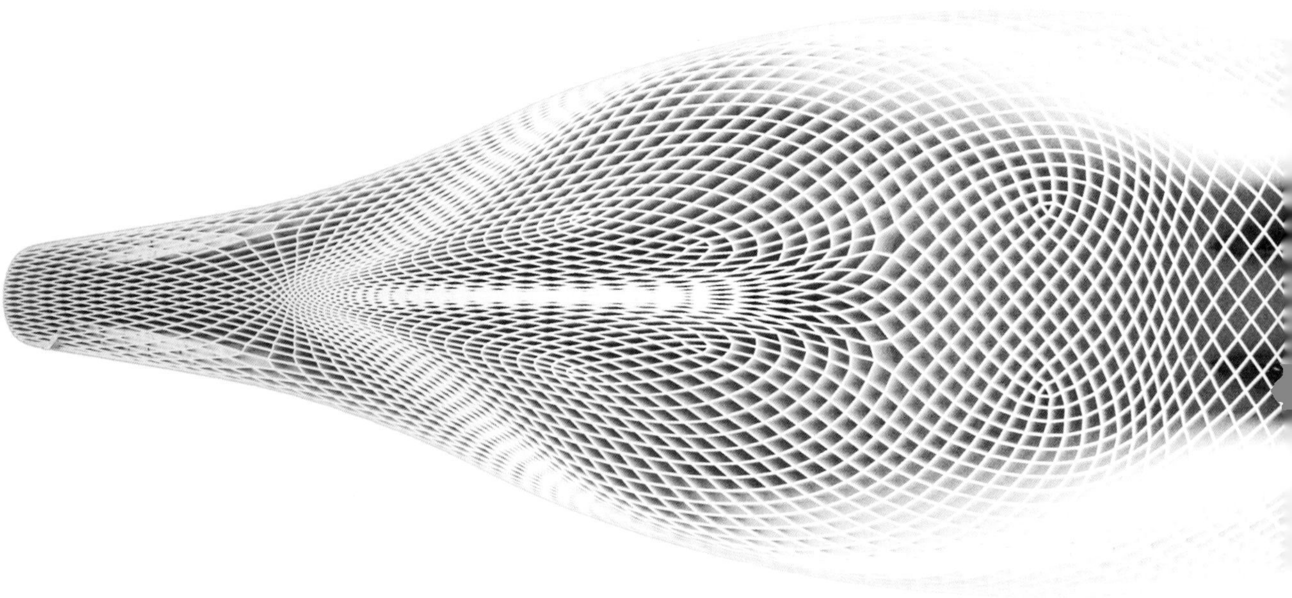

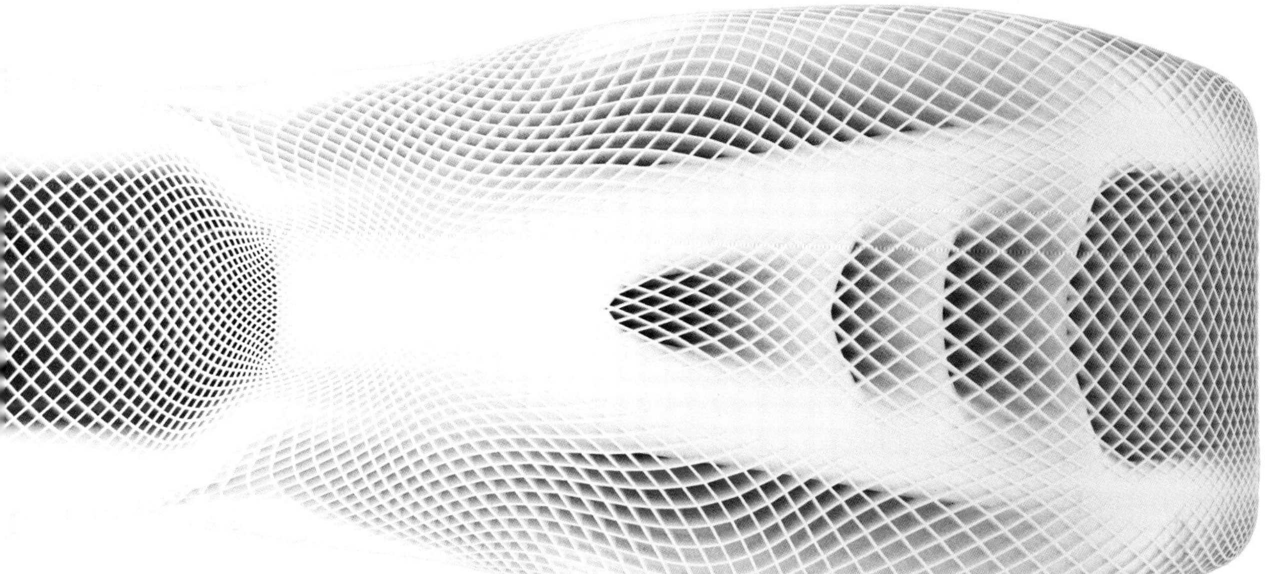

Bika Rebek
Bank
2008

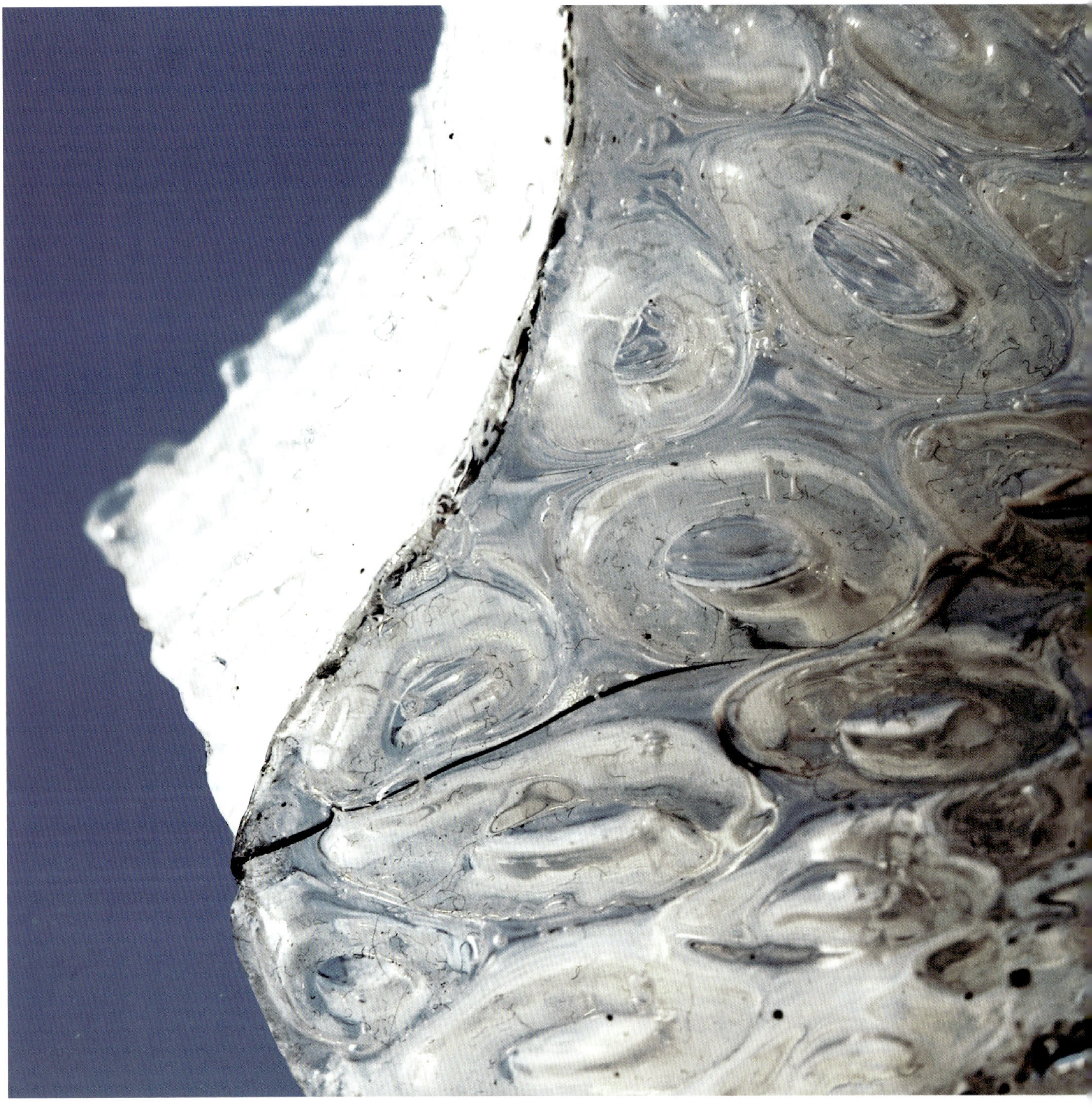

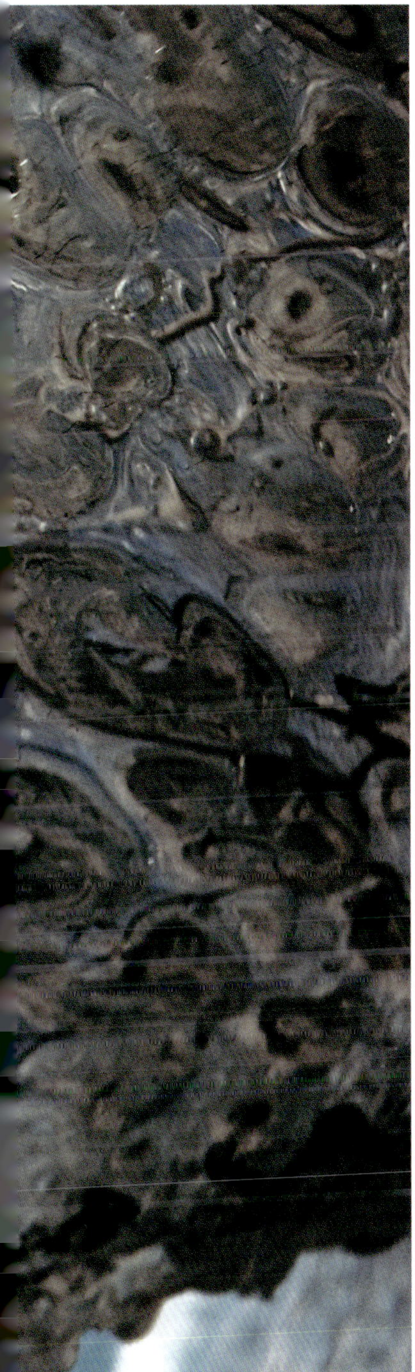

Julia Körner
Bank
2008

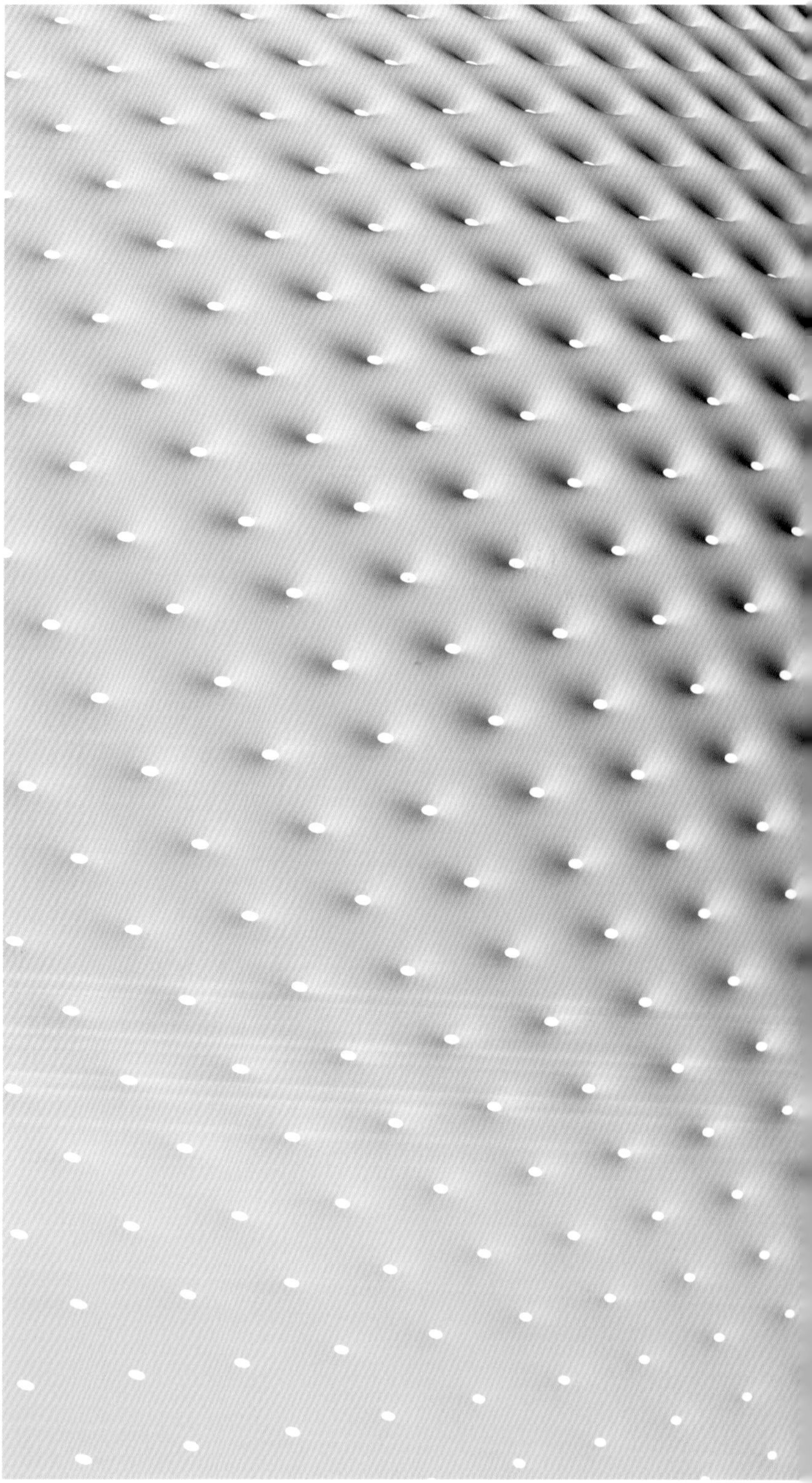

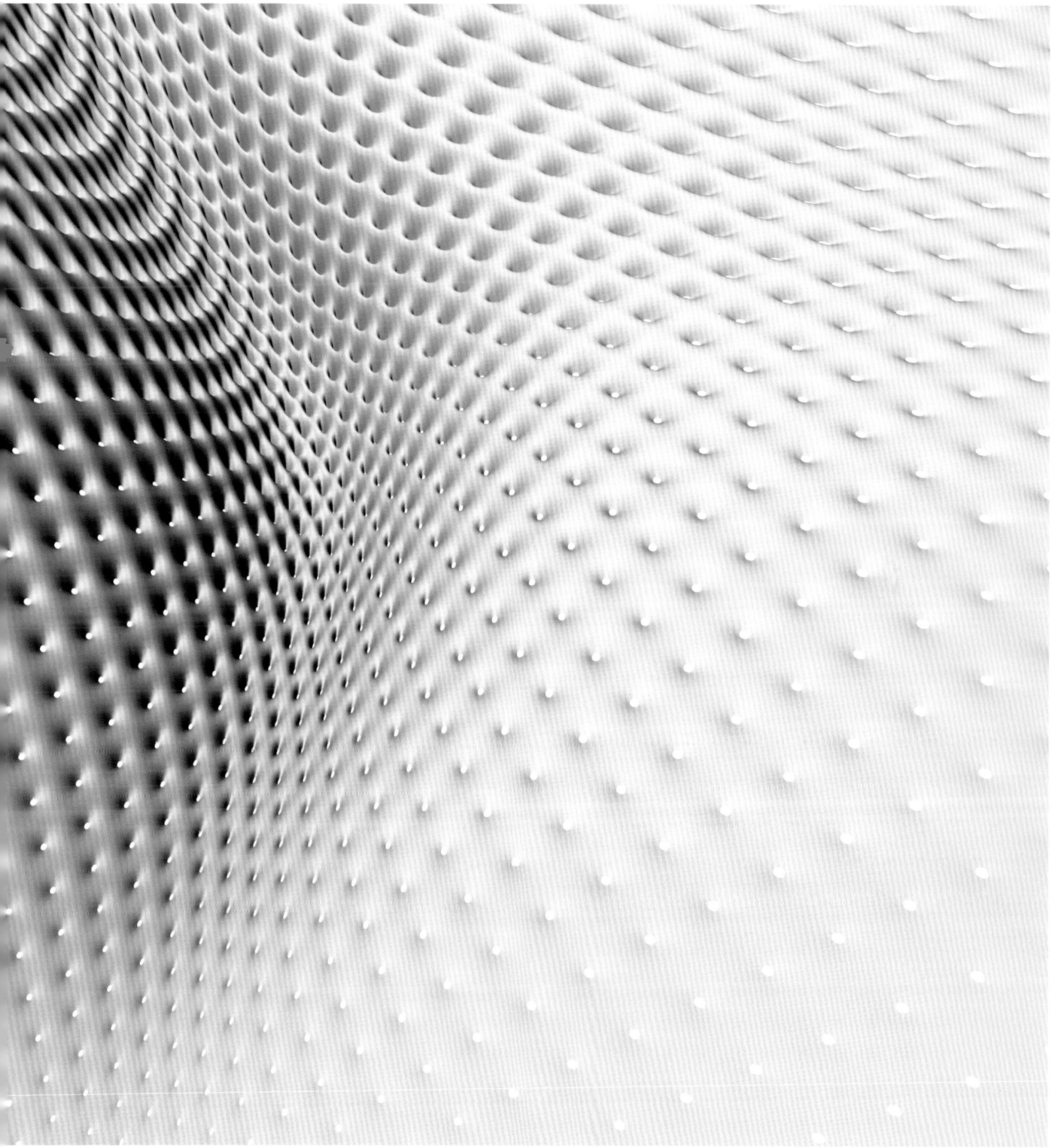

SELECTED EXCERPTS

A Culture of Surface
Chris Bangle
Greg Lynn Form
New York: Rizzoli, 2008
p.44

Given that our product must be unmistakably emotional it follows that its surfaces must likewise be so. The methodologies of car surfacing were invented and codified during the second great paradigm of car design, which lasted from the late 1920s until the 1970s. Before that time car design was about post-and-lintel constructions of much wood and little steel, stiff "houses on wheels" with porch steps on the side, an eave hanging out from the front, and a garden statue out on the end of the fence (the cab, with a running board, roof visor, and hood ornament). Not that this was inadequate, the whole industry was just beginning to climb the Maslovian charts and most customers were happy for an alternative to ol' Dobbins. Vehicle formalism owed more to Pullman trains than to carriages, which often featured complex curved shapes, colorful surfacing, and an amazing proportional variety. Carriage flamboyance was not suited for mass production as it was practiced at the time.

The skill sets of the naval draftsman were needed to direct even the hand-formed coachworks from the horse-power days, but it was the transition in car design to clay or plaster modeling in the 1930s that created modern surfacing techniques. These combined the mathematical precision of hull lofting with the expressive formal freedom of the sculptor. The new economic and social customer context was fast paced and future oriented, and exciting hydrodynamic forms were translated into sweeping lines and aerodynamic steel teardrops. If it was good for yachts, it must be good for cars, and form enthusiastically followed function. As new visual references appeared—Fighter plane tail fins! How speedy can you look?—they were adapted to the symmetrical barrel-like hulls of the vehicles. The first real car design studios came into existence in which the precision of orthographic projection was meshed with the exploratory nature of clay carving. Sculpture and lofting are only compatible if masterful discipline is exercised, and a tradition of "highlighting" for reflection control and "theoreticals" for geometrical construction was passed along from generation to generation within the studios. This surfacing culture lives on in modern car design studios in both their handwork and computer-modeling practices.

Atmosphere
Helene Furjan
Crib Sheets
New York: Monacelli Press, 1995
p.71

The contemporary explosion of digital media has generated a twofold erosion of Guy Debord's culture of spectacle: an "overexposure" to the flows of information and images that creates a loss of registration (a kind of digital ADD); and a shift away from spectatorship toward immersion and interaction, which breaks down the authority of the viewing subject and engages other senses—an experiential understanding of space concerned with atmosphere and effect.

Such a sensory understanding of architecture has its links to the interest in 'effect' manifested in Baroque and Enlightenment architecture, which was rediscovered by its theorists in Gothic cathedrals. From mysterious lights and moody atmospheres to the kinetics of light and shade on three-dimensional surfaces, effects were tied to temporal or climatic changes and the mobility of the spectator. Such "architectures of shadow" or sensation reached their maturity only recently, in the interactive multimedia environments of the Eameses' exhibitions, in Constant's New Babylon and its legacy in the works of Archigram and Koolhaas, or in the vibrating color-fields of Verner Panton's interiors: a flux of tunic, erotic and strongly affective atmospheres, immersing their visitors in a psychedelic vibe (architectural "happenings"). All of these "environments"—what they are more than they are spaces—in their very deployment of multisensory effects, operate in a perceptual paradigm that rejects the authorizing mode of the spectacle: distraction.

Distraction, posited by Walter Benjamin so many years ago as the mode of architectural perception, is not so much a peripheralizing inattention as it is a mood.

Countering absorption, a state of observation matched to a much older visual paradigm, with a synesthetic form of perception that is optical and tactile, distractive and immersive, a distracted attention requires an active engagement with the matrix of information flowing toward the viewing subject. An organization that operates like the rapid jump cut of an MTV kind of attention, distraction is created by flooding the visual field with information, demanding, as a result, not a hyperconcentration, but an absorption that pushes perception to its limits: a distracted concentration, or a concentrated distraction. Like the diffuse fields of Diller and Scofidio's Blur building, such a perceptual mode is at once oversaturated and undersaturated, "overexposed" and "underexposed" in Paul Virilio's terminology.

What You Surface is What You Get
Sylvia Lavin
Log 1
New York: Anyone Corporation, 2003
p.103—104

In his attempt to evict subject matter from what he called avant-garde art, Clement Greenberg focused attention on the surface of painting. It's not that the surface didn't exist in the discourses on art before Greenberg, but Greenberg made the surface isomorphic with painting for the first time. He considered everything extraneous to medium specificity unless it could be brought to bear on the surface Greenberg, in fact, made painting into a surface. Although the intellectual achievement of this reformulation of the history of painting has always been recognized and grappled with, Greenberg's narrow formalism has largely been discredited within art history and within the field of painting itself. As panting recaptured content, became three-dimensional, and morphed into new genres, Greenberg's surface got covered over with a whole host of new materials, issues, and problems.

But as painters were leaping into other territories, architecture began to give Greenberg a second wind. Architects have been discovering the surface that painters abandoned. From Sigfried Giedion to Colin Rowe, writers have often described architecture as a race to keep up with the other arts and with painting in particular; both Giedion and Rowe understood modern architecture to be perpetually seeking to reproduce the inventions of cubist painting. But this is not another speculation on why architecture is slower than other disciplines or why it always moves at a losing pace behind painting, or technology, or other supposedly more advanced timekeepers. Rather, it is an attempt to return to the question of discipline and medium specificity in terms that work with rather than against the surface accumulations that repulsed Greenberg. Architects and artists are today increasingly interested in the extra-expressive effects of their mediums and in the very superfluousness that Greenberg denigrated as kitsch and thus as nondisciplinary. This shift in sensibility neither resolves nor renders questions about disciplines irrelevant; it only makes them more pressing and numerous. Is the new architectural interest in surface concerned with the same old surface of painting that Greenberg uncovered? Could there be more than one surface that lies in a single plane but that is driven by dissimilar discursive traditions? Can we theorize disciplinarily when differences between disciplines appear to occupy exactly the same surface?

SURFACE: EFFECT

DIE CUTTING

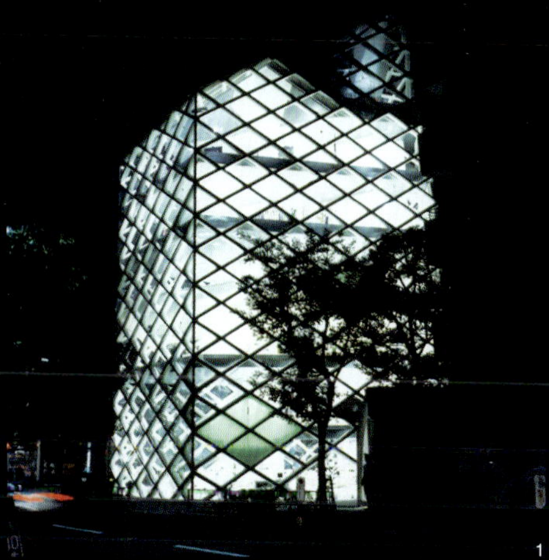
1

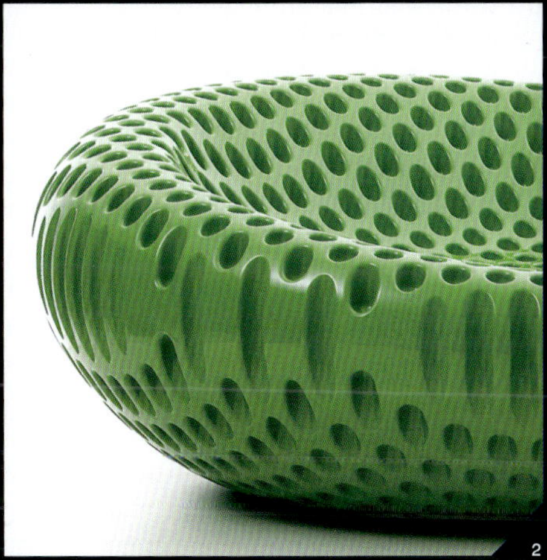
2

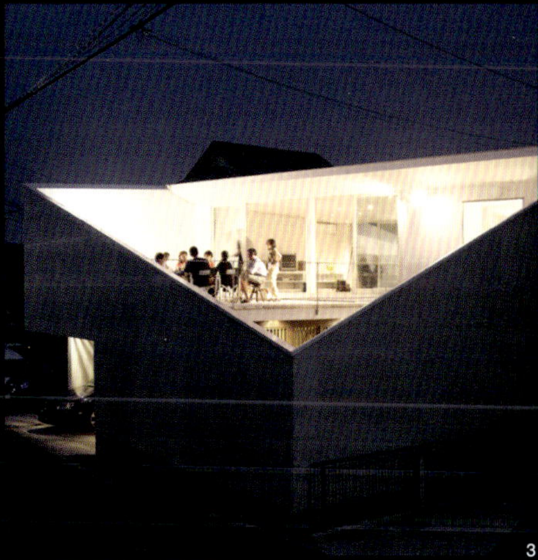
3

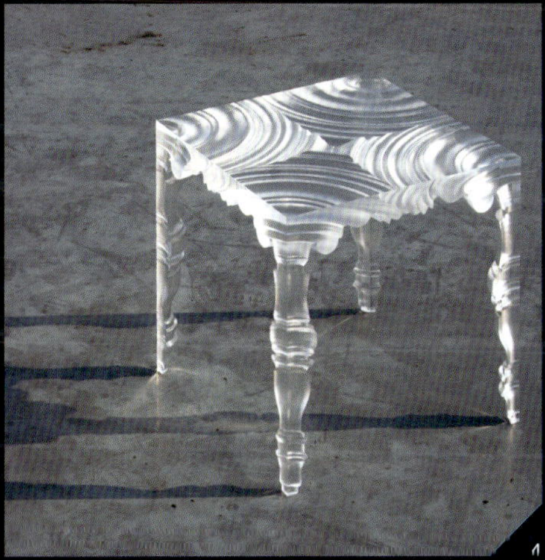
4

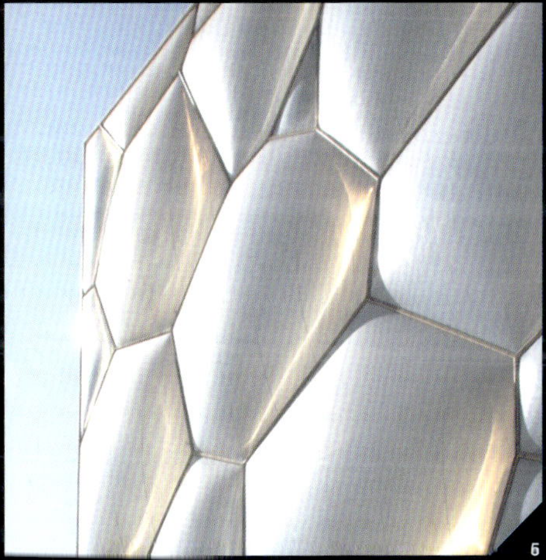
5

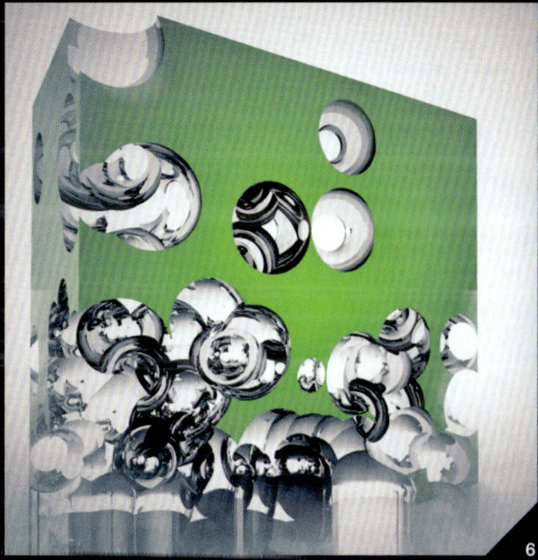
6

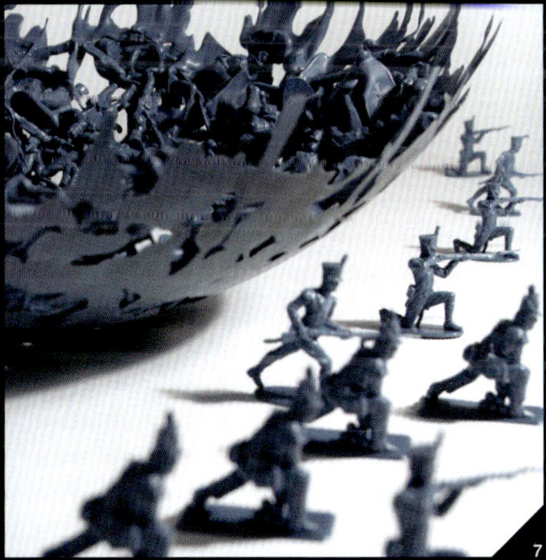
7

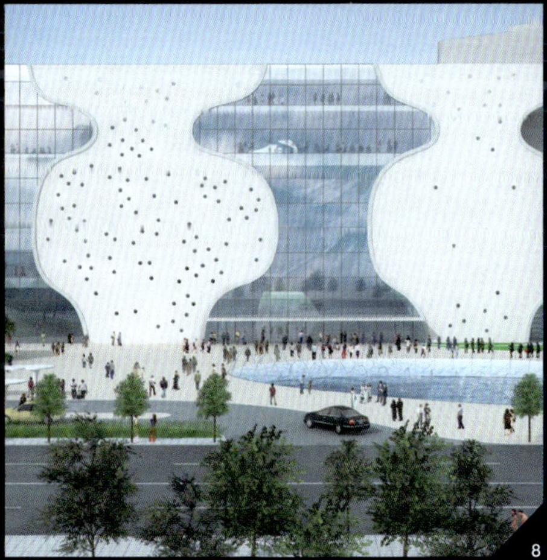
8

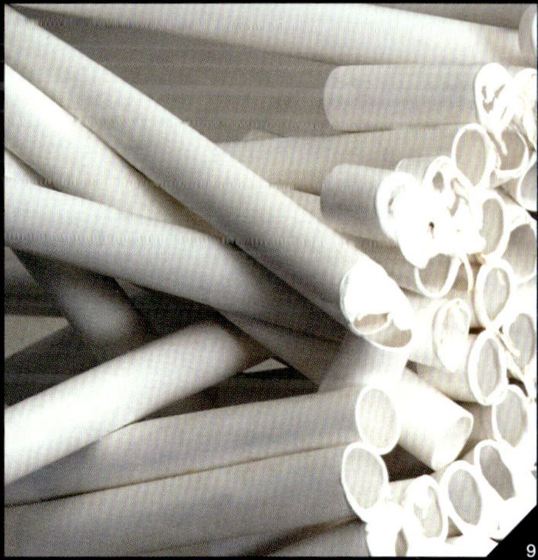
9

Miklos Deri
Vertical Case Study
2004

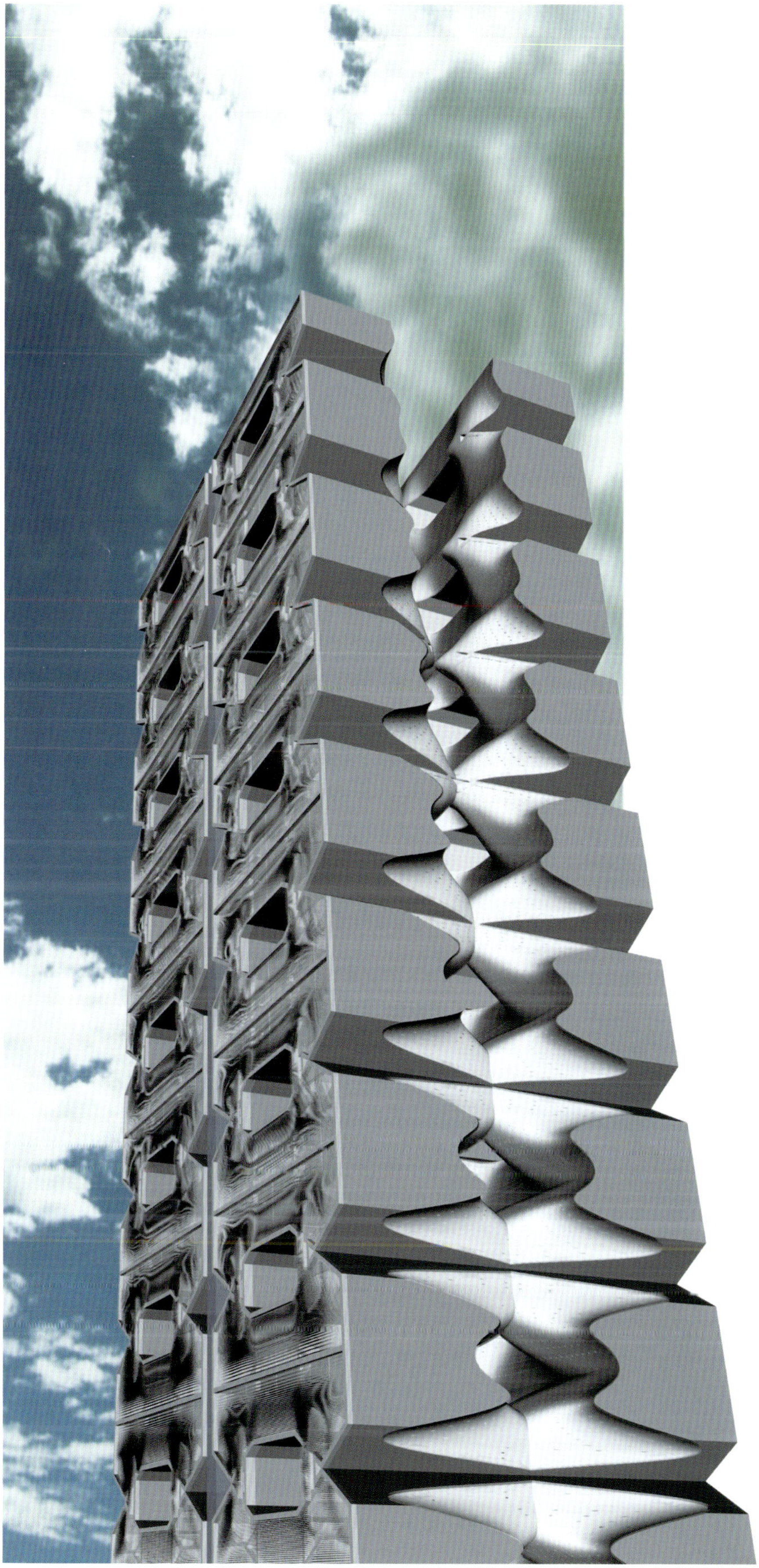

Anna Edthofer and Maja Ozvaldic
Car Design Center
2006

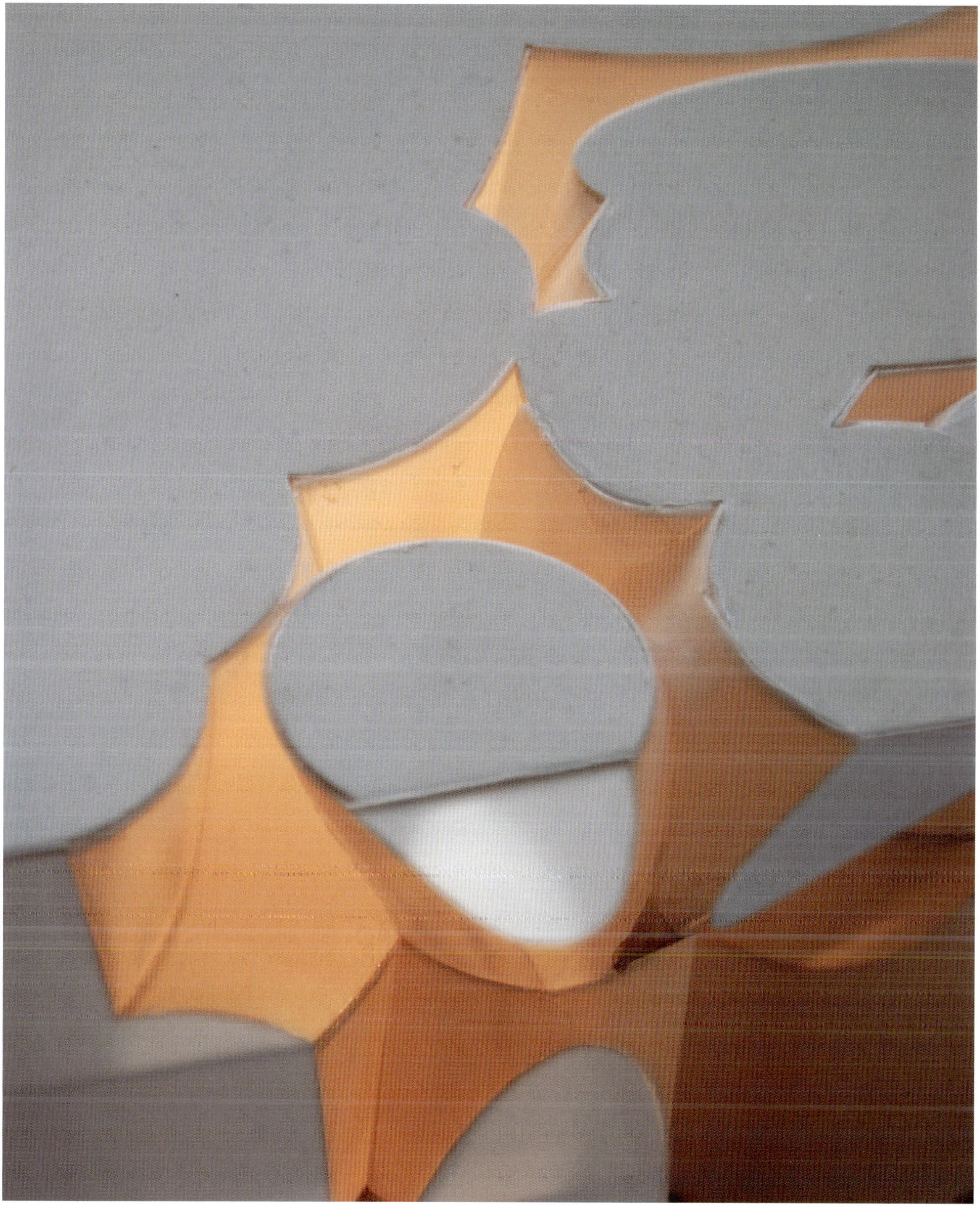

Cornelia Faisst
Diploma: City Centre TV, Vienna
2006

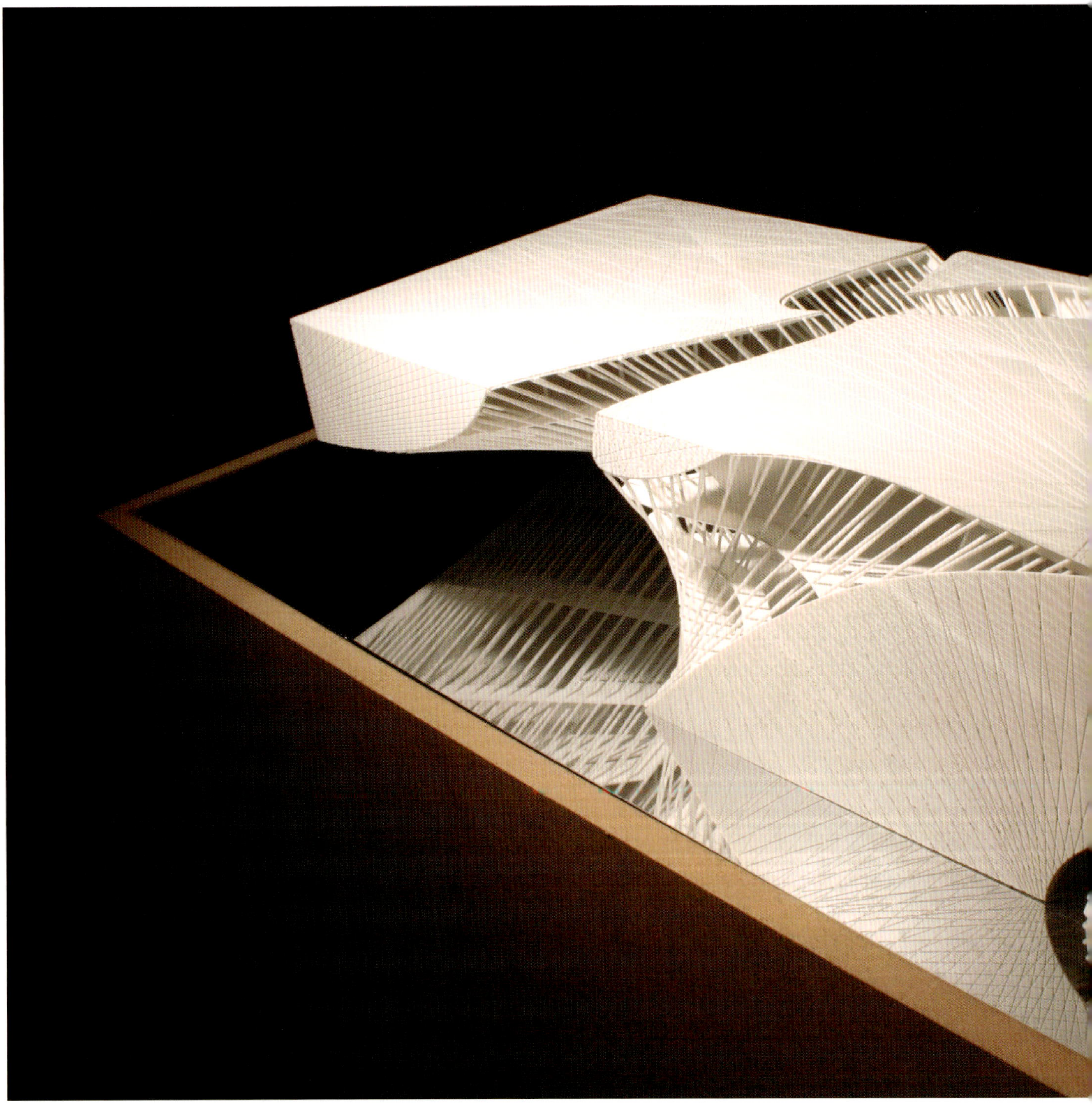

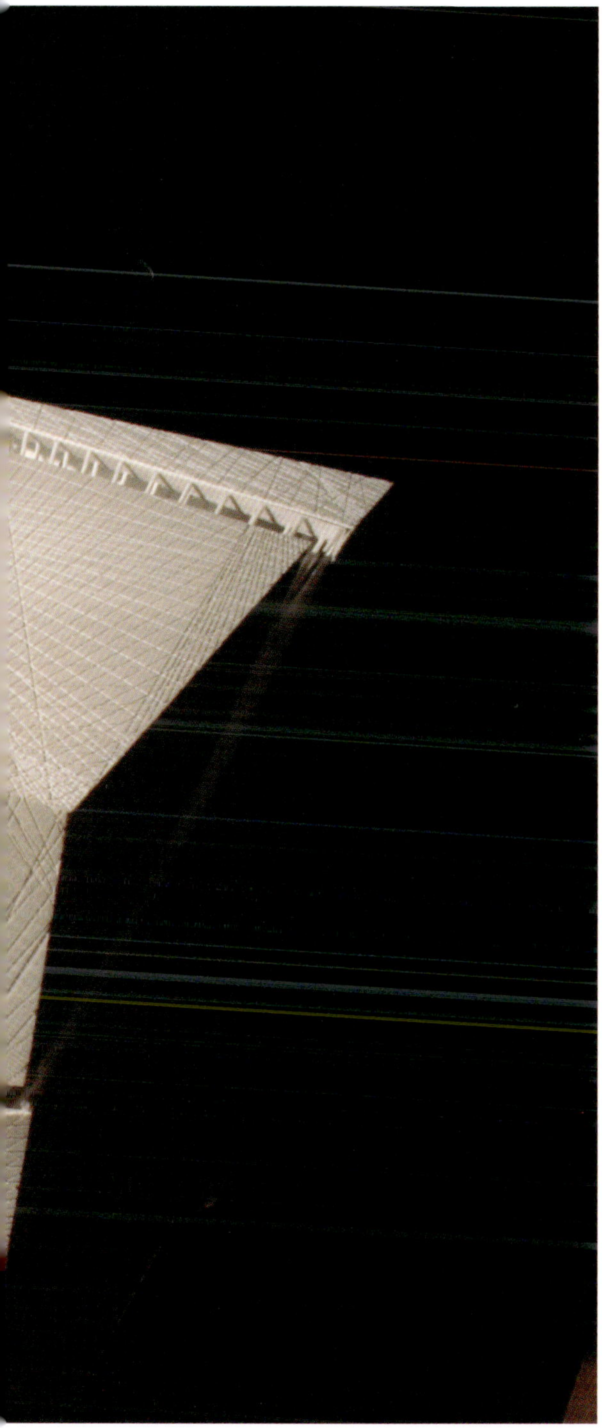

SELECTED EXCERPTS

Geometry
Preston Scott Cohen
Crib Sheets
New York: Monacelli Press, 1995
pp. 127–128

It is possible today for the architect to conceive of a precise relationship—one, moreover, that is wholly unprecedented—between the configurations of geometry and architecture, a relationship marked by mutual agitation and reciprocal alteration. But at present, this remains a provisional hypothesis. Foundationalist nostalgias aside, it must be admitted that without a firm conception of the epistemological grounds of architecture, no such inventive agitation can take place. For, unlike previous periods when this kind of interaction was able to develop, the absolute foundations of architecture and geometry can no longer be taken for granted.

To begin a new project involving a fertile agitation of architectural forms by means of geometry, it is useful to look at advancements in geometry that began during the Renaissance. The development of seventeenth-century projective geometry can be traced in part to this period when there were indications of an alternative vision of the architecture/geometry interaction: the instrumental, technical advancements in representation and construction-perspective, orthogonal projection, axonometry, stereotomy. This vision could not be realized in practical terms in the succeeding two centuries because projective geometry in the seventeenth century and descriptive geometry at the end of the eighteenth were disembodied and disassociated from architecture. While Renaissance architecture required axiality and grids to manifest hierarchical, centralized forms through perspectivel convergence, projective geometry, for the most part, advanced remotely from the space and discipline of architecture.

Between the Baroque era and the Enlightenment we see two connected developments: the codification of these forms of geometric knowledge—the period that gave birth to the means of intersection between cylinders, cones, ellipsoids, and spheres—and in architecture, the gradual disappearance of nonorthogonal forms as a reflection of the commitment to programmatic standards. The result for architecture was that basic shapes predominated, and in the nineteenth century, though complex geometric techniques were taught to architects, they were hardly used by them. It was in the field of engineering that the techniques of intersection, enabled by stereotomy and projective geometry, were used for the design of machines, ships, trains, etc. In the twentieth century these forms would be transferred back into architecture as iconography and analogy (as opposed to geometric technique) mimicked as a new "machine aesthetic."

There have been several other nostalgic revisions to geometry as an iconographic program in architecture. The fragmentary forms of Deconstructivism set against normative elements such as floors and structural components—thought by architects and theorists to be necessitated by developing technologies, or by the fluidity and indeterminacy of modern life—remain as arbitrary, vague, or imprecise as the compositional methods that lead to “normal” architecture. The claims that these developments are inevitable and necessary or due to advancing technologies in our time are spurious. Indeed, I would argue, those who seek to guarantee the legitimacy of architecture through such claims behave as if they are metaphysicians. Nevertheless, among academic architects today, there is a movement afoot that maintains that the changing circumstances of contemporary life find their implicit architectural equivalence in the form of a blob.

Would it be possible for digital media to shift the emphasis from the iconographic programs of architecture to the development of alternative methodological foundations? True, architecture cannot provide axiomatic foundations comparable to those of complex geometry.

Nevertheless, it is possible today to recognize the autonomy of geometry, and to understand the consequences of disrupting it according to the circumstances of architectural conventions. For example, can the architect intervene in the world of inviolable geometric autonomy? Can the arbitrary (conventional) lines and spatial divisions of practical Euclidean forms merge with the necessary tines and spatial indivisibility of nonorientable geometric figures and their linear intersections? By seeking similar degrees of surface curvature between independent geometric figures—primitive forms such as cones, spheres, cylinders on the one hand, and nonorientable self-intersecting rectangles, self-intersecting one-sided surfaces such as helicoids, and catenoids, on the other—near-tangencies can be achieved, invoking a possible but ultimately unattainable synthesis. This discord parallels the perennial disagreement between geometry and materiality. Only now, what happens to the relationship between inside and outside? How do we contend with this problem programmatically? What are the thermal and material implications and consequences? Finally, do these conditions need to be shaped explicitly or inexplicitly, according to geometric principles that beg these questions? It is the promise of order and the evident struggle under-taken to realize it that is of interest. Perhaps there will be a new “near miss” between the disciplines, another iteration in the ongoing contest: architecture v. geometry.

SURFACE: EFFECT

INJECTION MOLDING

An aggregation of continuously varying modular elements that maintain a hint of the plastic, candy coated aesthetic of the mass production technique.

Injection molding is used to manufacture pieces from thermoplastic by injecting molten plastic into a mold at high pressure. Evoking the trash cans or frisbees made this way infuses architecture with an element of fleeting contemporary pop culture rather than the modernist goal of staid timelessness. The technique inspires a desire for high gloss and minimal seams, but its driving implication is an aesthetic of aggregated nonstandard small-scale parts. Fundamentally, these parts are not based on an ideal model; the variation and movement within the series is as noteworthy as similarities between repeated parts.

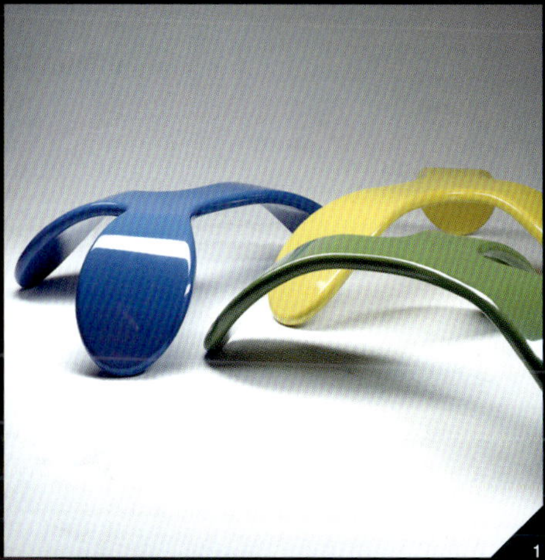
1

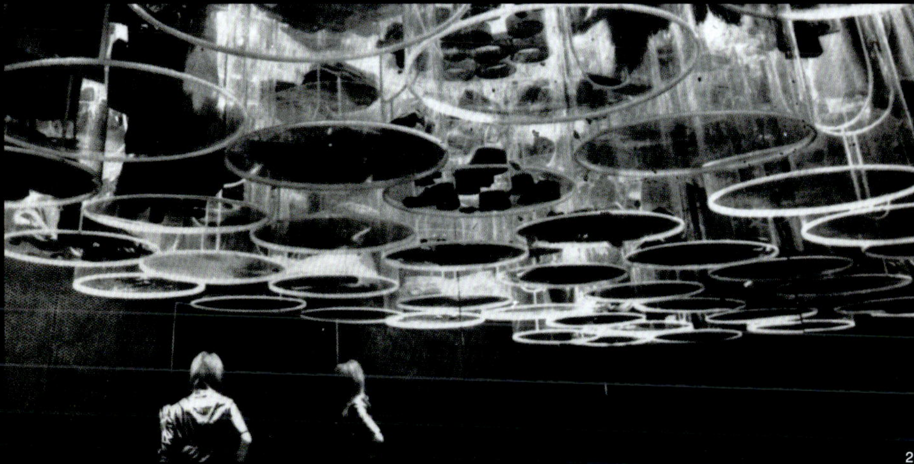
2

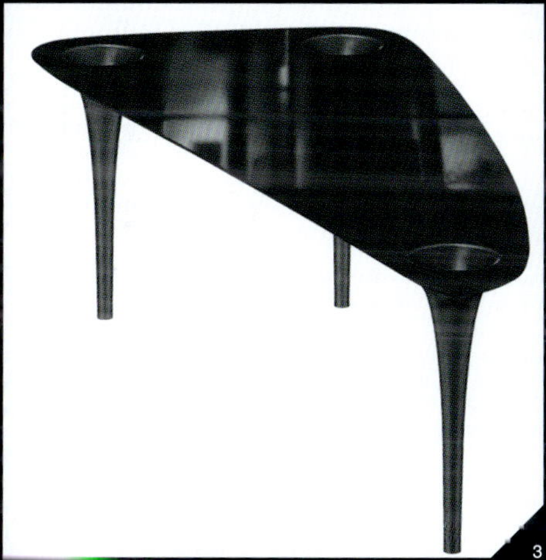
3

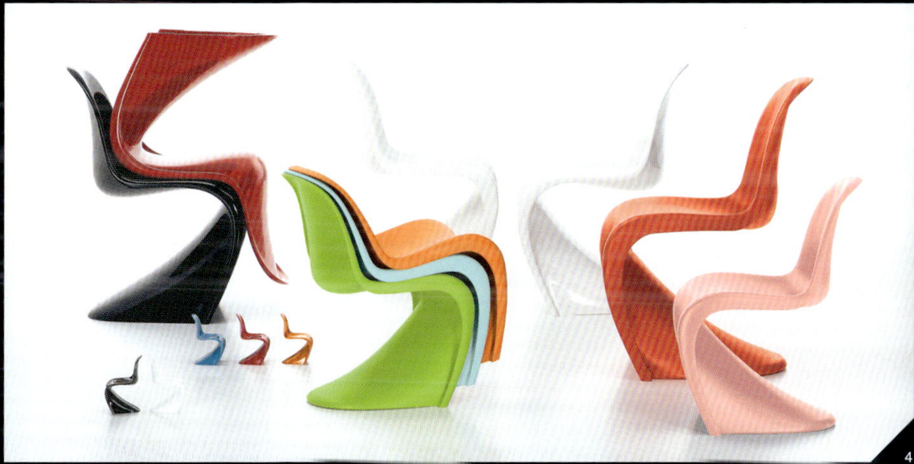
4

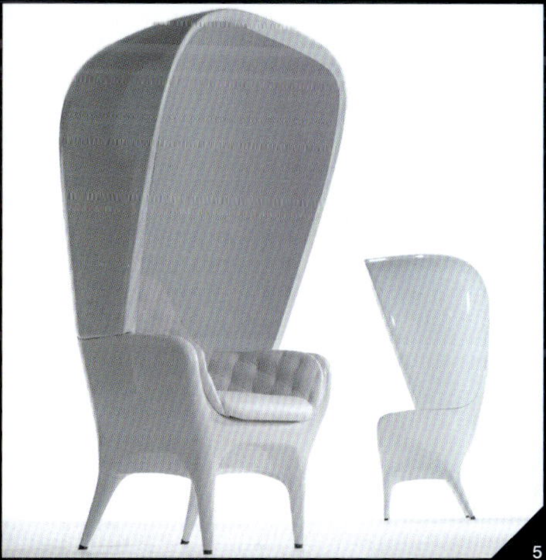
5

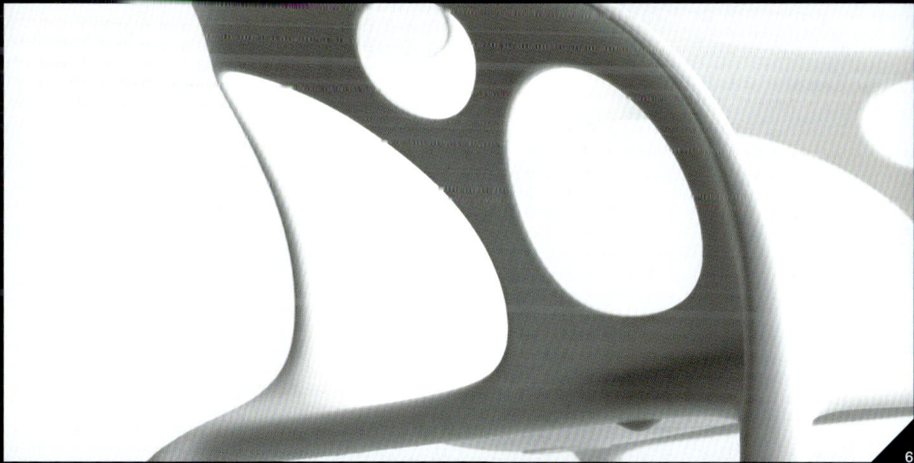
6

Mirko Daneluzzo, Igor Szuba and Verena Lihl
Factory for Today
2008

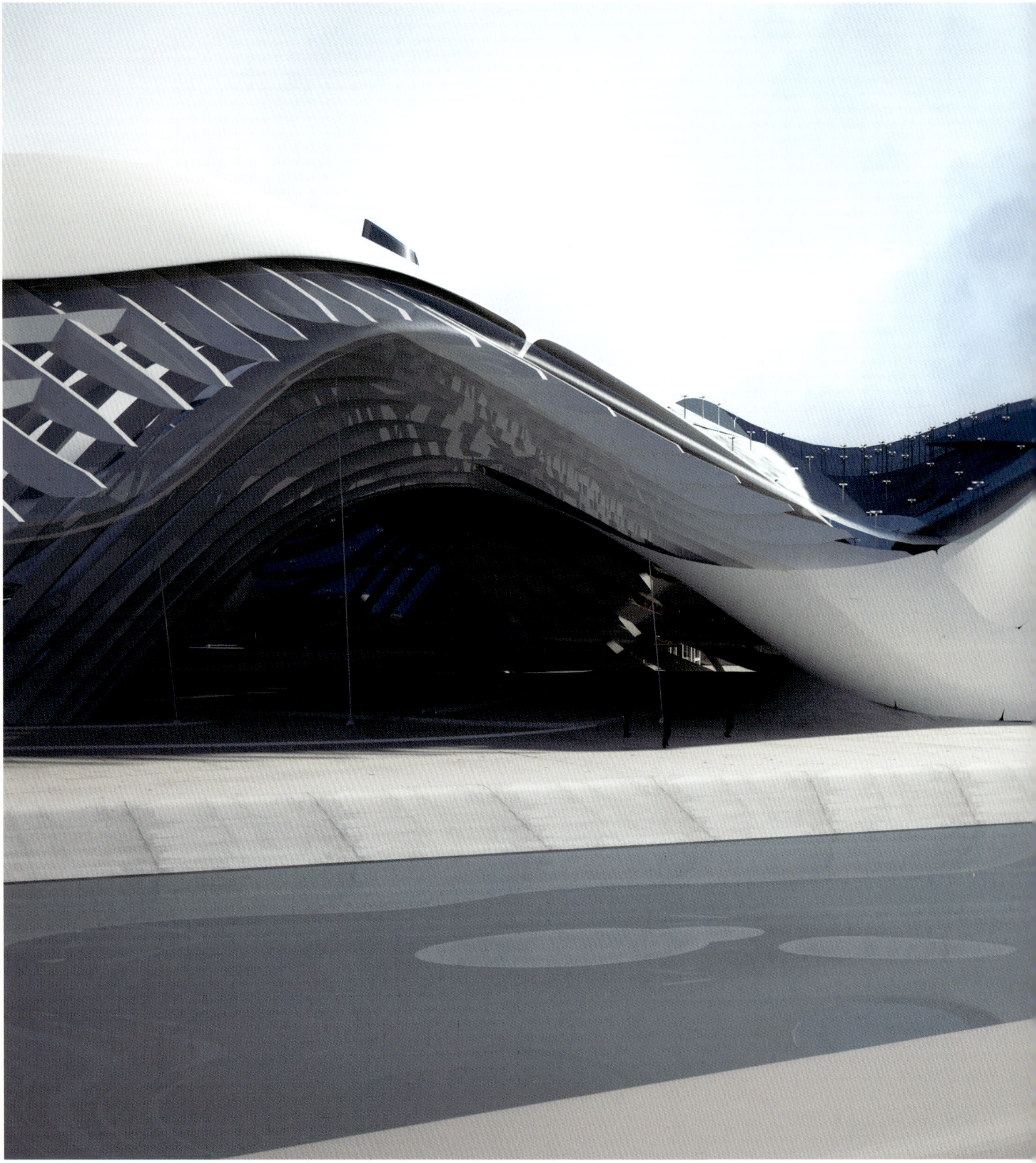

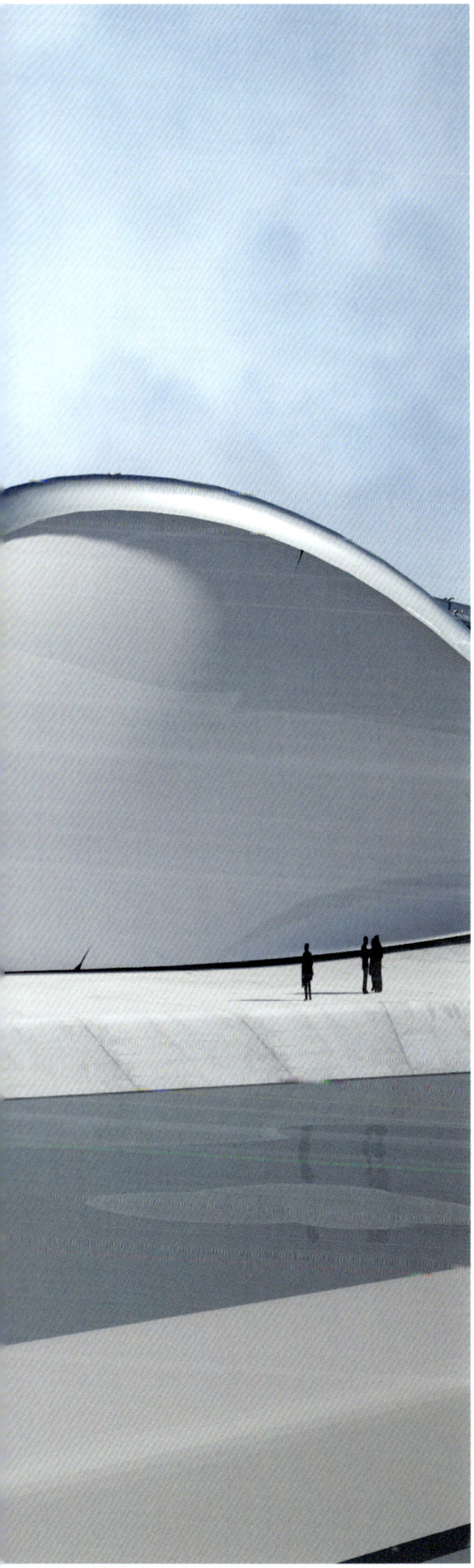

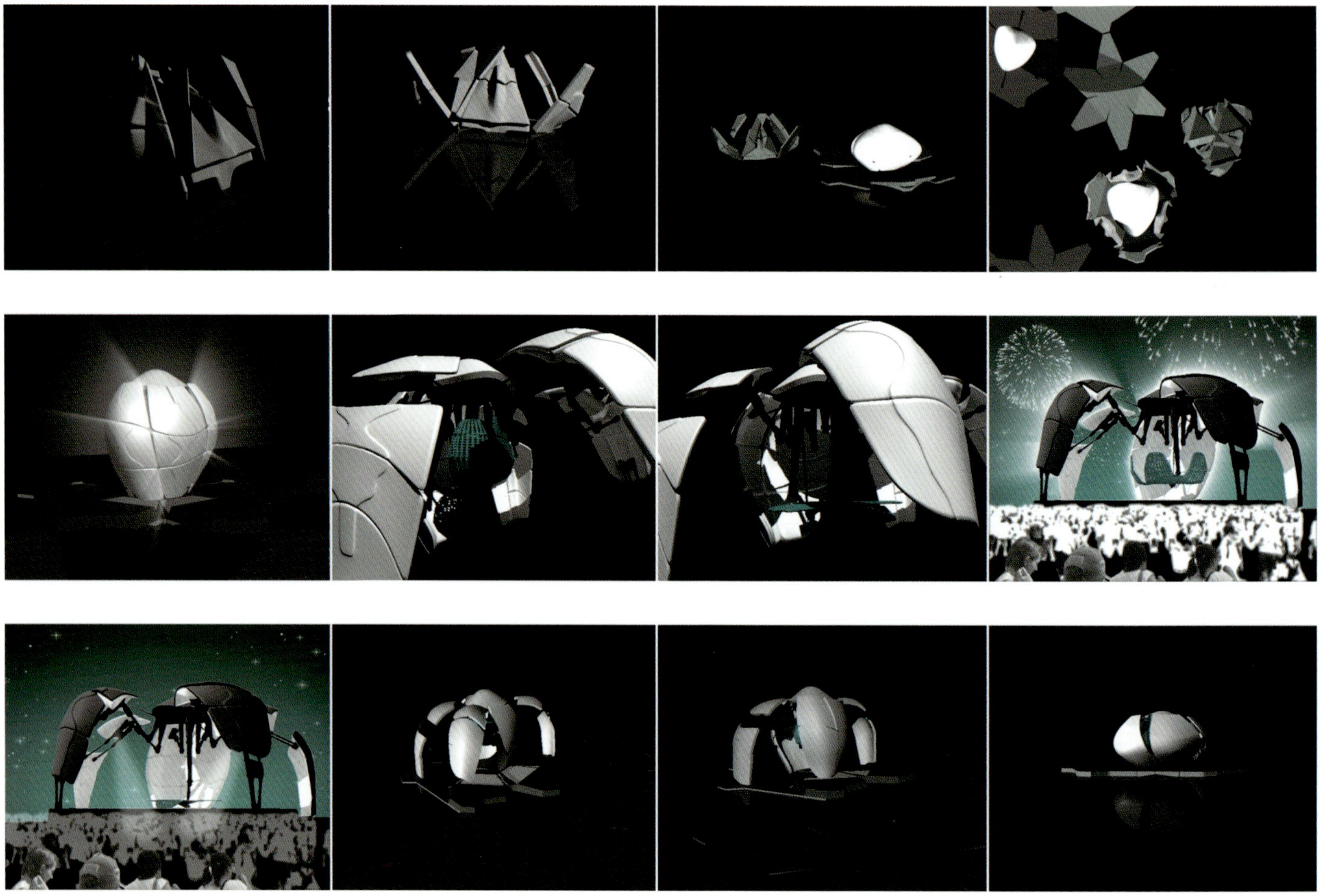

Maja Ozvaldic and Sarah Schneider
Giant Robot (video stills)
2006

Bence Pap
Giant Robot (video stills)
2006
(Photo credit: Getty Images)

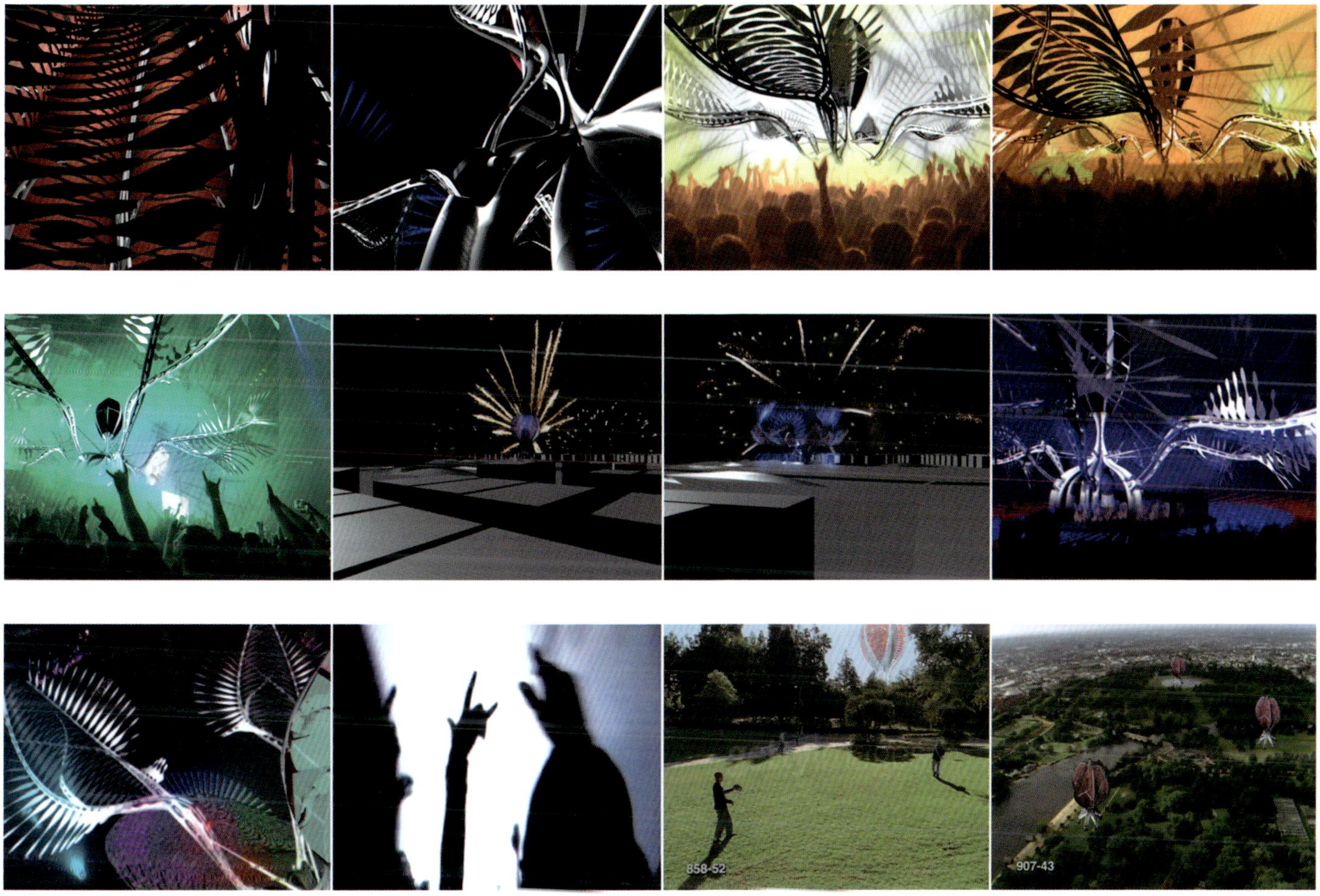

Claudia Cavallar
Diploma: Piscine Jackson Pax
2005

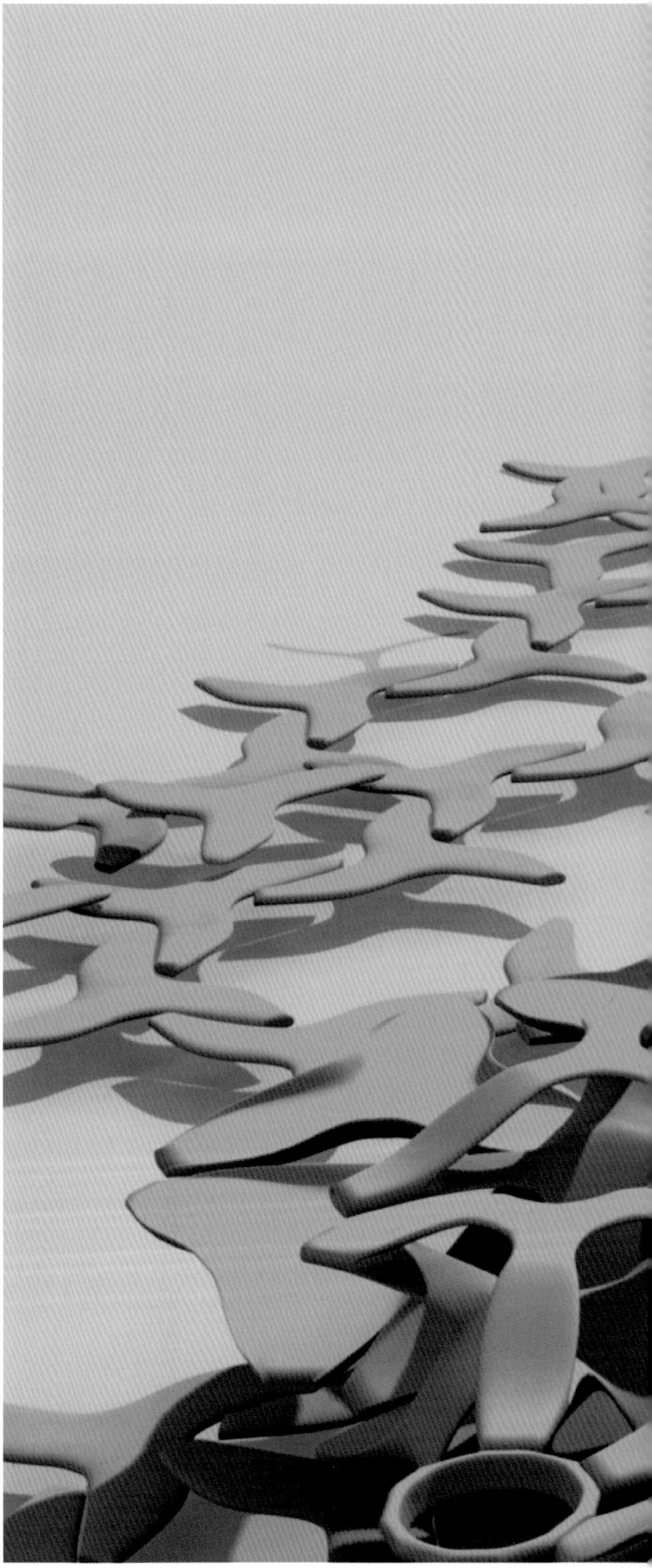

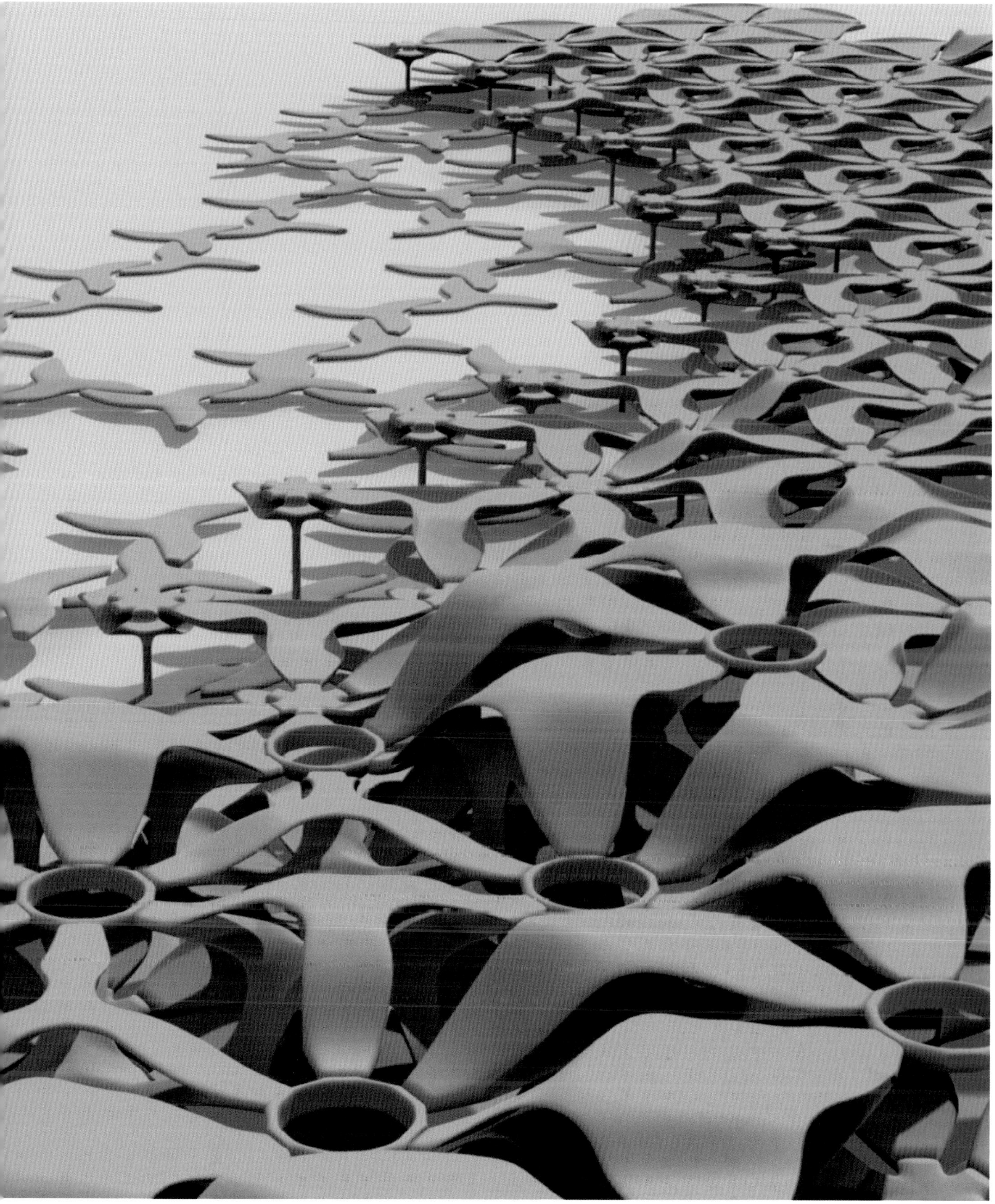

SELECTED EXCERPTS

Mutant Materials in Contemporary Design
Paola Antonelli
New York: Museum of Modern Art, 1995
p.120

Plastics represent the distance that a century of technological progress has put between craftsmanship and industrialization. Polymers are the artificial materials par excellence and can only be formed in a malleable state. Unfortunately, the production processes almost always require expensive tools. Among the exceptions are polyurethane resins, which are cured at ambient temperatures and shaped with simple composite or wood molds... But the processing of polymers often involves a more costly and complex technology. Nevertheless, today's manufacturers have been able to achieve some degree of freedom within a specific production cycle in order to create more distinctive objects and better satisfy market needs. In addition, computer-aided design and computer-aided manufacturing (CAD/CAM) programs simulate the flow of the materials in the molds and predict the final outcome prior to production; they are a virtual-reality version of the craftsman's exploratory work and mitigate the burden of industrialization.

Injection molding—suitable for the most common polymers, such as polystyrene, high density polyethylene, polypropylene, and ABS—is the most frequently employed technology. Objects are produced one at a time from granules that are liquefied under heat and pressure and injected into steel molds. Similarly, continuous techniques, such as calendering and extrusion, employ open-ended molds, and blow or rotational molding form objects through centrifugal pressure, which causes the plastic material to adhere to the mold walls.

Form's second coming
Jeffrey Kipnis
The State of Architecture at the Beginning of the 21st Century
New York: Monacelli Press, 2004
p.59

Our tacit approach in architecture today is to treat the same as equivalent to identity, that is, as a defective form of difference, or difference equals zero. Such a categorical (essentialist or typological) notion of the same at best tolerates small differences and is therefore inherently conservative, as followers of Leon Krier's argument will appreciate. Yet in other fields, in mathematics and biology, for example, something else is afoot. As we track the evolution of geometry from descriptive to analytic and projective to topology, we see another notion of the same developing. Descriptive geometry, like Krier, sought to establish categories and to construct membership and equivalence tests in order to control difference. With triangles, descriptive geometry gave us definitions—scalene, right, isosceles, and equilateral—and tests for congruence and similarity. Projective geometry abandoned that apparatus in exchange for the power to transform any triangle into another, giving rise to a dynamic rather than categorical theory of the same. Topology took that evolution one step further, abandoning even the originating primitive or elemental shape (the "triangle") in favor of a general manifold—a geometric figure or solid that is not changed by homeomorphisms, such as stretching or bending, as illustrated by the proverbial equivalence of the doughnut and the coffee cup. Topology thus theorizes mathematical sameness in yet more powerful dynamic terms, Deleuze's choice of the term "multiplicité" is a nod to that project; it is from the French mathematical term for what in English topology is called a manifold. Look at the faces and figures around you: all variations, no original theme. There is the idea of the face to be sure, but no ideal face.

A New Understanding of Difference
Jesse Reiser
The Atlas of Novel Tectonics
New York: Princeton Architectural Press, 2006
pp.62–64

If idealist difference is understood as deviation from a transcendental model, then essentialist difference is understood as serial accident, like the variations in blush in a crate of peaches. If you buy one thousand tiles, or one thousand mass-produced custom teapots, you will see this kind of variation in the form or patina of each.

Sanford Kwinter introduces a third idea in his example of how one reads facial expressions. The smile is not a deviation from a straight face but a whole in and of its own. Neither do we see the face in a nominalist way, entirely unique and disconnected from other faces, nor is its expression accidental and thus referred back to an essence.

It is instructive to look at how variation enters the social field for an analog. Mass-customization is most successful when mobilized in some larger construct rather than as individualized units marketed and released into society in isolation from the rest of the series.

In the latter case their differences only bear an abstract relationship to the whole. Whereas when you start to look at variations in a field, difference is no longer isolated but forms emergent wholes not reducible to the sum of their parts. That is their abstract status, but it is their deployment that is the crucial issue. Granted, such variation can be deployed at any scale, but there is a range outside of which the system becomes invisible. At micro scales they merely act as decorative texture; conversely, at an extreme macro scale such difference becomes imperceptible and in that sense meaningless. It would, for example, be absurd to suggest continuous variation in the joints of superhighways. It is at the middle to large scale-the space of mass reception-that there seems to be both an economy and a need for variation.

This notion of difference applies across a range of scales, from the very small to the very large. The proper use of continuous variation consists in taking a molecular population and deploying it as a molar or large-scale aggregate, thus making the statistical variation comprehensible and visible for a certain quantity. In this way it becomes a living datascape.

VOLUME: POCHE

PETTICOAT LAYERING

Light, fluffy voluminous surfaces created by the addition of many layers or the folding pleating or ruffling of the surface.

The layered fabrics of a Victorian petticoat and the fluffy structure of whipped creams and froths both generate volume through repeated bubbles, folds, coils, and convolutions. But while petticoat layering can create structures that are light, airy and fluffy, it can also project “costumes of moods” in Benjamin’s terms through an excess of structure. The translucency and the cloudy depth of petticoat layering create richness and illusory atmosphere as well as a supple interiority.

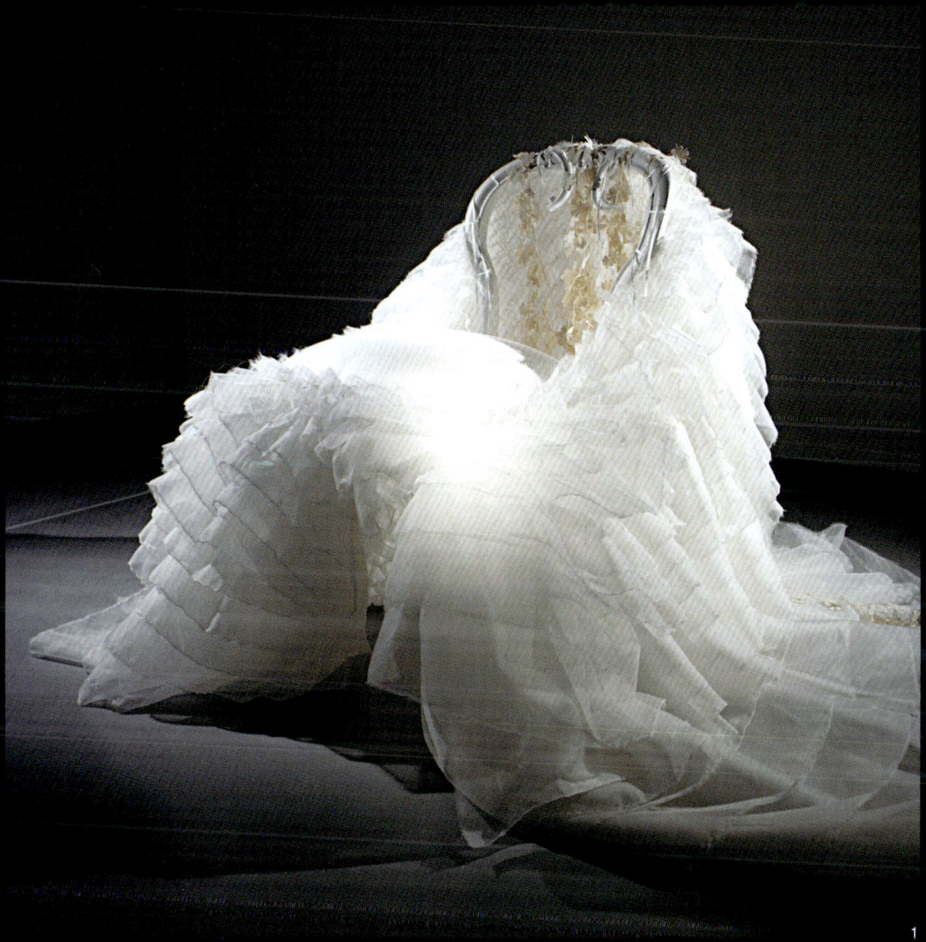

1

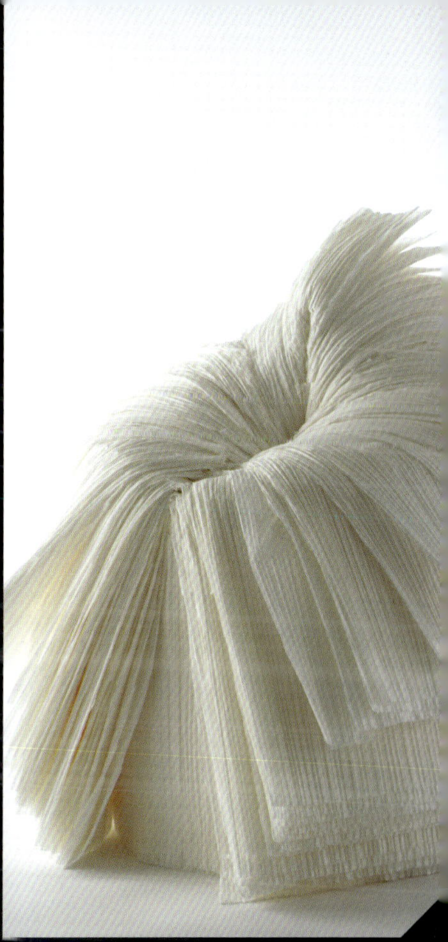

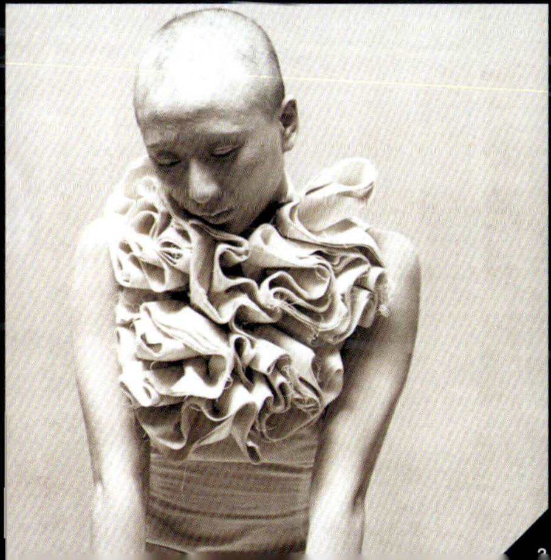

2

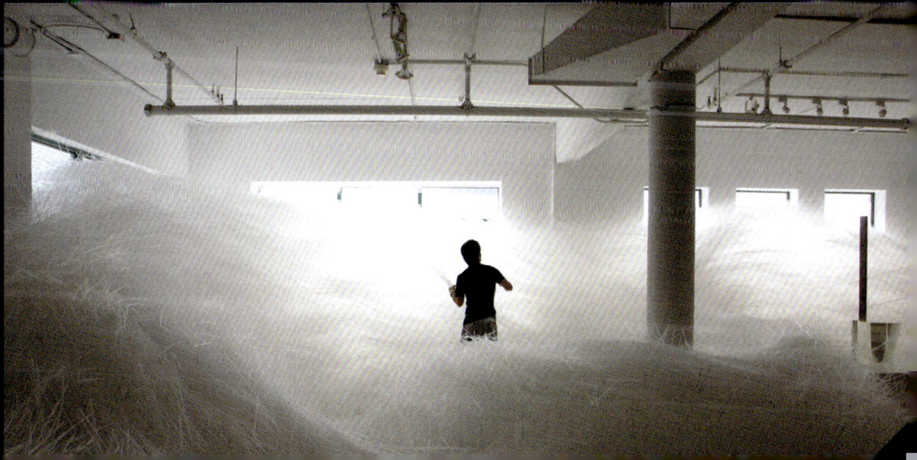

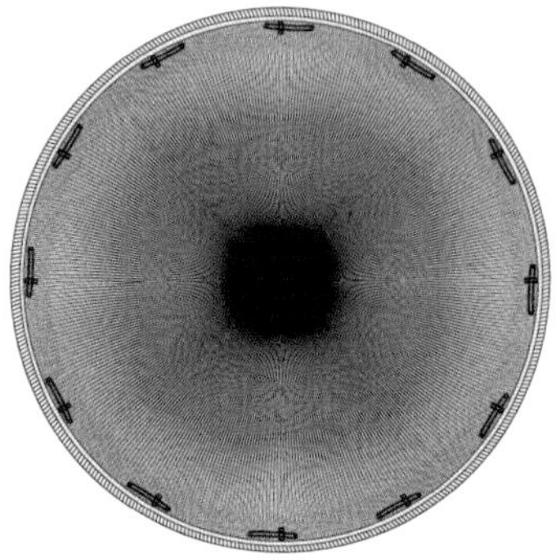

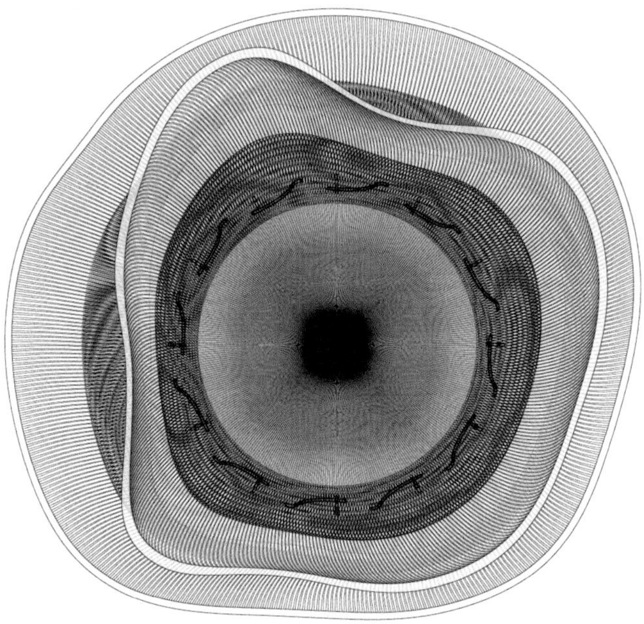

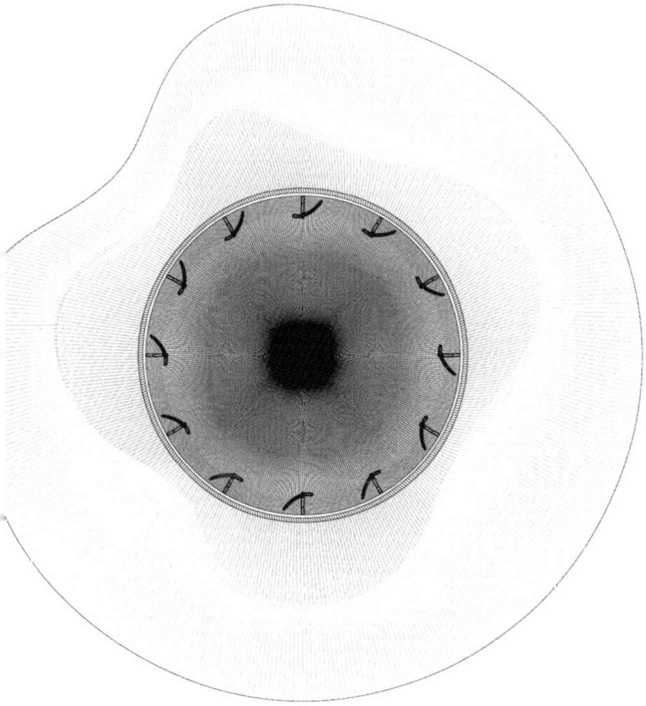

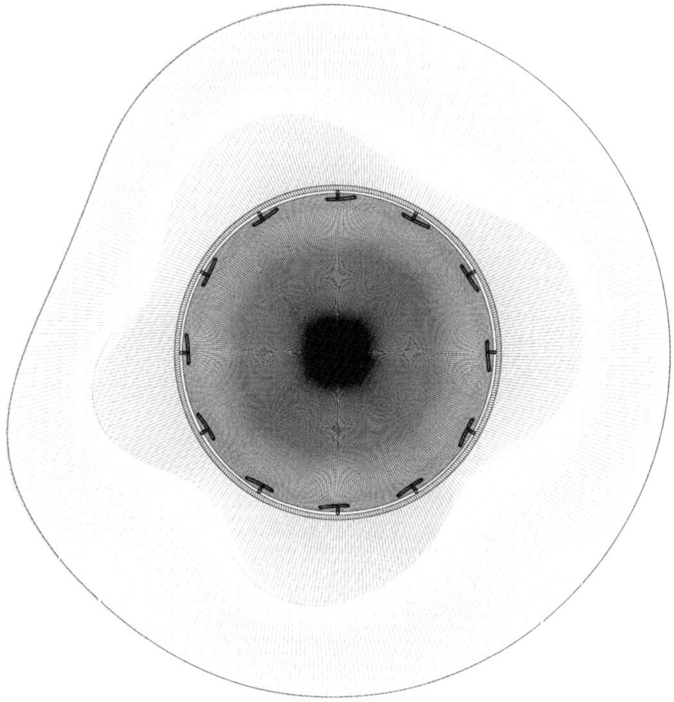

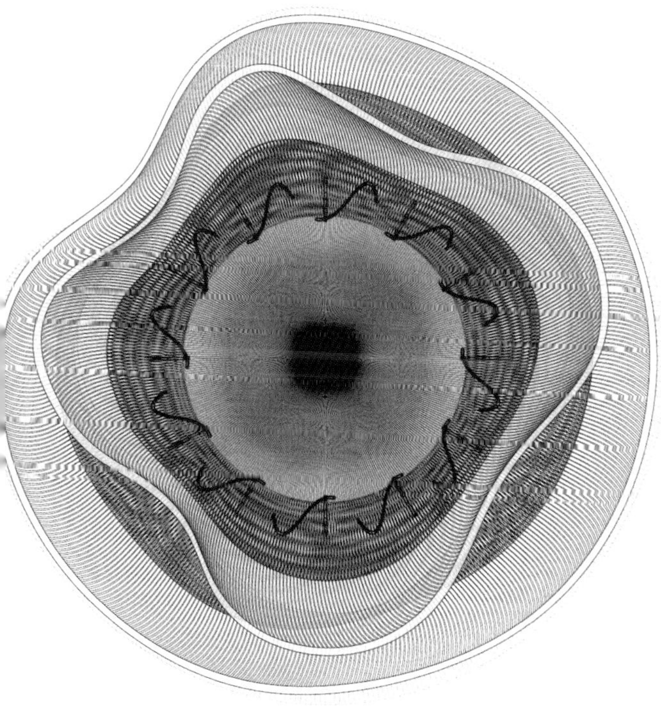

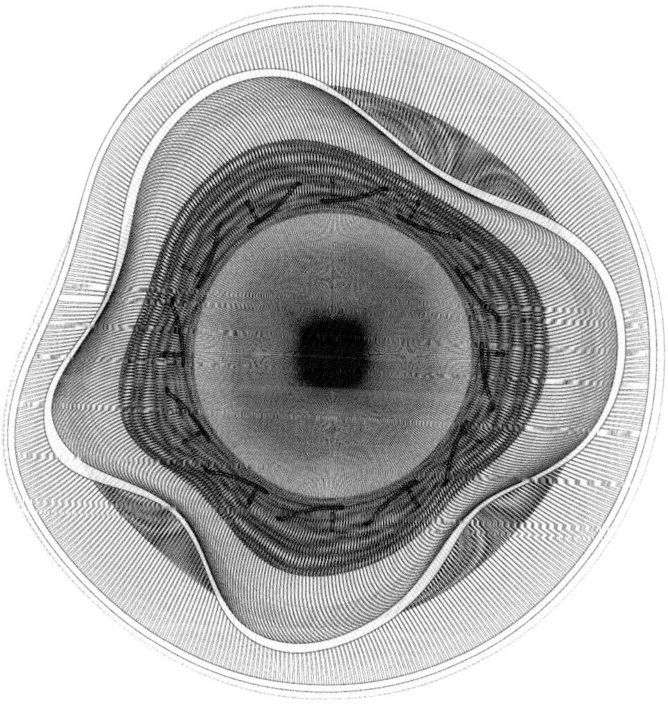

Anna Psenicka
Red Bull Pavilion
2005

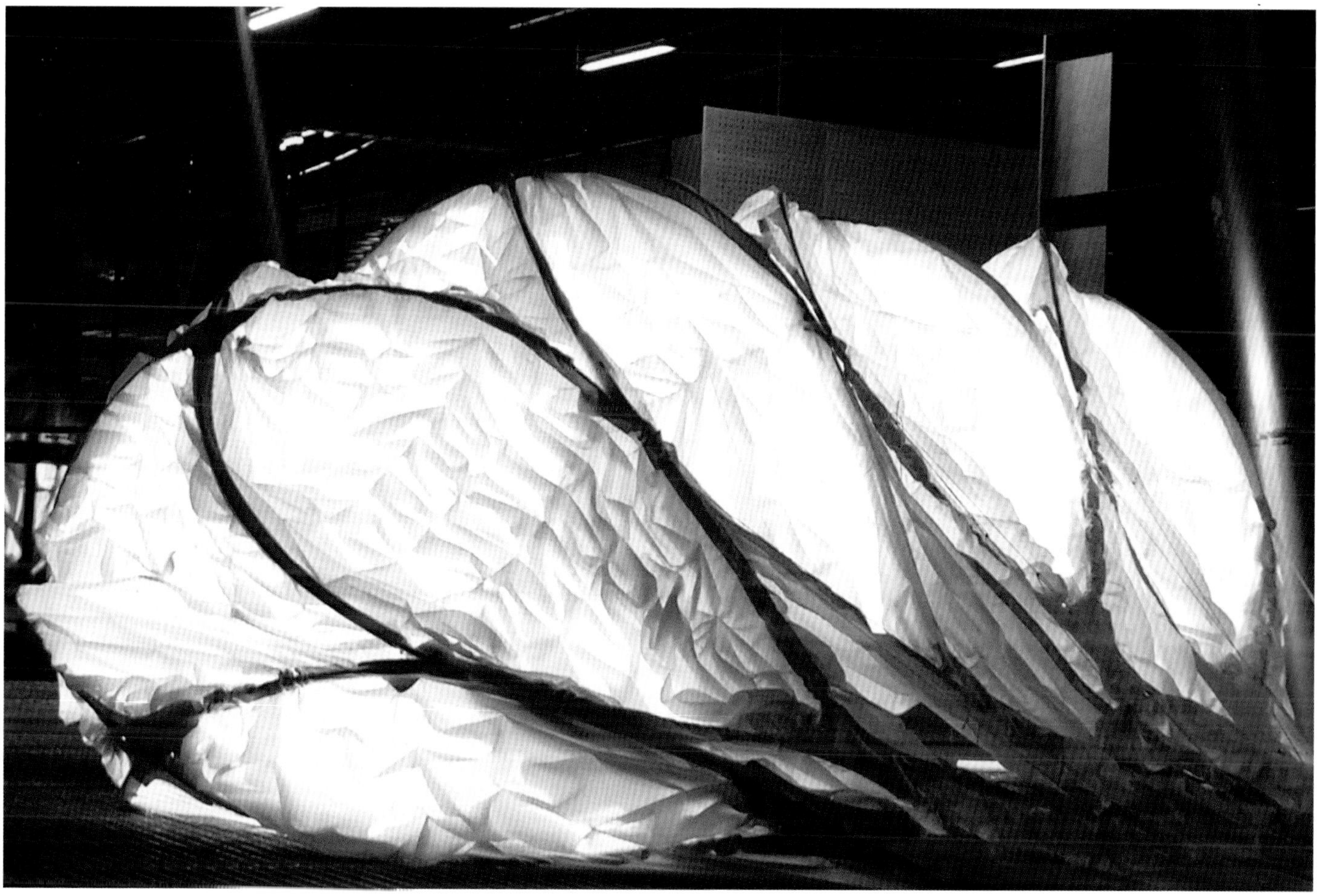

Peter Vikar
Red Bull Pavilion
2005

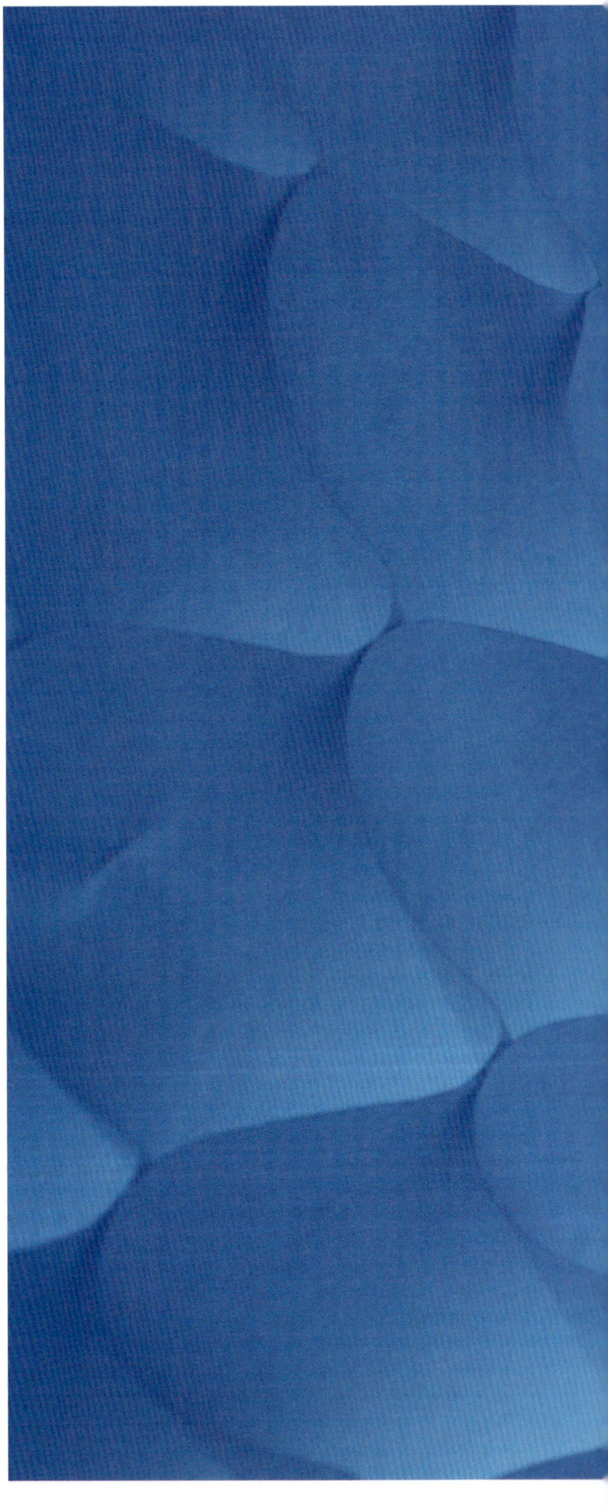

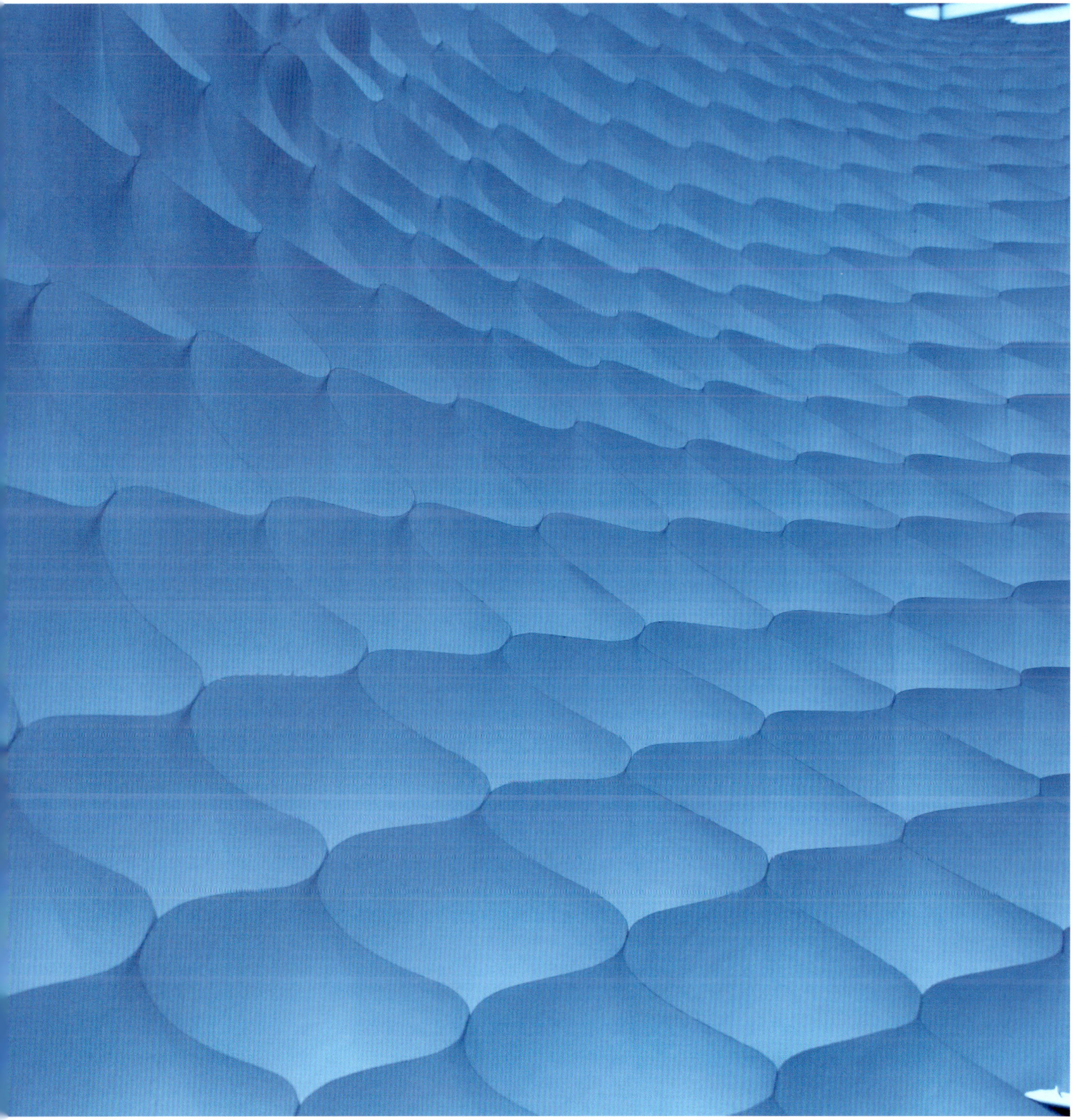

SELECTED EXCERPTS

The Four Elements of Architecture: A contribution to the Comparative Study of Architecture (1851)
Gottfried Semper
The four Elements of Architecture and Other Writings, trans: Harry Francis Mallgrave and Wolfgang Hermann
Cambridge: Cambridge University Press, 1989
p.104

The weaving of branches led easily to weaving bast into mats and covers and then to weaving with plant fiber and so forth. The oldest ornaments either derived from entwining or knotting materials or were easily produced on the potter's wheel with the finger on the soft clay. The use of wickerwork for setting apart one's property, the use of mats and carpets for floor coverings and protection against heat and cold for subdividing the spaces within a dwelling in most cases preceded by far the masonry wall, and particularly in areas favored by climate. The masonry wall was an intrusion into the domain of the wall fitter by the mason's art, which had evolved from building terraces according to very different conditions of style.

The Interior, The Trace
Walter Benjamin
The Arcades Project, trans: Howard Eiland and Kevin McLaughlin
Cambridge, Mass and London: Harvard University Press, 1999
p.216

Nineteenth-century domestic interior. The space disguises itself—puts on, like an alluring creature, the costumes of moods. The self-satisfied burgher should know something of the feeling that the next room might have witnessed the coronation of Charlemagne as well as the assassination of Henri IV, the signing of the Treaty of Verdun as well as the wedding of Otto and Theophano.
In the end, things are merely mannequins, and even the great moments of world history are only costumes beneath which they exchange glances of complicity with nothingness, with the petty and the banal. Such nihilism is the innermost core of bourgeois coziness—a mood that in hashish intoxication concentrates to satanic contentment, satanic knowing, satanic calm, indicating precisely to what extent the nineteenth-century interior is itself a stimulus to intoxication and dream. This mood involves, furthermore, an aversion to the open air, the (so to speak) Uranian atmosphere, which throws a new light on the extravagant interior design of the period. To live in these interiors was to have woven a dense fabric about oneself, to have secluded oneself within a spider's web, in whose toils world events hang loosely suspended like so many insect bodies sucked dry. From this cavern, one does not like to stir.

Atmosphere
Heather Roberge
Crib Sheets
New York: Monacelli Press, 1995
p.70

More and more, contemporary culture embodies an atmosphere of flows and rhythms that are becoming overtly apparent, expressed everywhere. While highly organized as discrete entities, flows and rhythms never entirely consume their surrounding material. Always suspended within their medium, flows never resolve into disconnected bodies.

The making of architecture in this context requires a method of inquiry that saturates environments with structure, which thereby produce not truthful structure but rather atmosphere.

VOLUME: POCHE

SURFACE POCHE

Set of interwoven surfaces which create another continuous implied surface at their collective edge.

One principle ambition of the studio is the intricate relation of surface geometry and patterns of seams, edges, openings and structural elements. Surface poche removes the actual surface and implies it only through the stacking and weaving of perpendicular structural surfaces. The geometry of the implied and actual surfaces are attuned to each other; any curve in the implied surface can only be produced by the twisting, gathering or thickening of the structural surfaces. These variations produce an ornamental effect and a synthesis that mitigates the traditional architectural dichotomy between structure and ornament.

1 **Mazda with Swift Engineering**
Furai, 2007
© (2008) Mazda Motor of America, Inc., used by permission.
www.mazda.com

2 **Patrick Jouin Design Team**
(L. Janvier, J-B. Auvray, R. Fischler, R. Perron)
Solid C1 Chair, 2004
photographed by Agence

4 **Tokujin Yoshioka**
Honey-pop Chair, 2001
image courtesy of Tokujin Yoshioka
www.tokujin.com

5 *Dowlatabad Gardens Main Building, Yazd*
photographed by M. Najafi

6 **Tara Donovan**

8 **Olafur Eliasson**
Your Mobile Expectations: BMW H2R Project, 2007
photographed by Jens Ziehe, image courtesy of Olafur Eliasson and BMW Group
www.olafureliasson.net

9 **Herzog & de Meuron**
Signal Box, Basel, 1999
photographed by Margherita

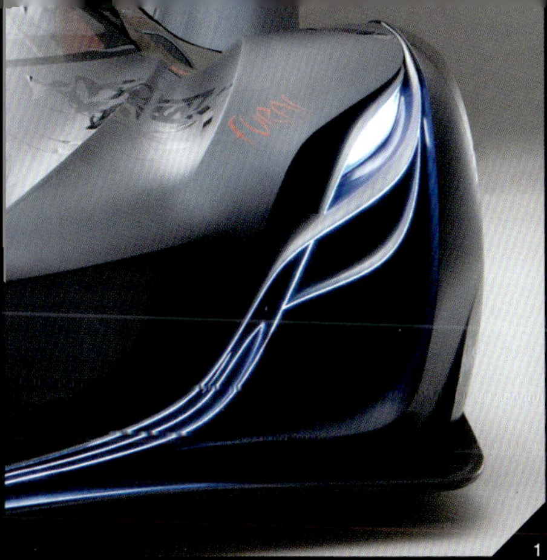
1

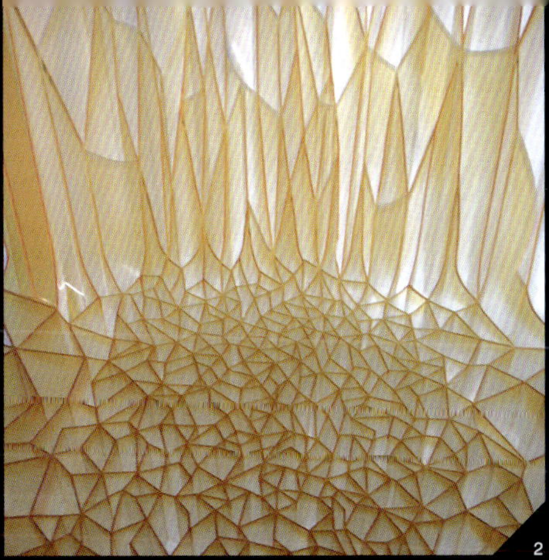
2

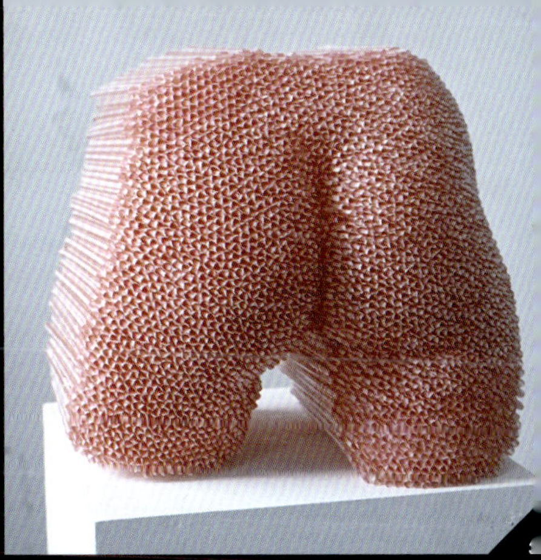

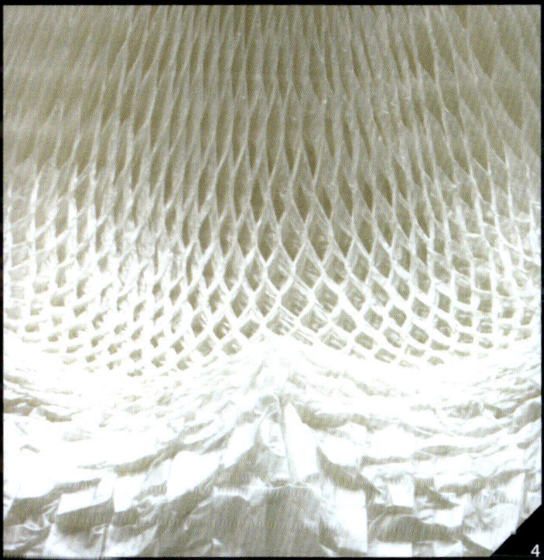
4

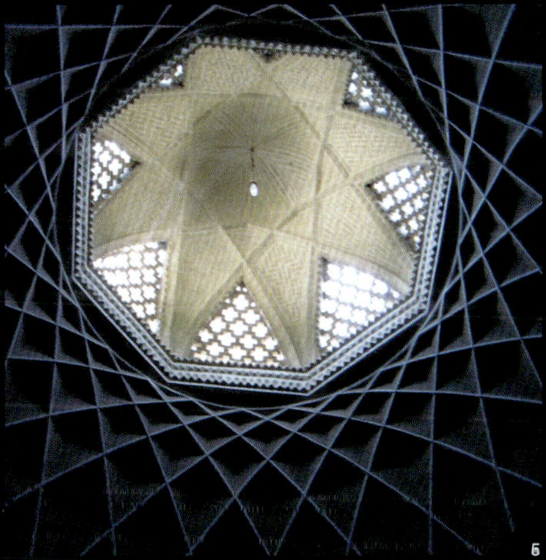
5

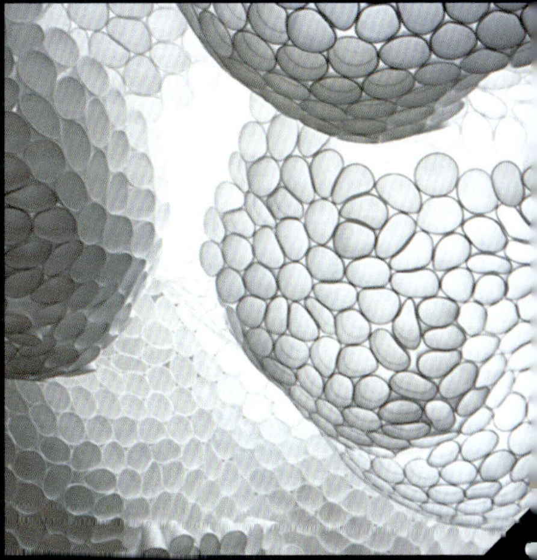

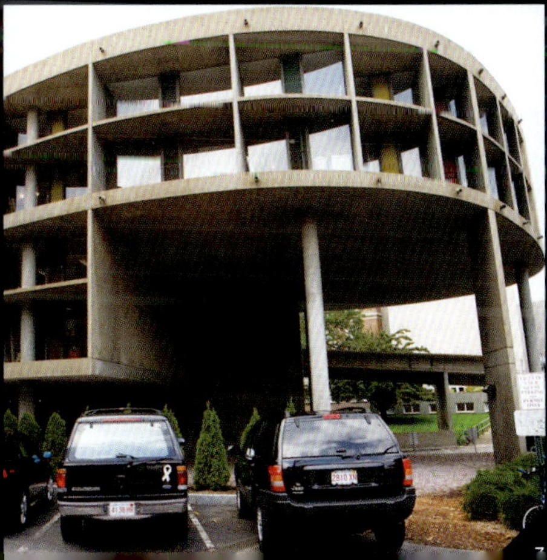

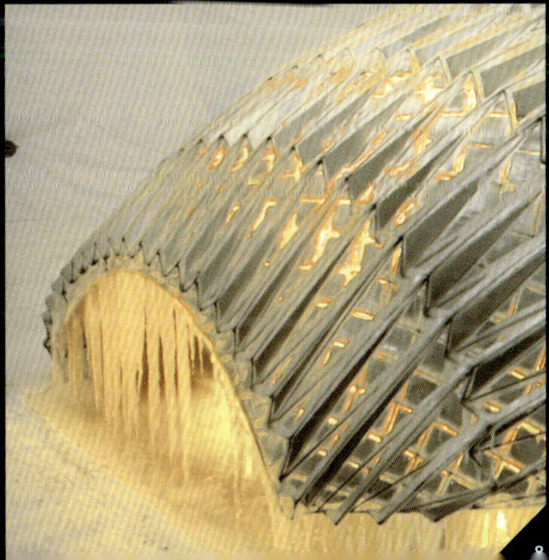

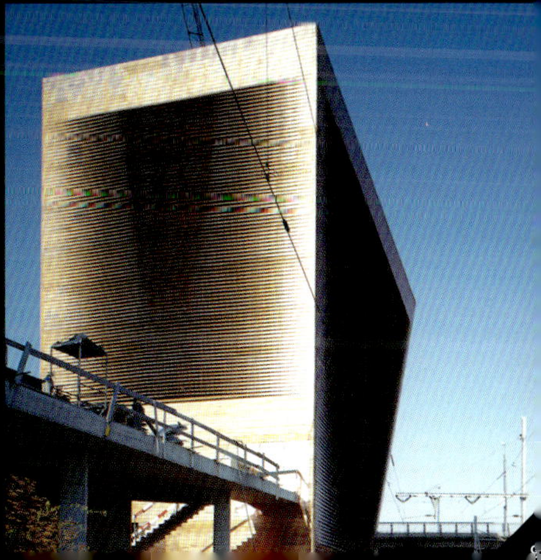

Anna Edthofer and Tina Tröster
Potato Problem
2005

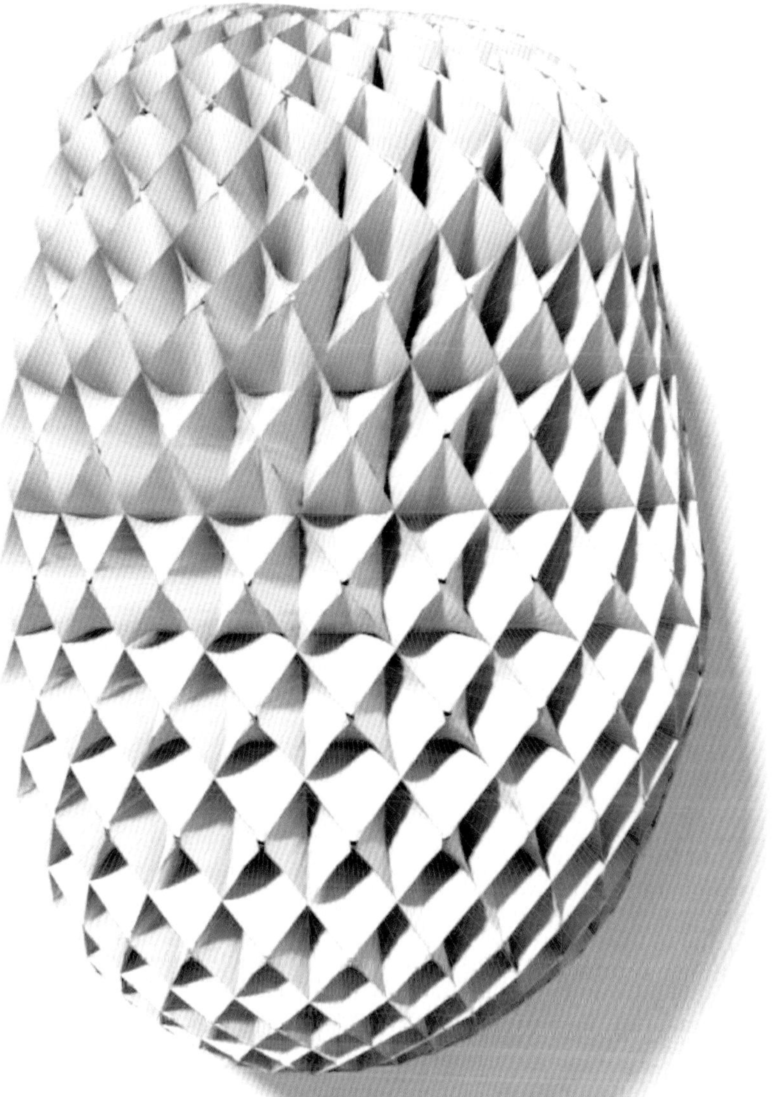

Nora Graw and Julia Körner
Car Design Center
2006

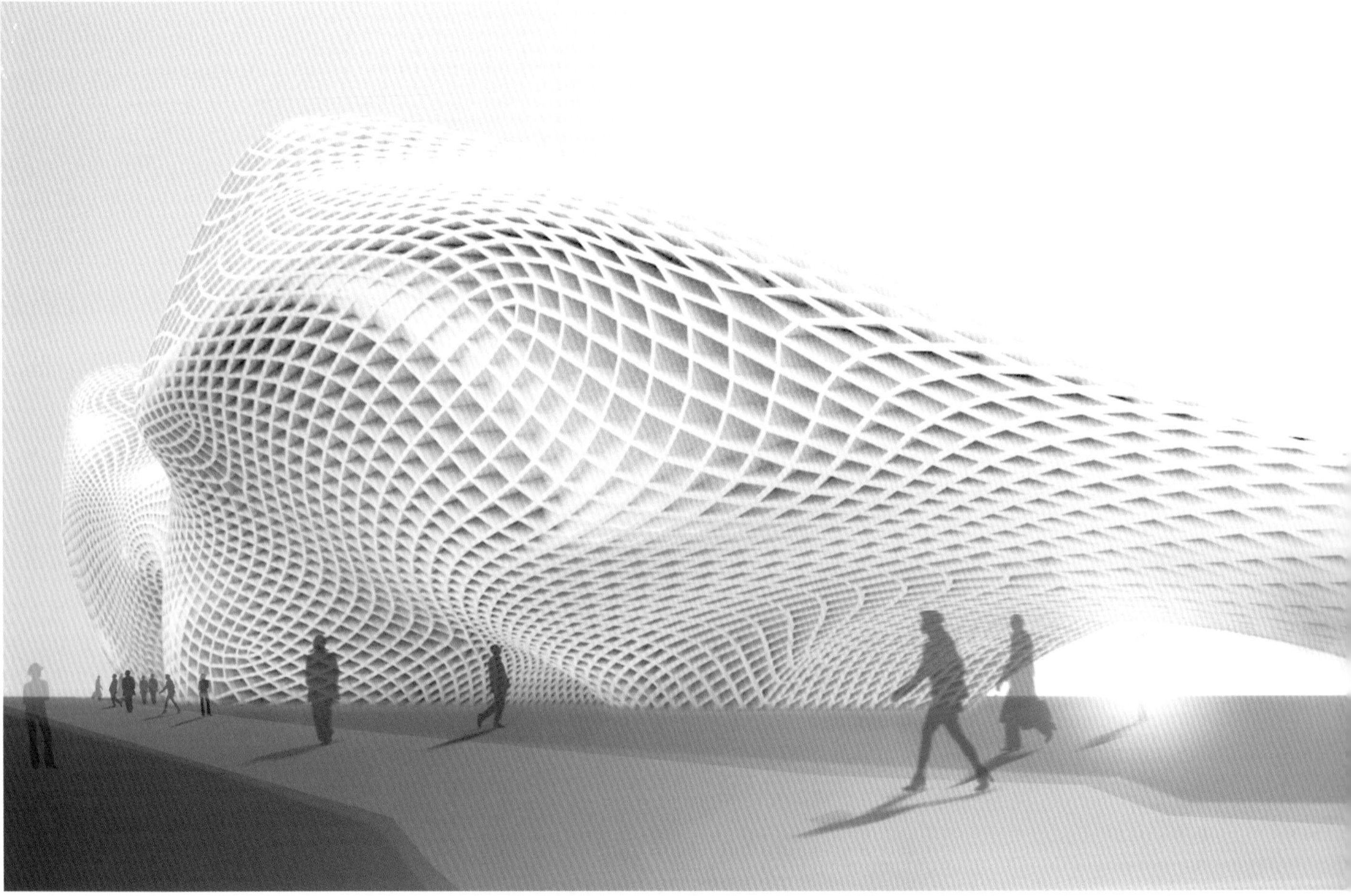

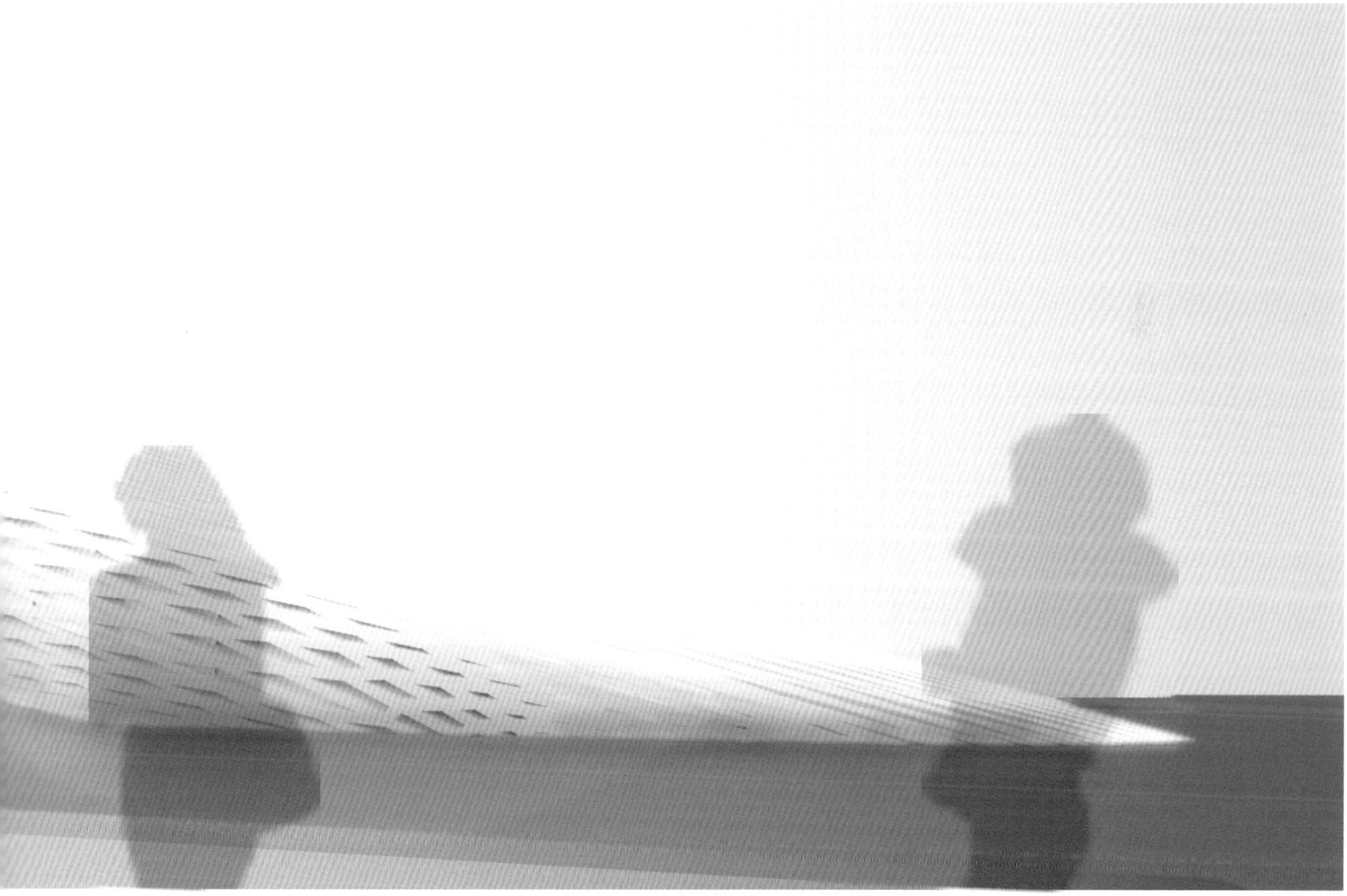

Nora Graw, Martina Lesjak and Maja Ozvaldic
Boat Factoy
2008

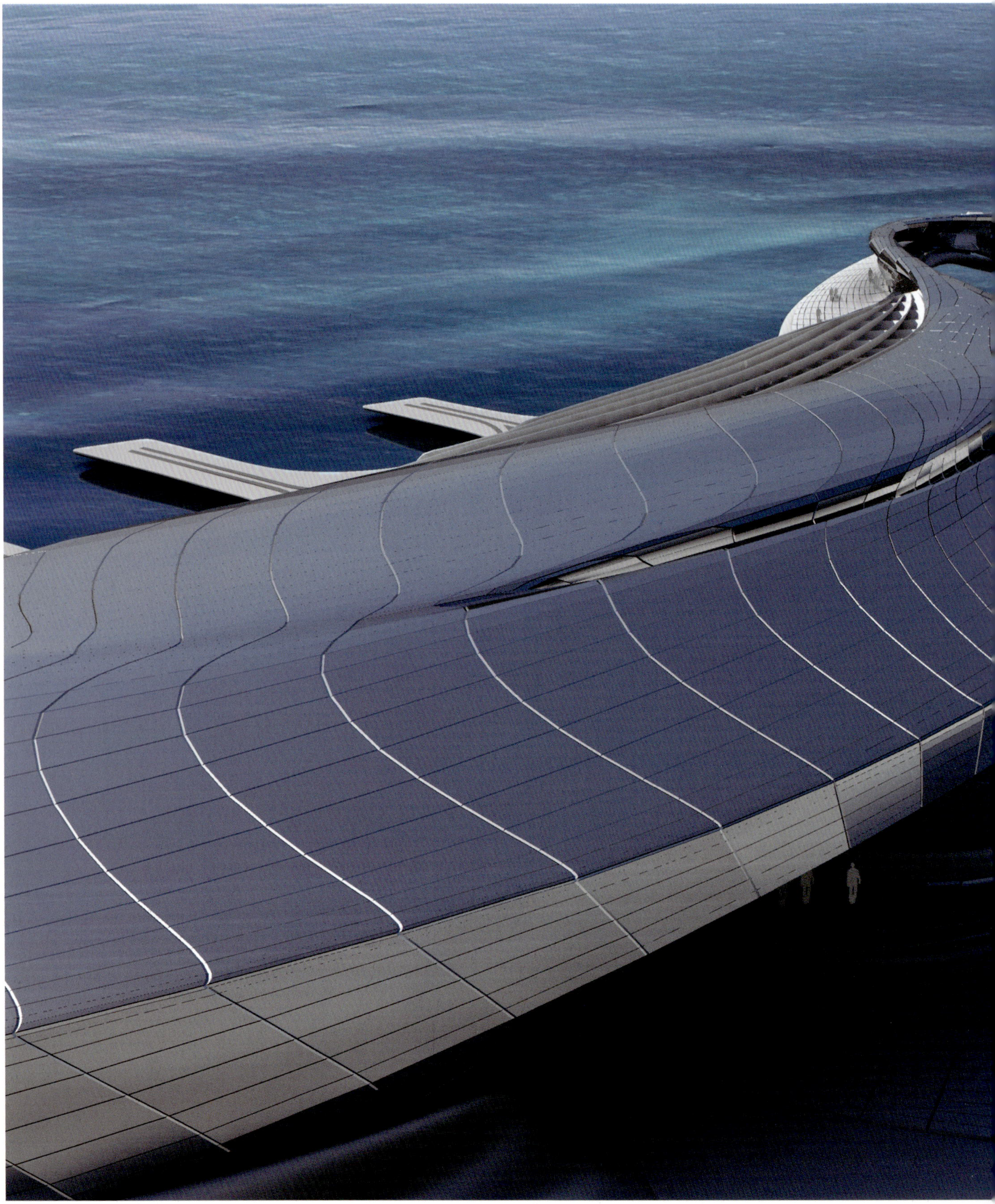

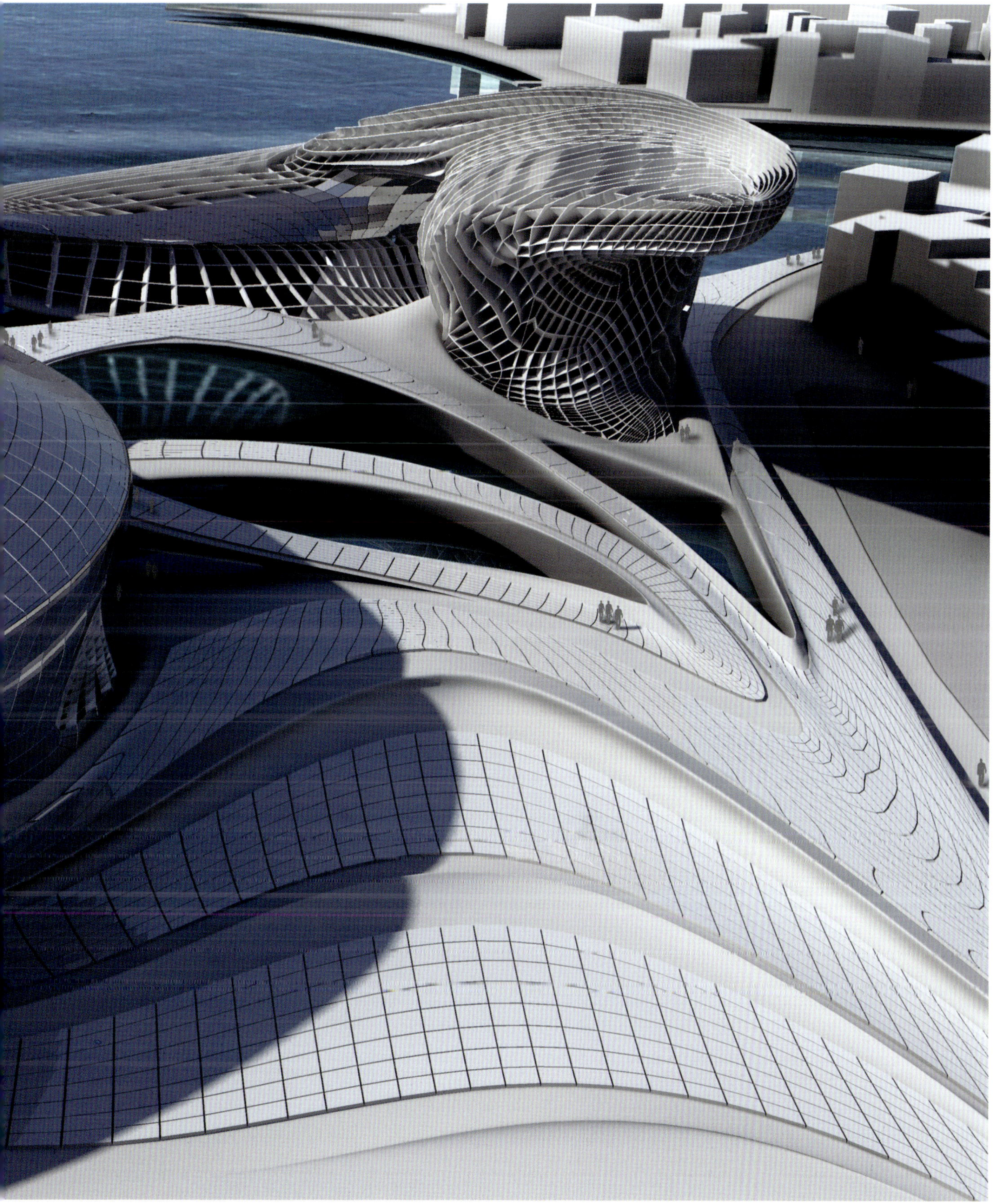

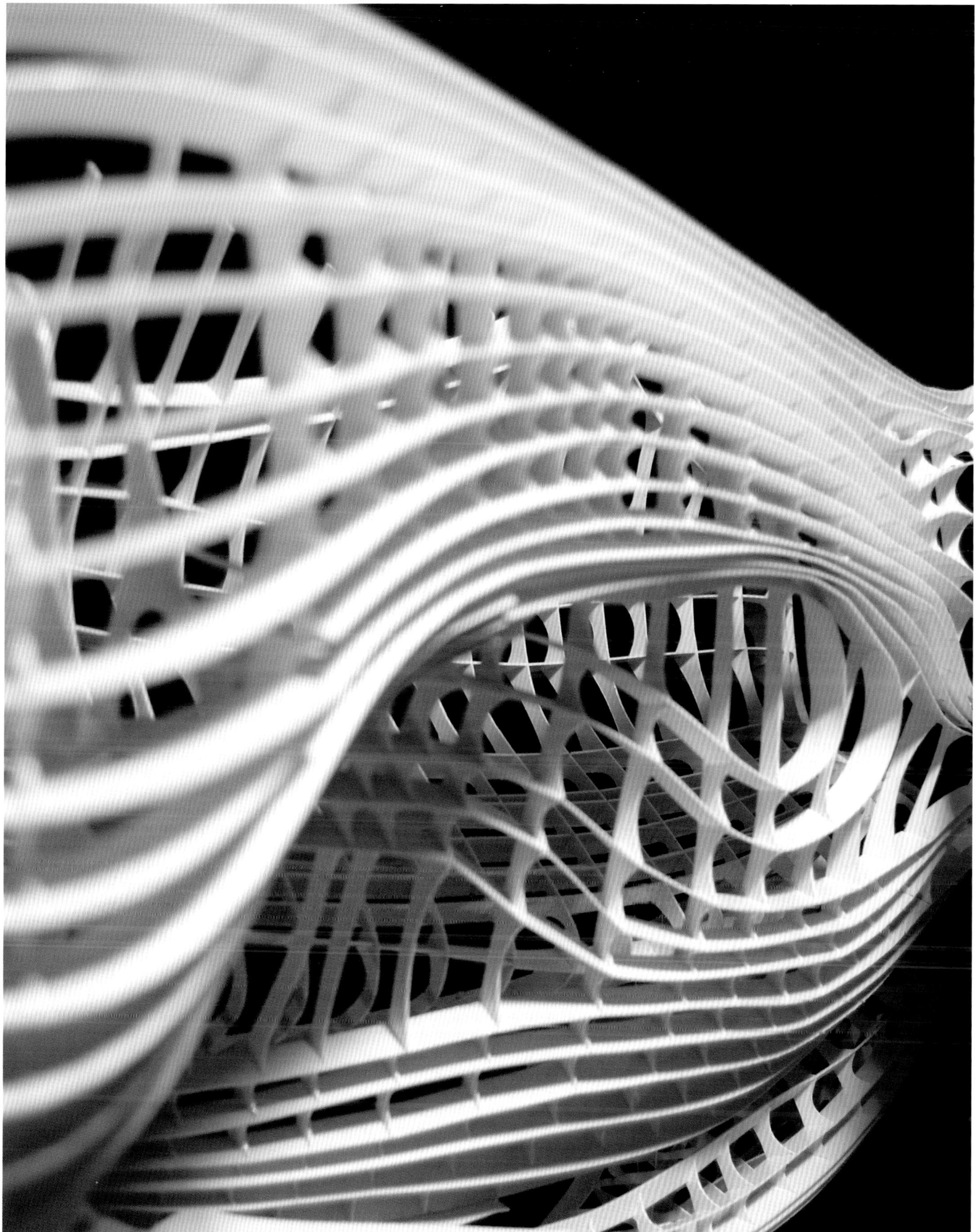

Peter Vikar
Red Bull Pavilion
2006

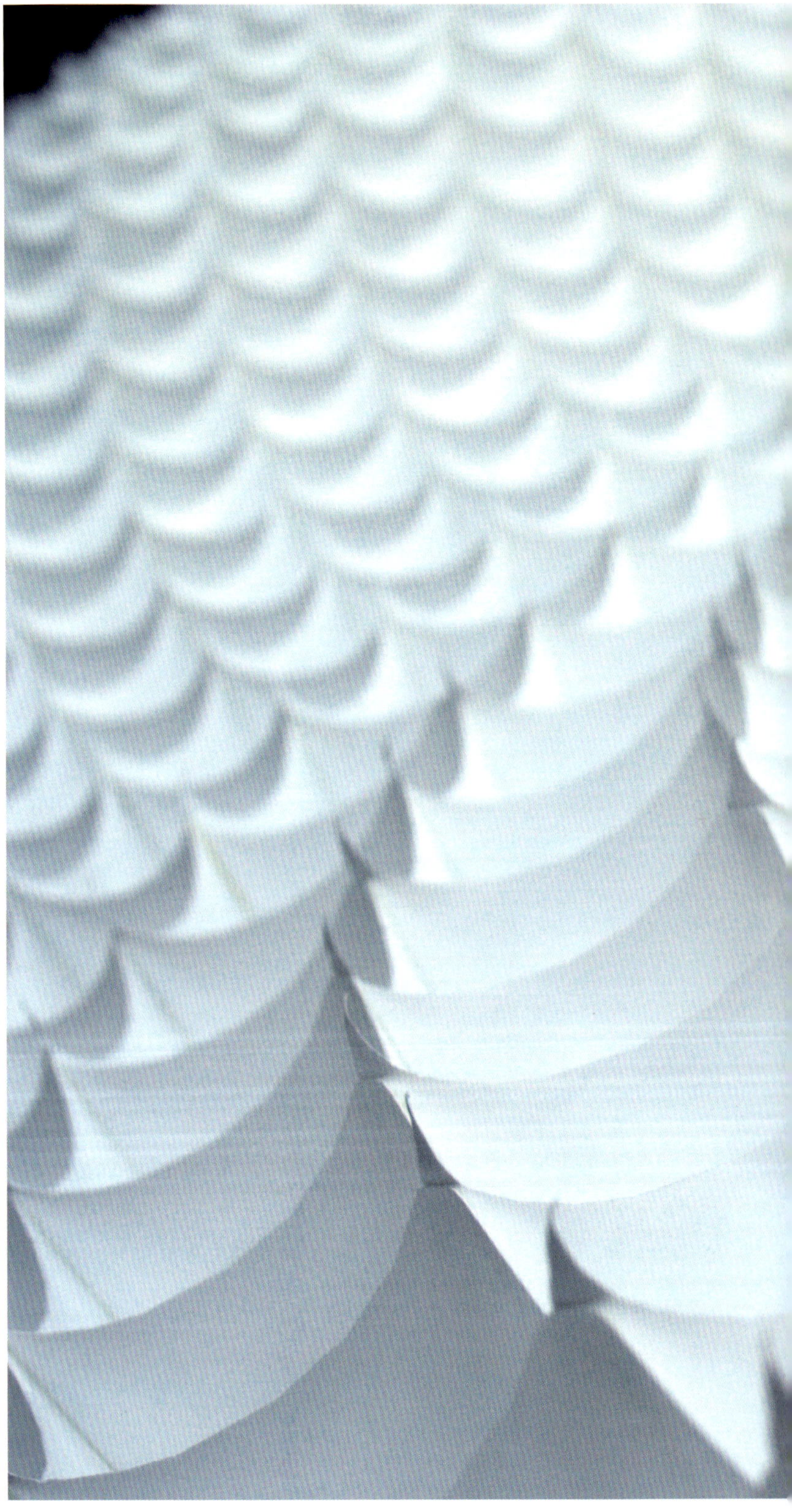

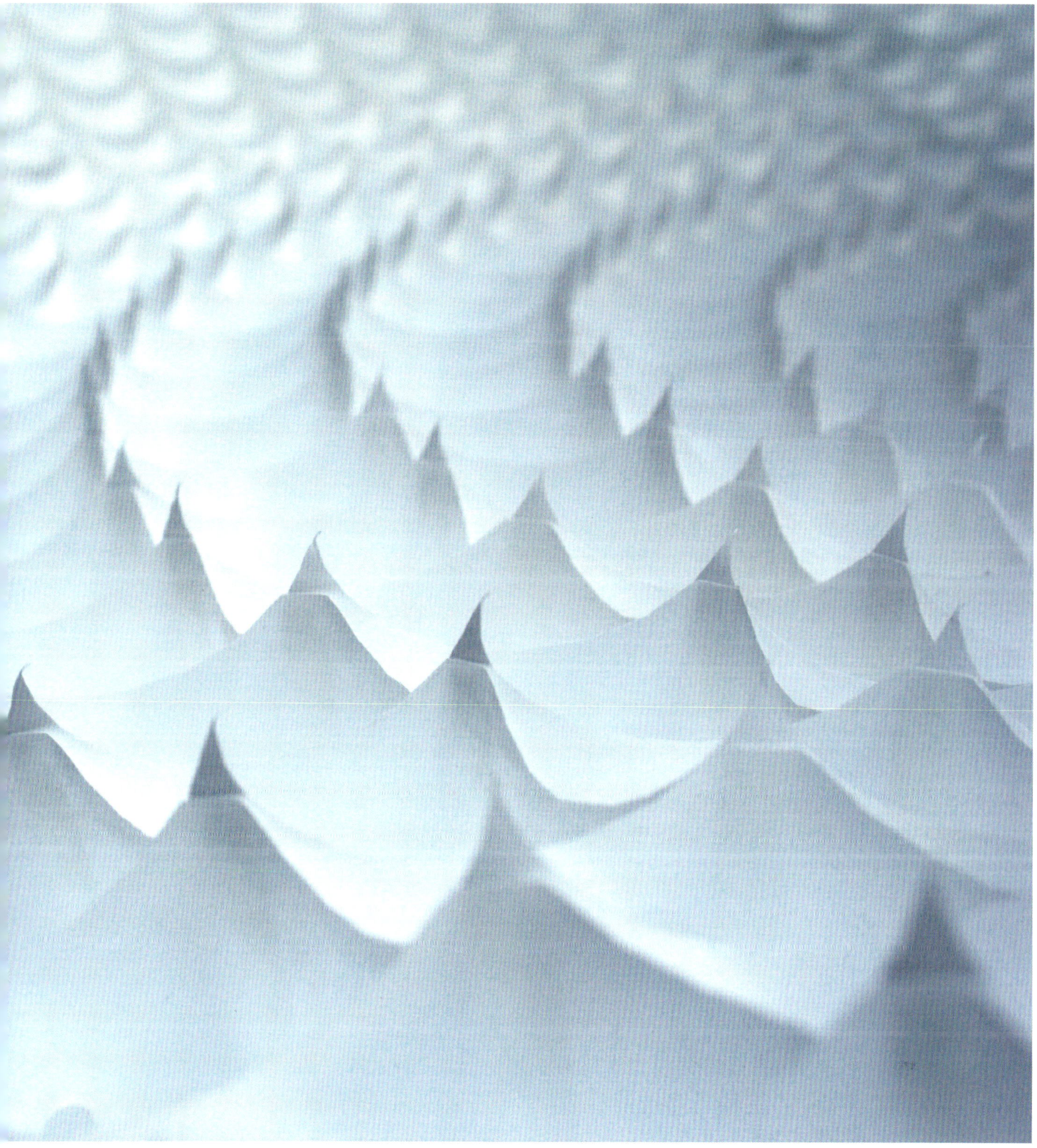

Tina Tröster
Toronto Dominion Tower
2004

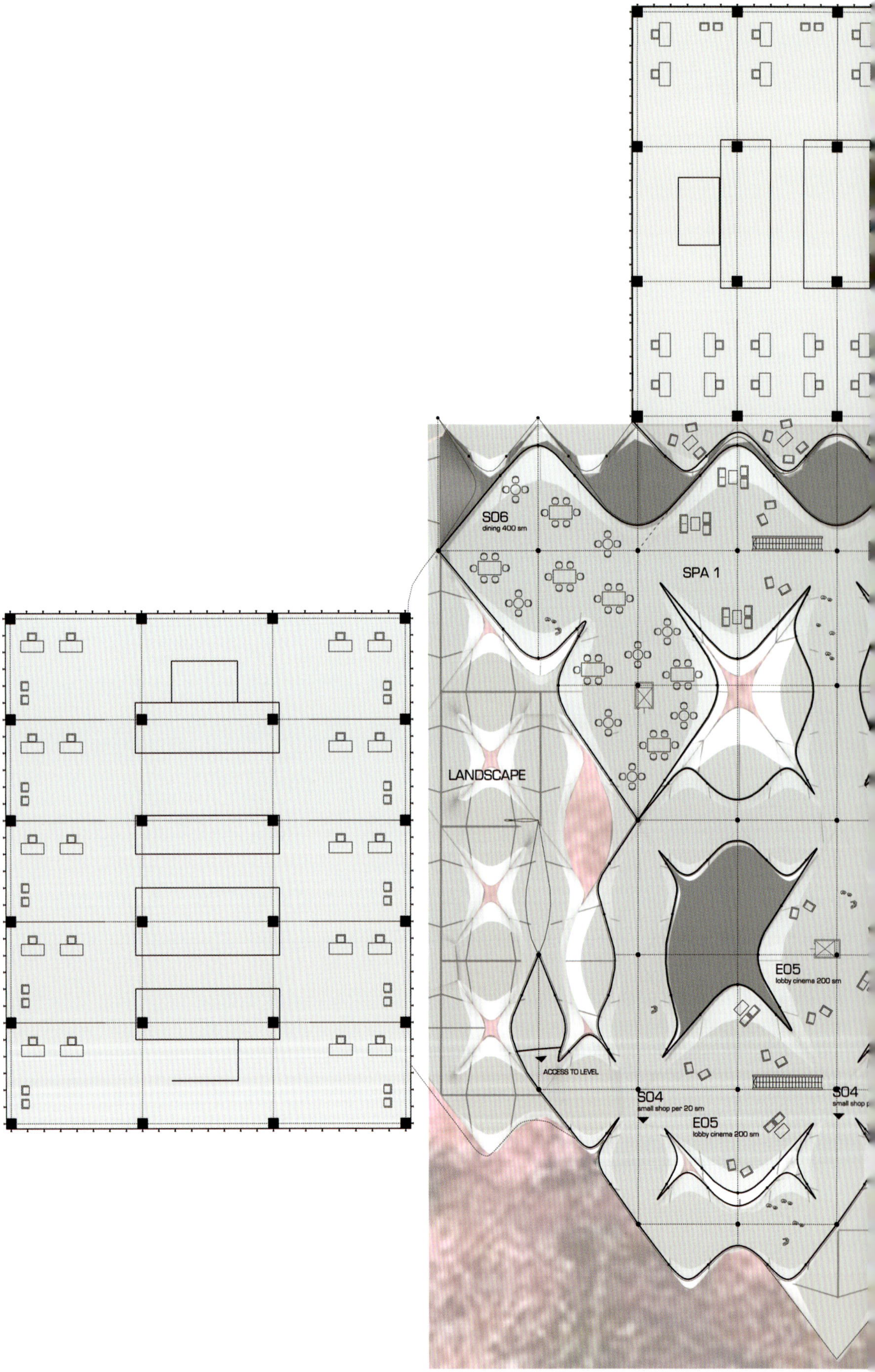

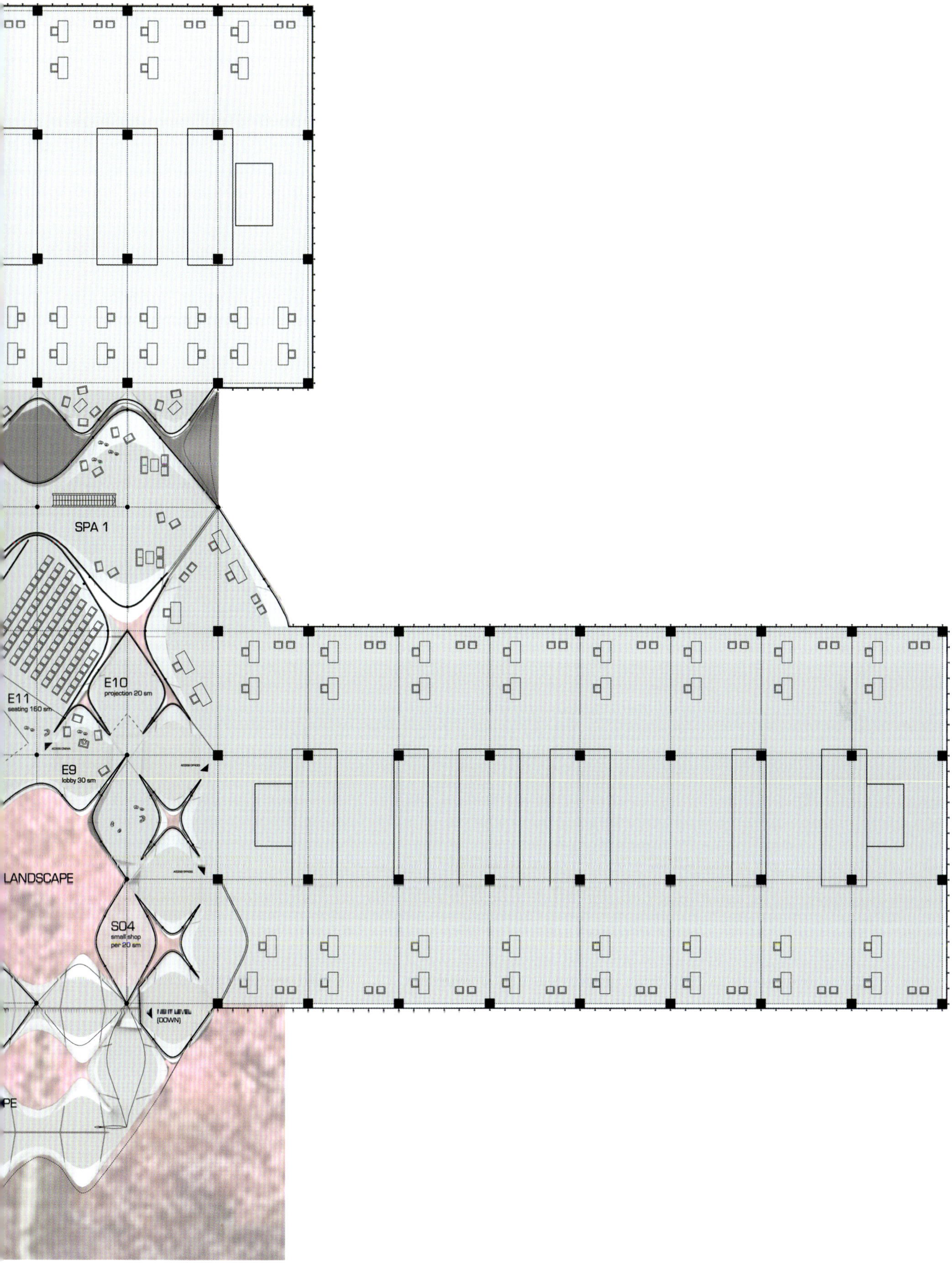
SPA 1
E10
projection 20 sm
E11
seating 150 sm
E9
lobby 30 sm
LANDSCAPE
S04
small shop
per 20 sm
(DOWN)

SELECTED EXCERPTS

Surface
Marc Angelil and Sarah Graham
Crib Sheets
New York: Monacelli Press, 1995
p.64

Flow-surface: exposing form to genesis, structure to flux, a conception of architectural morphology emerges where the object's discrete boundaries seem to dissolve. The incorporation of dynamic systems within the definition of the enclosure undermines the stability of the object as a condition of rest, fundamental to this understanding is the treatment of the object's surface as a figuration of fields.

By conceptually offering a flow of perpetual motion and of continuous multiplicity, heterogeneous yet coherent architectural assemblies are suspended in a temporal dimension—endlessly searching for another, then another, and yet another form. Intrinsic is the tendency to transgress physical perimeters, or to blur contour lines, a strategy capable of serving diverging tasks. On the one hand, it aims for disjunction by weakening holistic masses; on the other hand, it aims for coherence by linking disjointed organizations into a congruous while. The effect of indistinctiveness is pursued by way of surfaces that contain but do not define.

Introdution
Cecil Balmond
Informal
Munich, London and New York: Prestel, 2002
p.14

Geometry is never mentioned in the normal course of designing a building; it is taken for granted as a system of isolated bounded shapes. Appearance and externalities seem to be all that matters—there is no sense of interiorisation or working from a theoretical base of form towards a configuration; *symmetria* has turned into non-speculation. Space is left empty and barren, trapped in rigid containers. Seen as necessary evils out of a Cartesian logic, columns are placed in diminished regular grids. Structure is assumed to be a reduction and a regulation. The mindset is also the negative behind many a desperate underpinning of free-form; subtle transpositions of shape that fashion strength out of apparent feebleness are not well understood.

There is a lot more to structure than strict post and beam. Slabs may fold and act as lines of vertical strength, beams may bifurcate and change shape, columns can serve as beams, the ingredients are all there to evolve form in fascinating ways. The challenge is to make structure the new discipline in a re-examination of space.

Now the computer opens a door and gives unparalleled freedom to explore—the result is a bewildering and mind-bending free-for-all where anything goes. But cool new shapes and blobs are nothing more than mere facade if they are propped up by standard post and beam constructions. To create an integrity in the establishing of a free shape, a new method is needed for configuration with flexible start points. Instead of line—surface; instead of equi-support—scatter; instead of fixed centre—a moving locus; and instead of points—zones.

FIGURAL STRUCTURE

A composition of structural elements that detaches from or pushes through the building envelope, producing a massing of porous and variable figures.

Figural structure is read against the ground of the envelope. A monolithic compression of the two systems into a single layer is more easily read as a

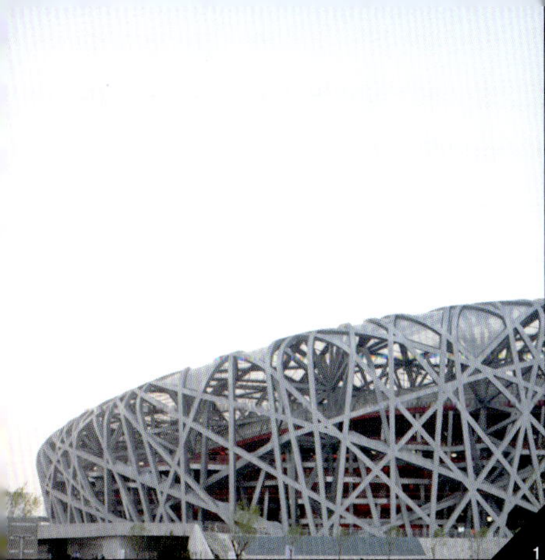
1

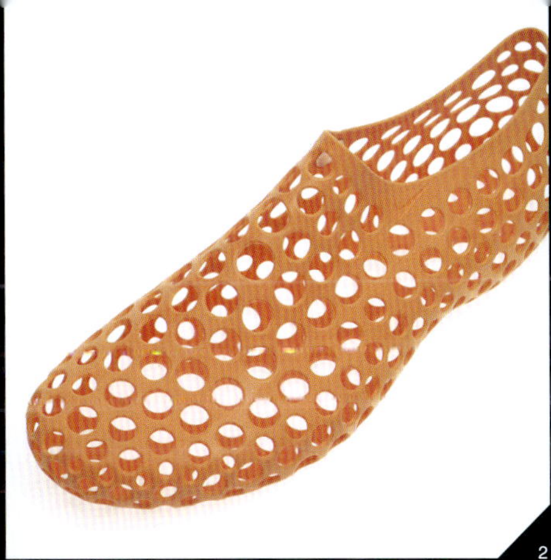
2

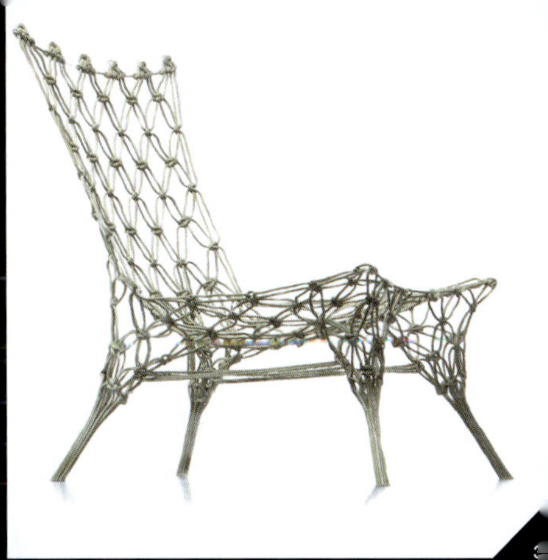
3

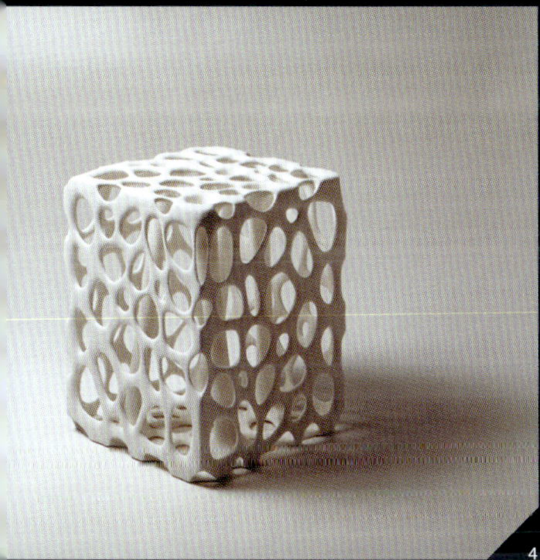
4

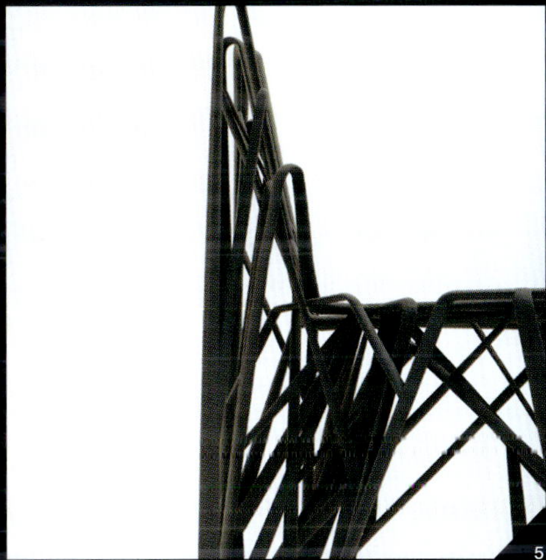
5

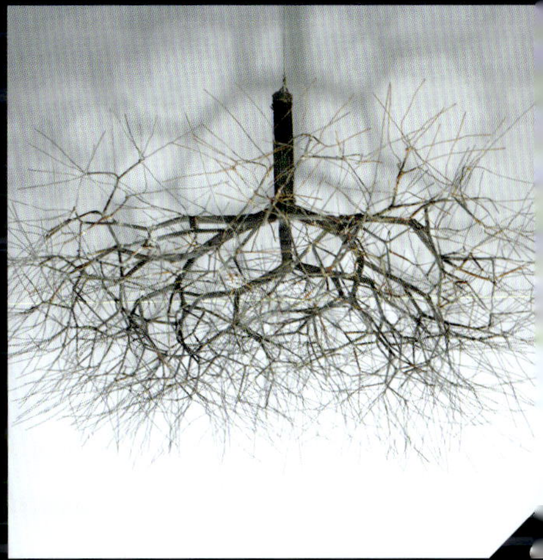

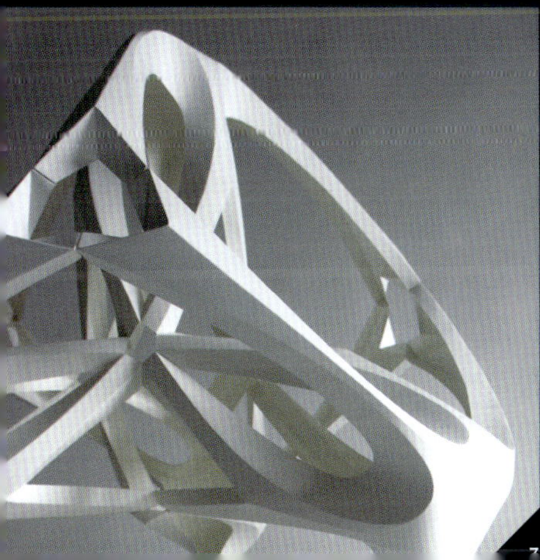
7

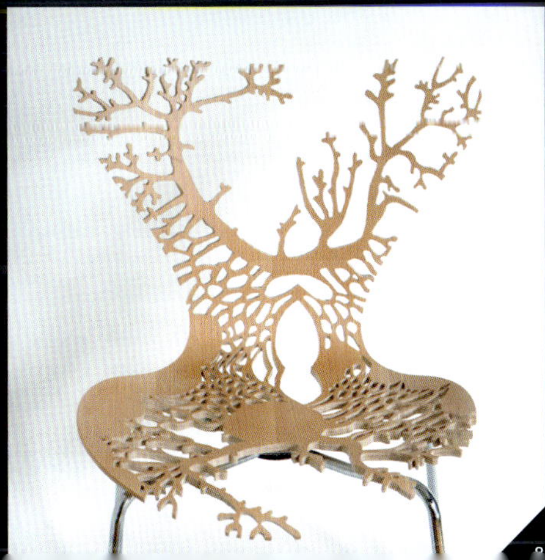
8

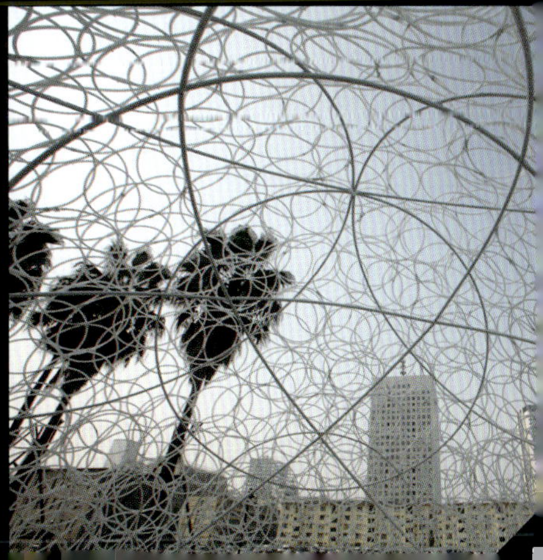

Dumëne Comploi and David Baum
Vertical Case Study
2004

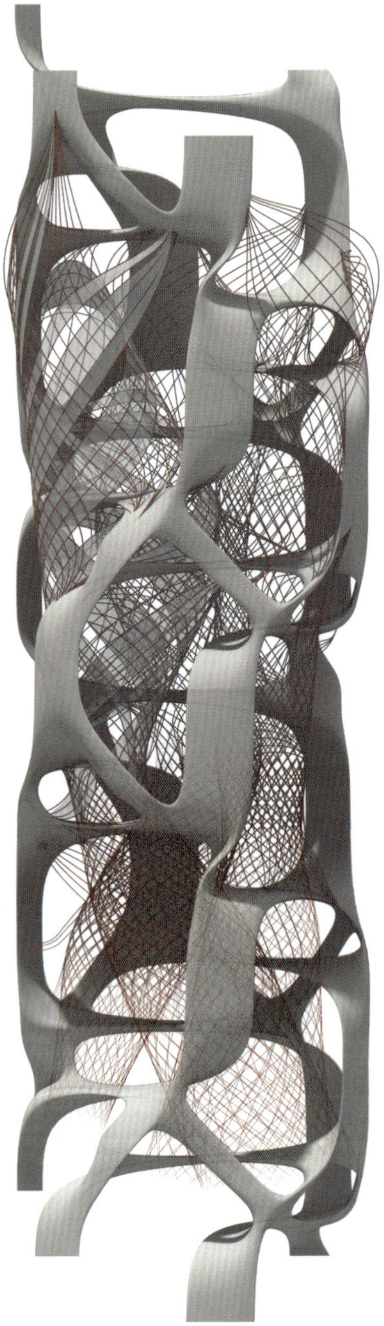

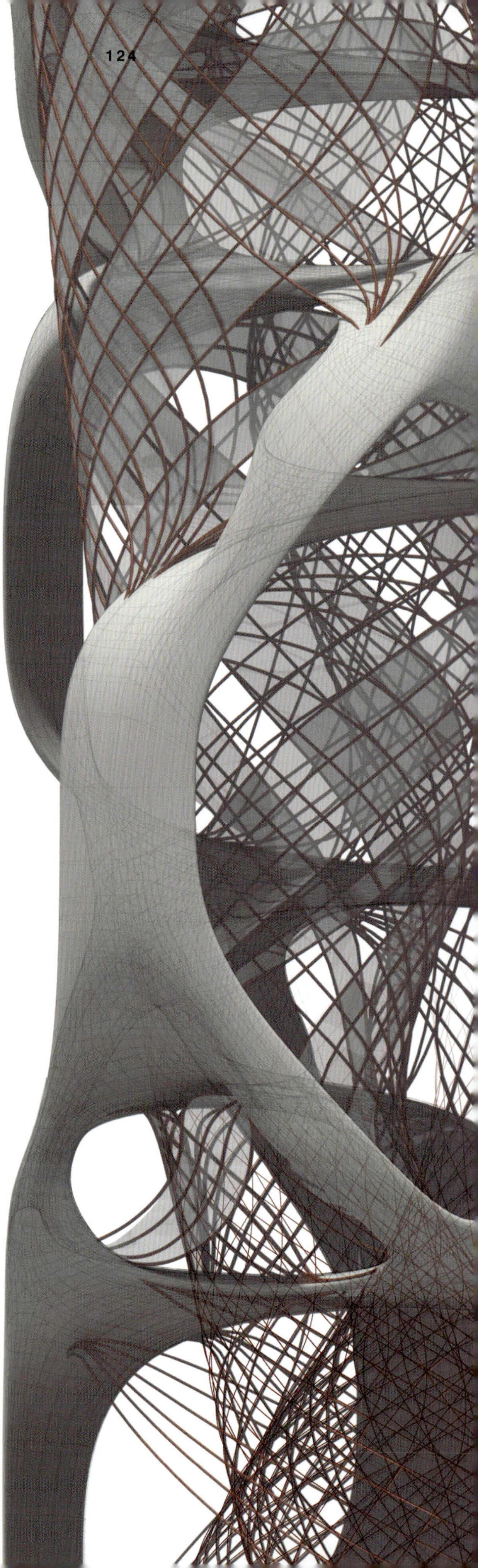

Andreas Krainer

Vertical Case Study

2004

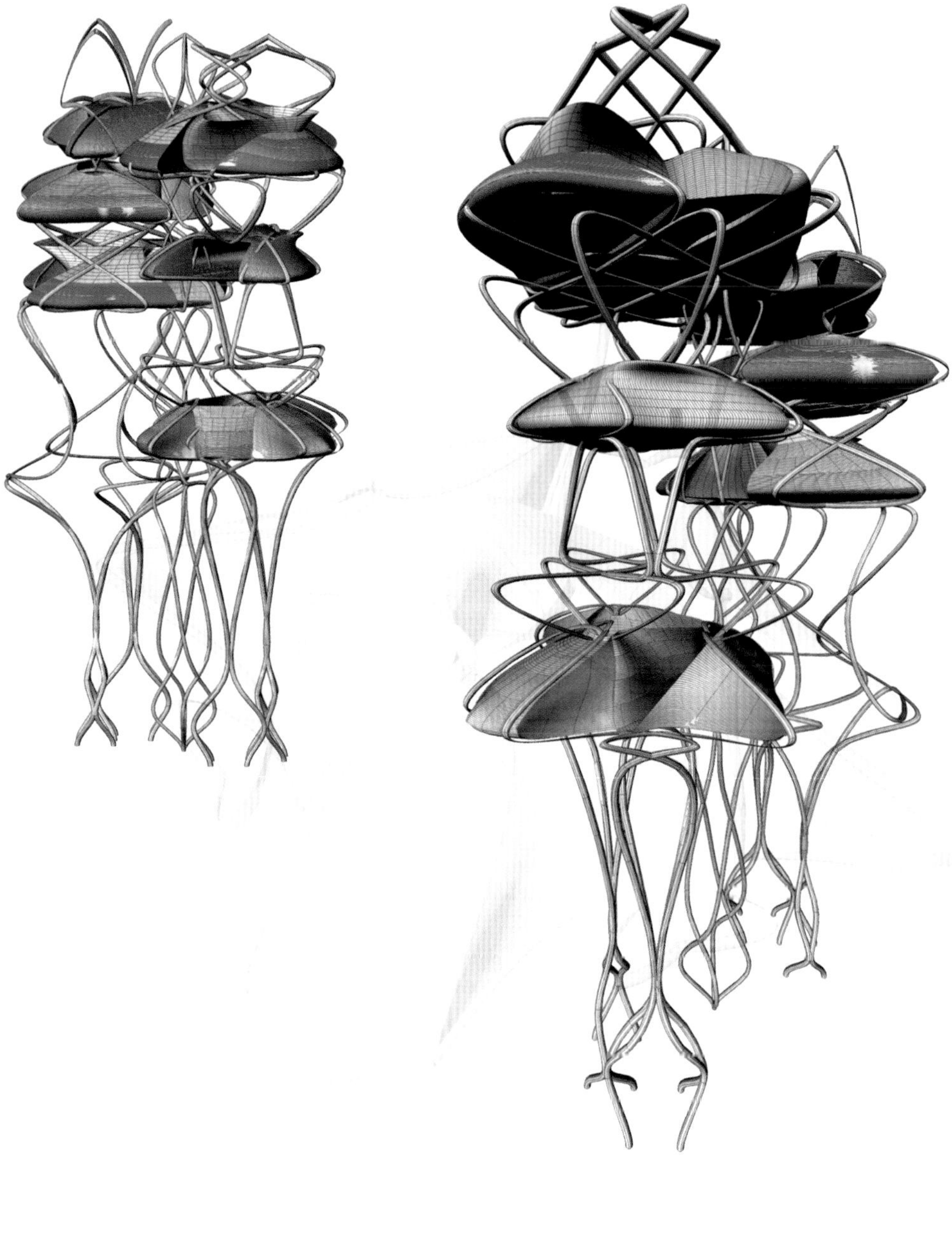

Julia Körner, Adam Vukmanov and Miljan Radojevic
Factory for Today
2008

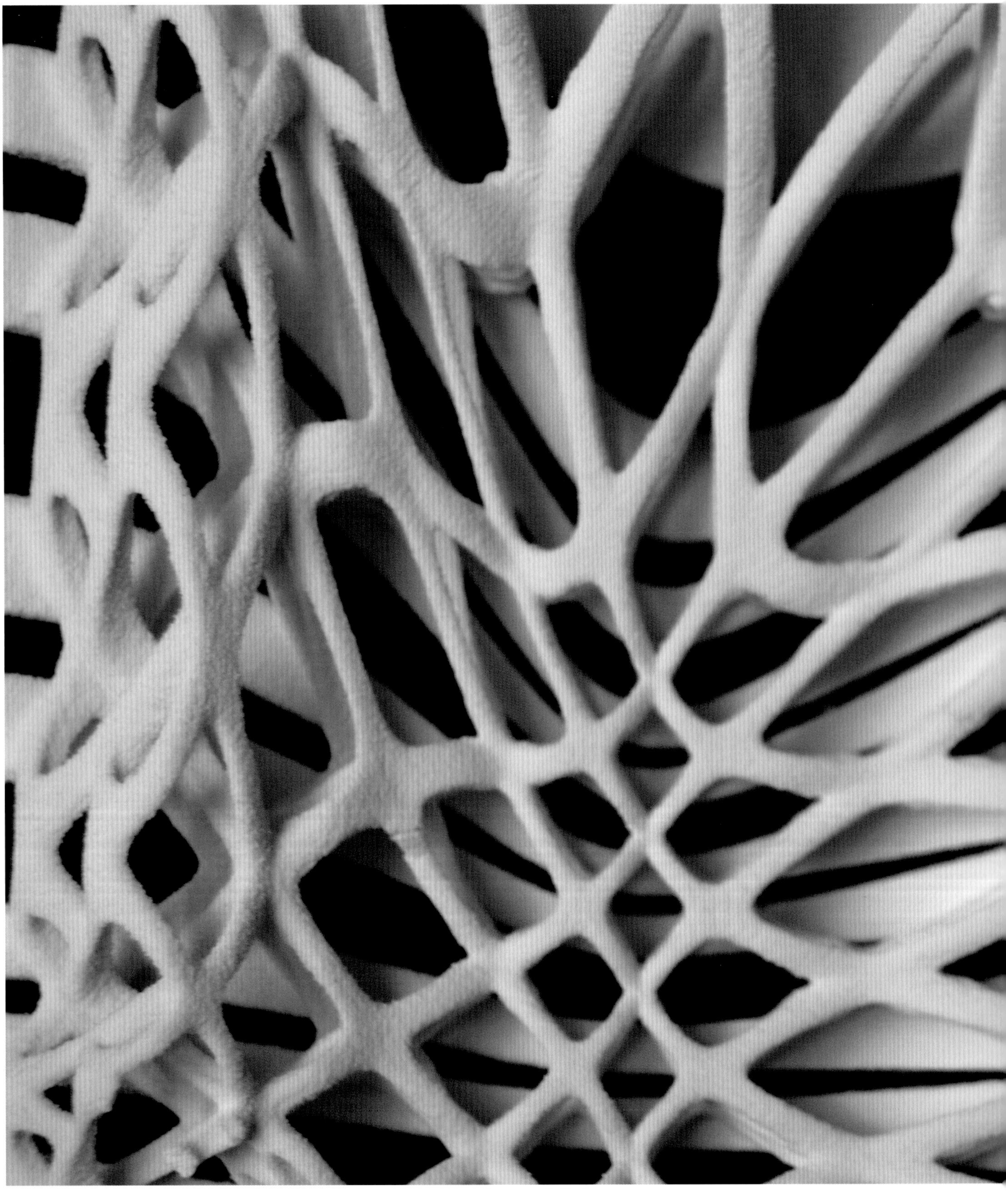

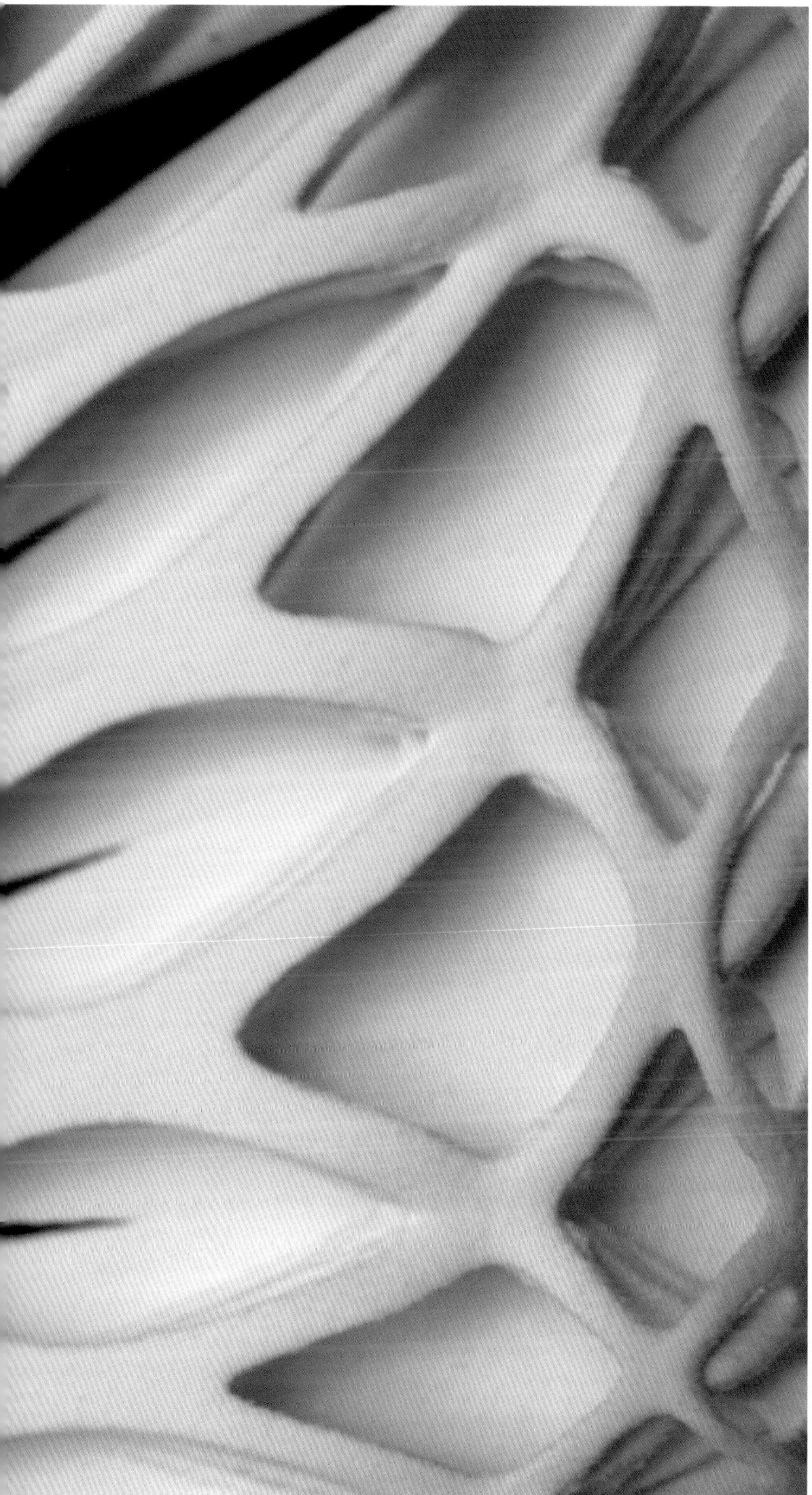

Nora Graw
Red Bull Pavilion
2006

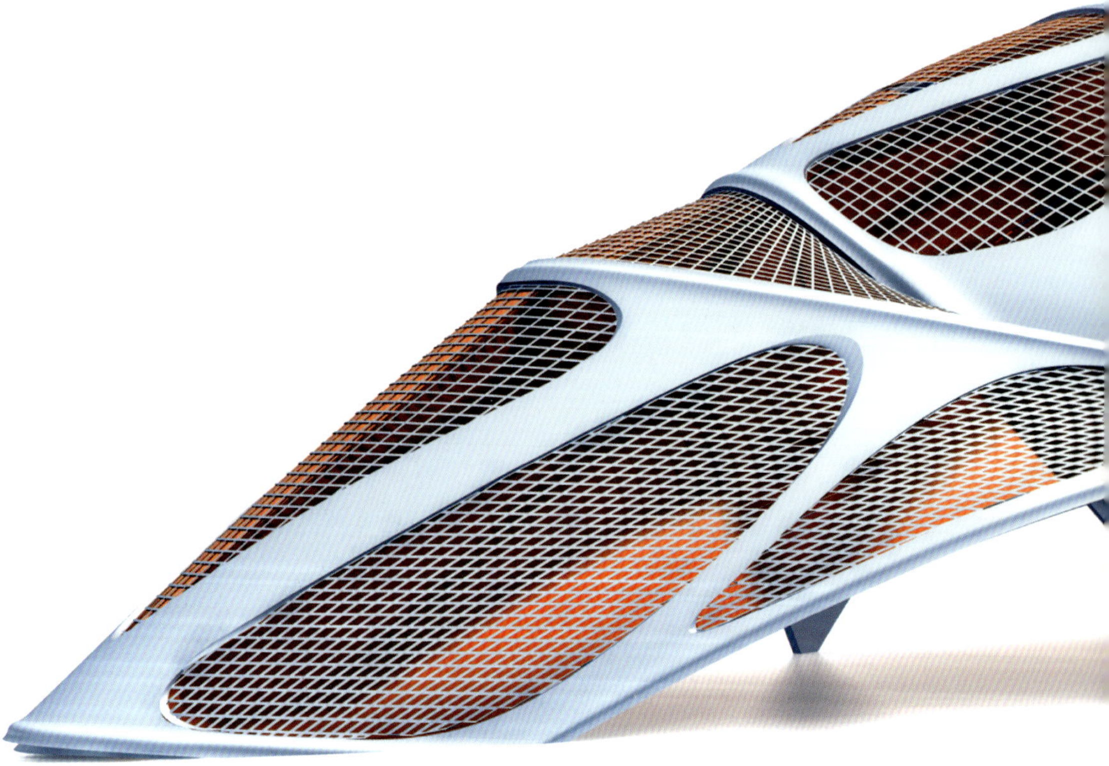

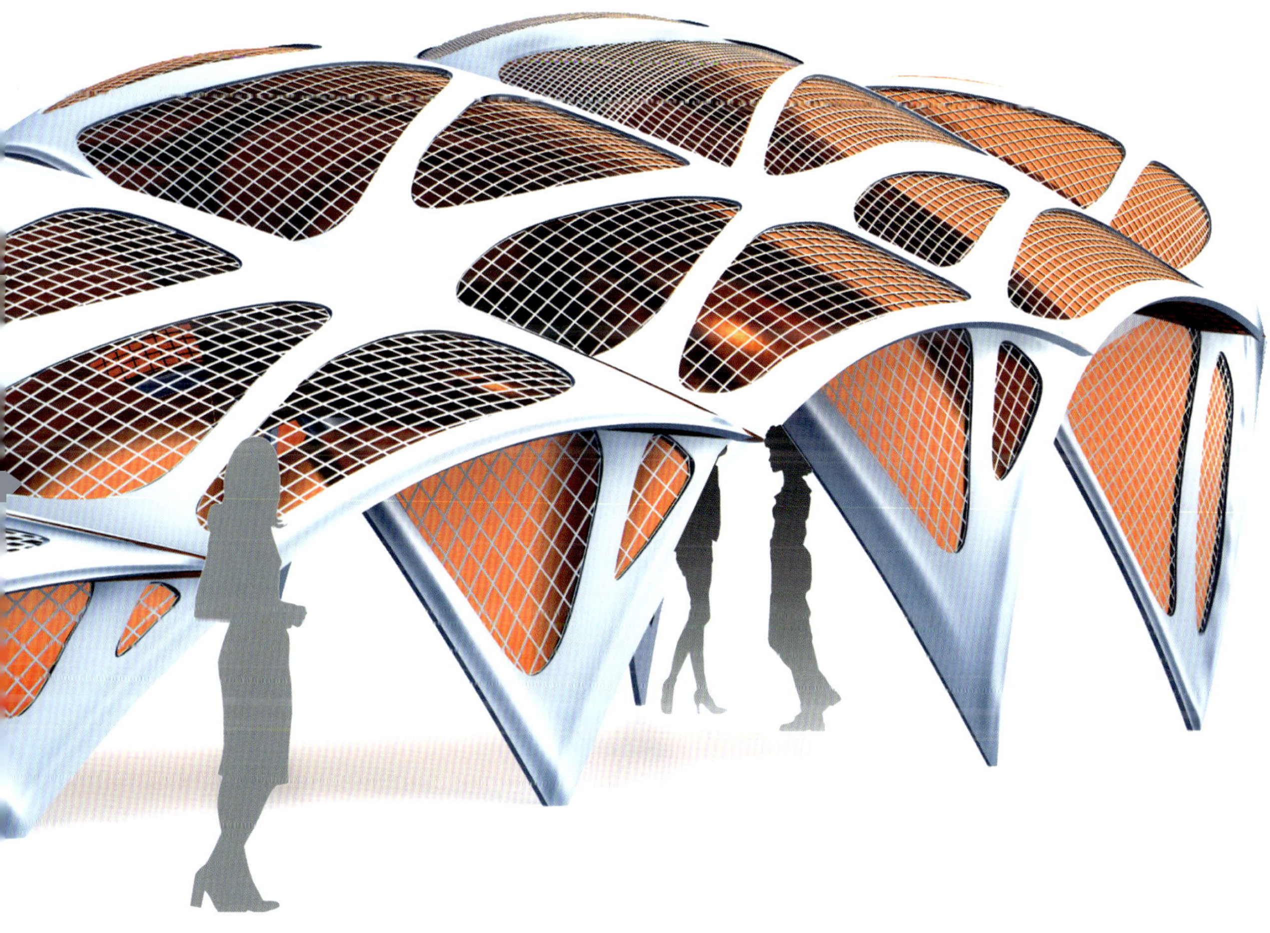

Julcsi Futo, Bika Rebek, Stefan Ritter
Factory for Tomorrow
2008

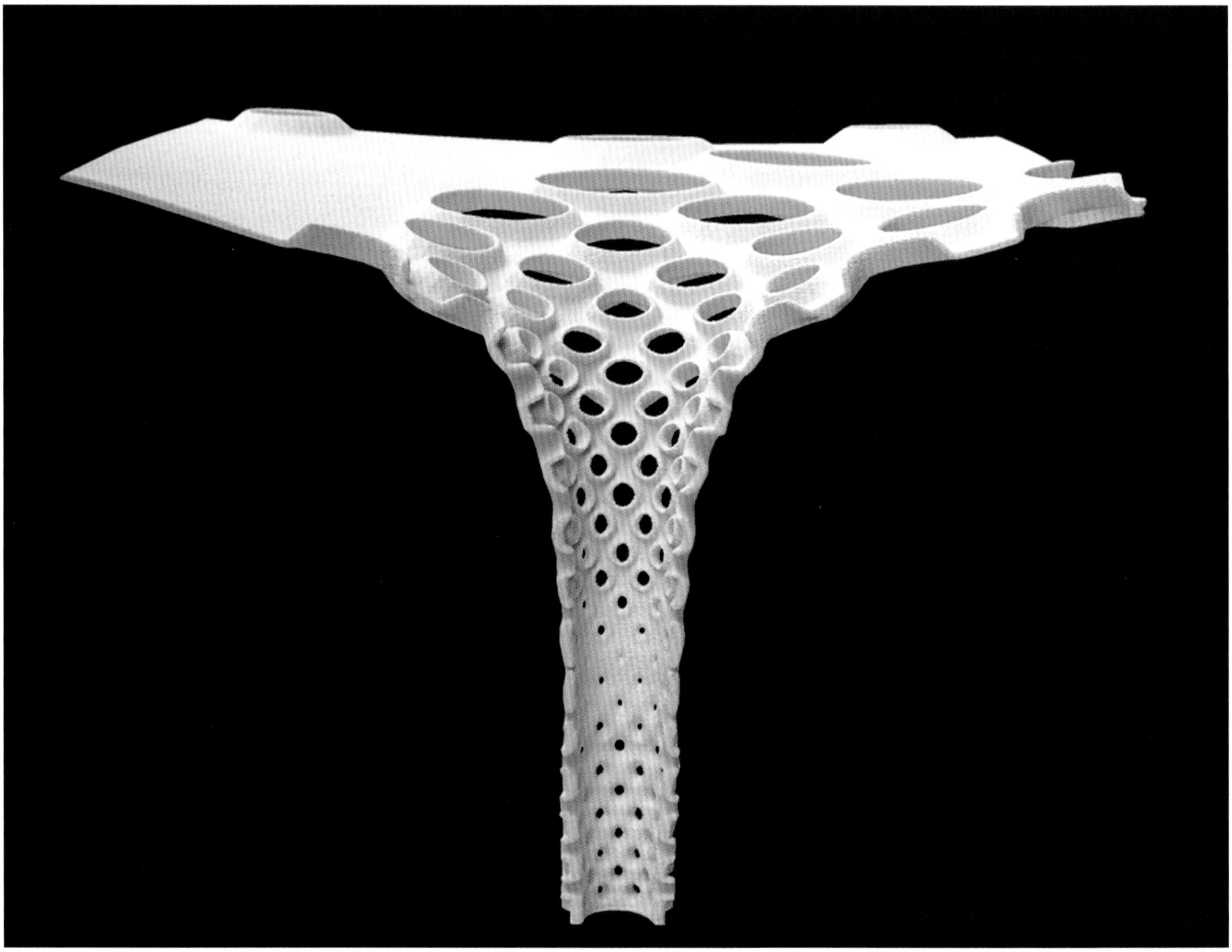

Dumëne Comploi

Multiplex

2005

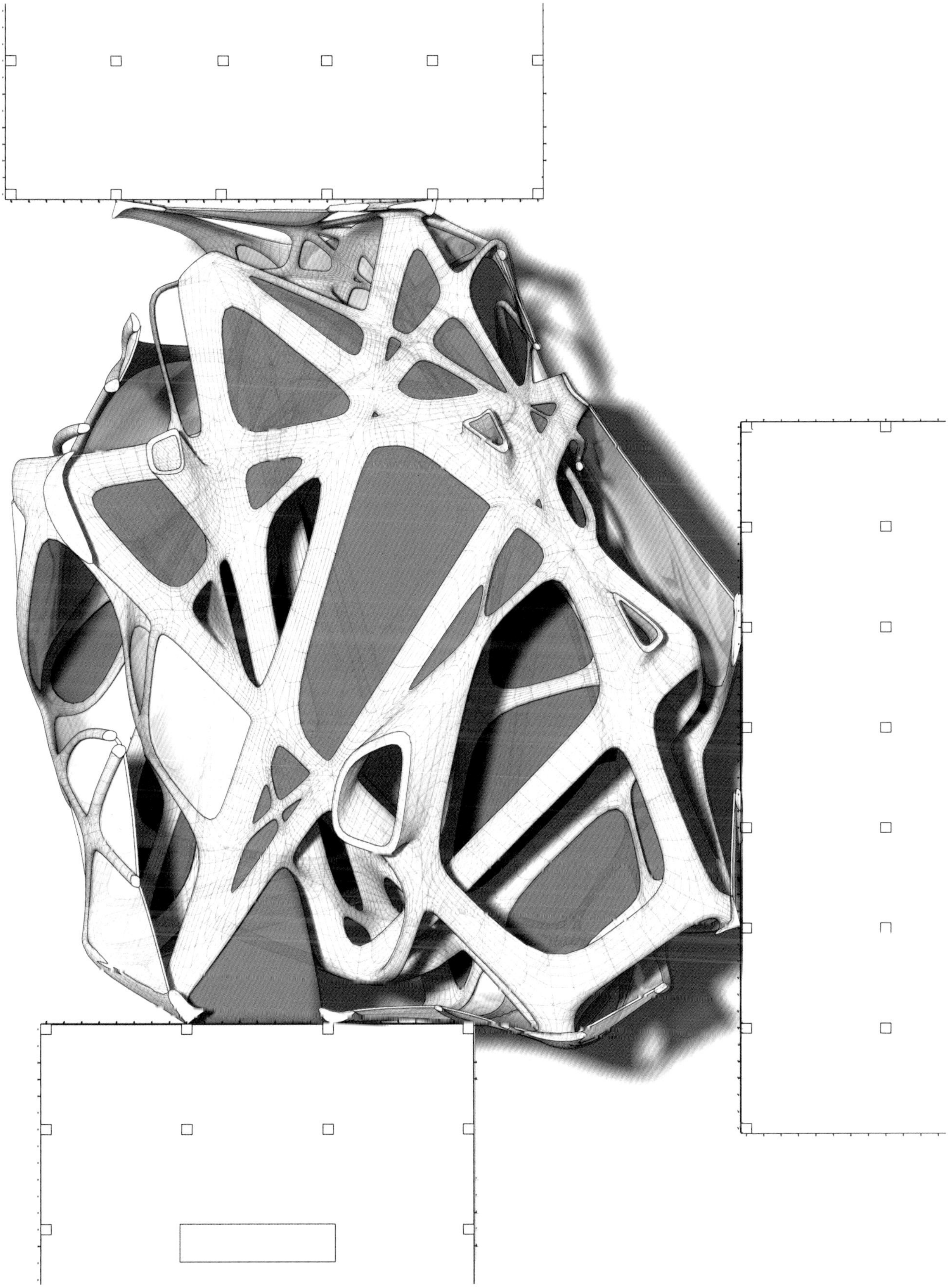

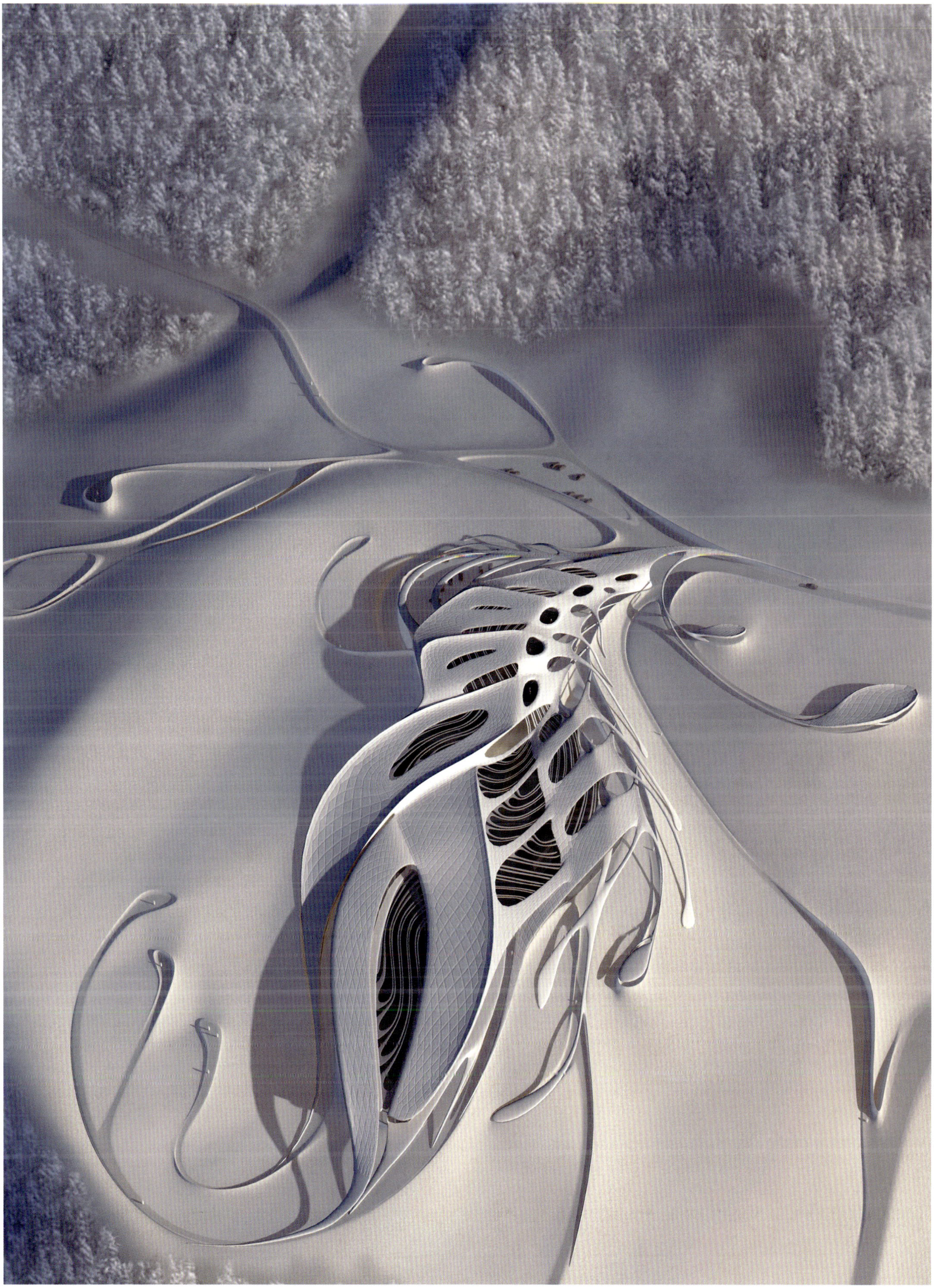

SELECTED EXCERPTS

Ornament and Conformity
Jesse Reiser
Reiser + Umemoto: Recent Projects
London: Academy Editions, 1998
p.32

Prominent among the dualisms that have regulated Western architectural thought has been the opposition between ornament and structure. Certainly, within the tendencies which may be associated with modernism that opposition has reached a critical and, one may say, even apocalyptic state; the most radical formulations attempting to erase one of the terms of the opposition (ornament), with the consequent movement of ornament into a covert or recessive condition within the prevailing structure. Postmodern practice, especially the historicist branch, promised to resuscitate ornament in response to what was perceived to be the sterility of a homogenous modernism. Both aspects of the classical relationship, however, continue to be upheld: the oppositional and the hierarchic domination of structure over ornament. On the one hand, ornament is detached from structure as a form of pastiche signage, and on the other, it manifests itself in the adornment of known types, especially in the collagist application of postmodern plan forms.

New architectural potential arises out of a fundamental reappraisal of the status of ornament and its implications for architectural organization. Axiomatic is the critique, and ultimately, the dismantling of the dualistic structure that has heretofore regulated these conceptions. First and foremost, it should be assumed, contrary to the classical formulation, that ornament is not subservient to structure, but that in fact, ornament is pre-eminently structure in itself; and furthermore, that what would classically be understood as structure is an inherent subset to, and of, the general ornamental organization. This collapsing of the duality has potentially far-reaching architectural consequences—though not, as one might immediately suppose, as a vehicle for producing yet another ornamentalised architecture. Rather, it employs the ornamental as a graphic instrument capable of engendering complex organizations and spatialities; in other words, those that would foster unforeseen irruptions of institutional forms and programmes.

Duck Soup
Peter Eisenman
Log 7
New York: Anyone Corporation, 2006
p.140

In the early 20th century, American pragmatist philosopher Charles Sanders Peirce put forward an articulate, three-part typology of signs: the icon, the symbol, and the index. The icon is distinguished by a similitude; it looks like its object, i.e.,a the hot dog stand that looks like a hot dog. The symbol is understood by convention or rule, like words in a sentence, or a classical facade symbolizing a public building. However, in a process of social transformation, forms, for example, the Greek colonnade, moved from being an icon to a symbol. In one sense, a symbol in architecture is a degraded icon, an icon that has become a cliché through repetition over an extended period of time. The history of classical architecture relies on symbolic conventions for its understanding. While some classical buildings became icons—in the visual sense of what a courthouse or a library was expected to look like—their primary resonance remained in the symbolic realm.

The last of Peirce's categories, the index, is understood as a record of a process or event, like the footprint that Robinson Crusoe discovers in the sand on the deserted island, which indicates human presence. Since architecture, because of its real presence and its need to resist gravity, will always look like architecture, it need not look like something else or represent something else; it can be merely an index of itself of its moment in time, of its process of becoming.

In one sense, since Alberti's critique of Vitruvius, buildings have always been iconic: they must not only stand up, they must also look like they are standing up. The operative words in this context are look like, that is, how they are seen.

Since the iconic relies more heavily than Peirce's other two sign categories on sight, its relationship to object buildings raises two issues concerned with seeing, the optical and the visual. The optical is a condition of sight that relies on direct sensory perception. It is the pure pleasure of seeing, like looking at an impressionist painting. The visual, on the other hand, requires not only physical evidence, but also the possibility in that physical evidence of something unseen, something that must be read into, like in a cubist painting. Thus, when an icon suggests a level of meaning or a metaphor, it can be understood as primarily visual. On the other hand, to the extent that an icon suggests a primary response to its shape or material, it is optical.

After-image

Ben van Berkel and Caroline Bos
Hunch 11: Rethinking Representation
Rotterdam: The Berlage Institute, Winter 2006–07
p.45

Images only partly work through meaning; the other part of their effectiveness resides in pure, physiological sensation, which exists separately from the world of signs of mental representations. The nature of vision, the optical system, ensures that the mind responds instantaneously to the eyes' actions. The eye is able to sense differences, to adjust, and to alert the mind.

This is why we decided to invest more in the longevity of our work by endowing our architecture with specific forms of intensity designed to generate the after-images that obstruct the onset of perceptual obsolescence. For, while the ideas, illusions, emotions, associations, and other mental constructs evoked by the sensations triggered by the optical system can be both stronger and longer-lived than any consciously created concepts of messages, they are not an intentional part of the architectural repertoire. Literally, the after-image refers to the lingering visual impression that is caused by intense or prolonged stimulation of the visual retina. To us, the after-image means something slightly different; we use the notion to include the entire scale of sensations and perceptions caused by intense impressions. We see design as the skeleton structure, which is clad with subsequent images, effects, and space-enhancing techniques. For centuries perspective has been used as a tool to stimulate perception, but perspectival distortion represents just one technique to enrich the awareness of space. Curved spaces go much further than only extending the forward-looking gaze; they open up a polycentric, camera-like perception of space into all directions and dimensions. Curved, continuous space, with its diagonal transecting areas, delivers unexpected spatial sensations. Ultimately, the concept of the after-image addresses the way architecture can continue to function as an art. The image of a building is not interesting anymore; architecture as art is about the image the viewer takes home. What do you remember? What was it all about?

VOLUME: VOID

SUPERFLAT LAYERING

The reduction of form to a set of two-dimensional layers arranged at varying depth. In relation to the Japanese art movement, the removal of 3-dimensional form places greater emphasis on flat figure and pattern but unlike superflat, depth is reconstructed through overlaid figure.

Superflat was coined by Takashi Murakami to describe representation that is devoid of perspective and hierarchy, with multiple components all existing equally and simultaneously. On many levels it references subculture, hyper graphics, the ultra cool, Japanese cartoon cultures of manga (comic books) and anime (animation). In architecture the technique is often employed in facades, to enhance the singularity of the façade with multiple readings that overlap and interrelate, blurring and distorting the depth of the façade. The skin appears both flat and voluminous; diverse effects transition from one to another continuously rather than discretely as panels and frames.

1 **Beat Zoderer**
Bulb No4 / 07, 2007
photographed by André Huber, image courtesy of Beat Zoderer

2 **Peter Callesen**
Holding on to Myself, 2006
photographed by Anders Sune Berg, image courtesy of Helene Nyborg Contemporary
www.petercallesen.com, www.helenenyborg.com

3 **Henri Rousseau**
The Equatorial Jungle, Chester Dale Collection in Washington, 1909
image courtesy of the Board of Trustees of the National Gallery of Art
www.nga.gov

4 **Gabriel Orozco**
Moon Axel, acrylic on linen canvas, 2005
image courtesy of Marian Goodman Gallery
www.mariangoodman.com

5 *Mosaic of Abraham*, Ravenna St. Vitale, 6th century

6 **Yayoi Kusama**
Dots Obsession, 1999
image courtesy of Yayoi Kusama
www.yayoi-kusama.jp

7 **Takashi Murakami**
Kansei Gold, acrylic and gold leaf on canvas, 160 × 151cm, 2008
image courtesy of Blum & Poe and Takashi Murakami/Kaikai Kiki Co.

www.kaikaikiki.co.jp

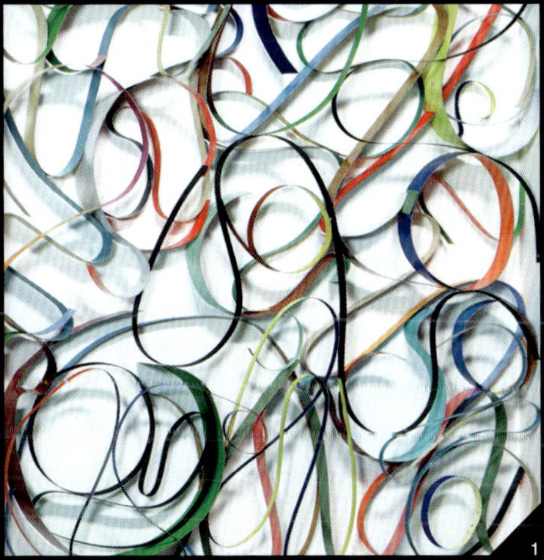

1

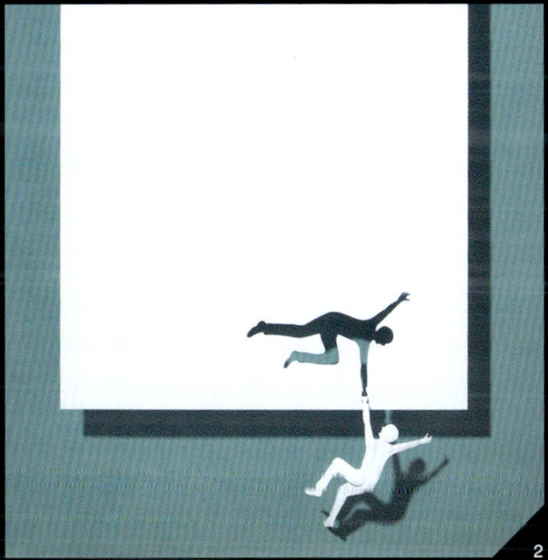

2

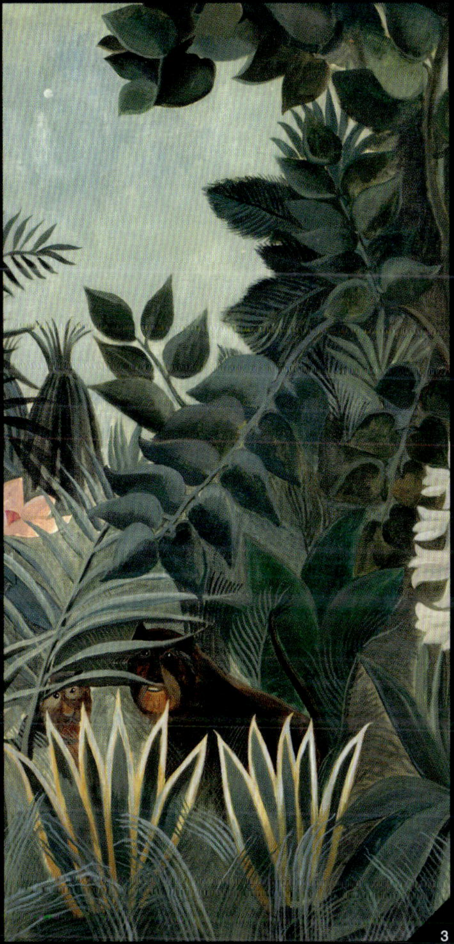

3

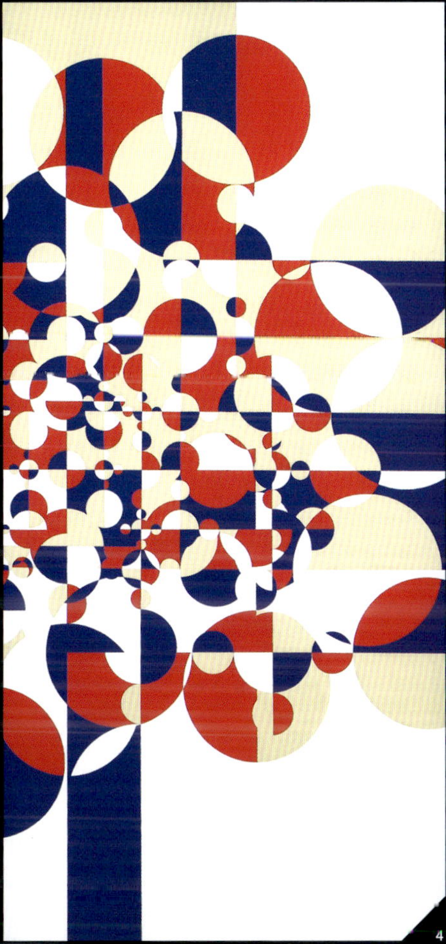

4

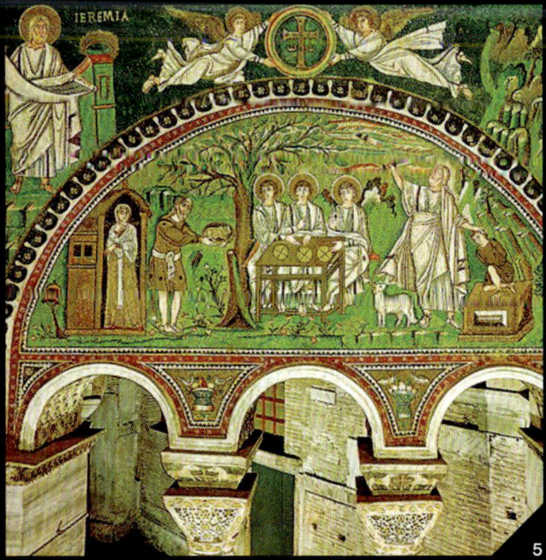

5

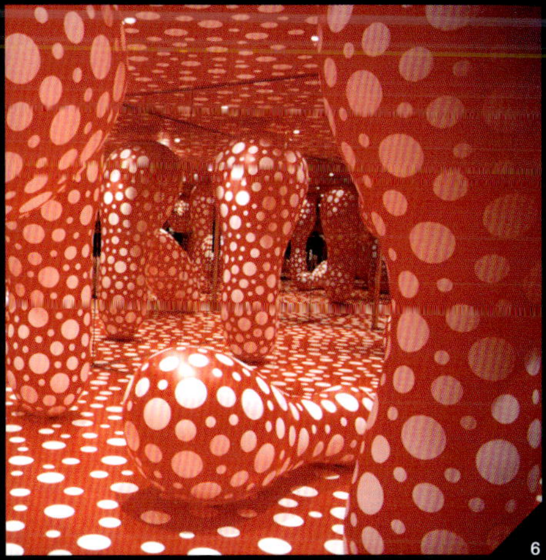

6

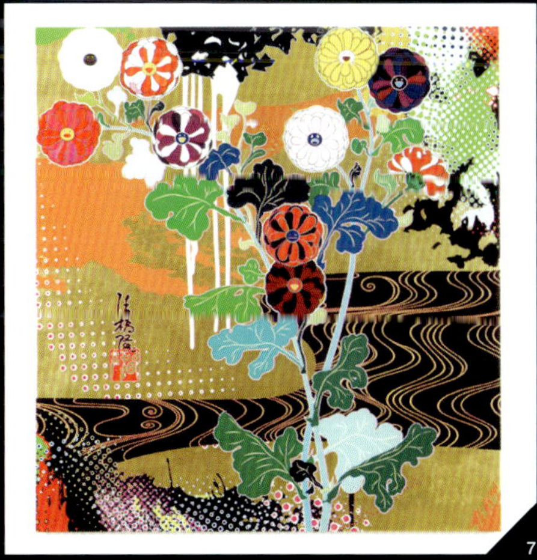

7

Bence Pap
Diploma
2006

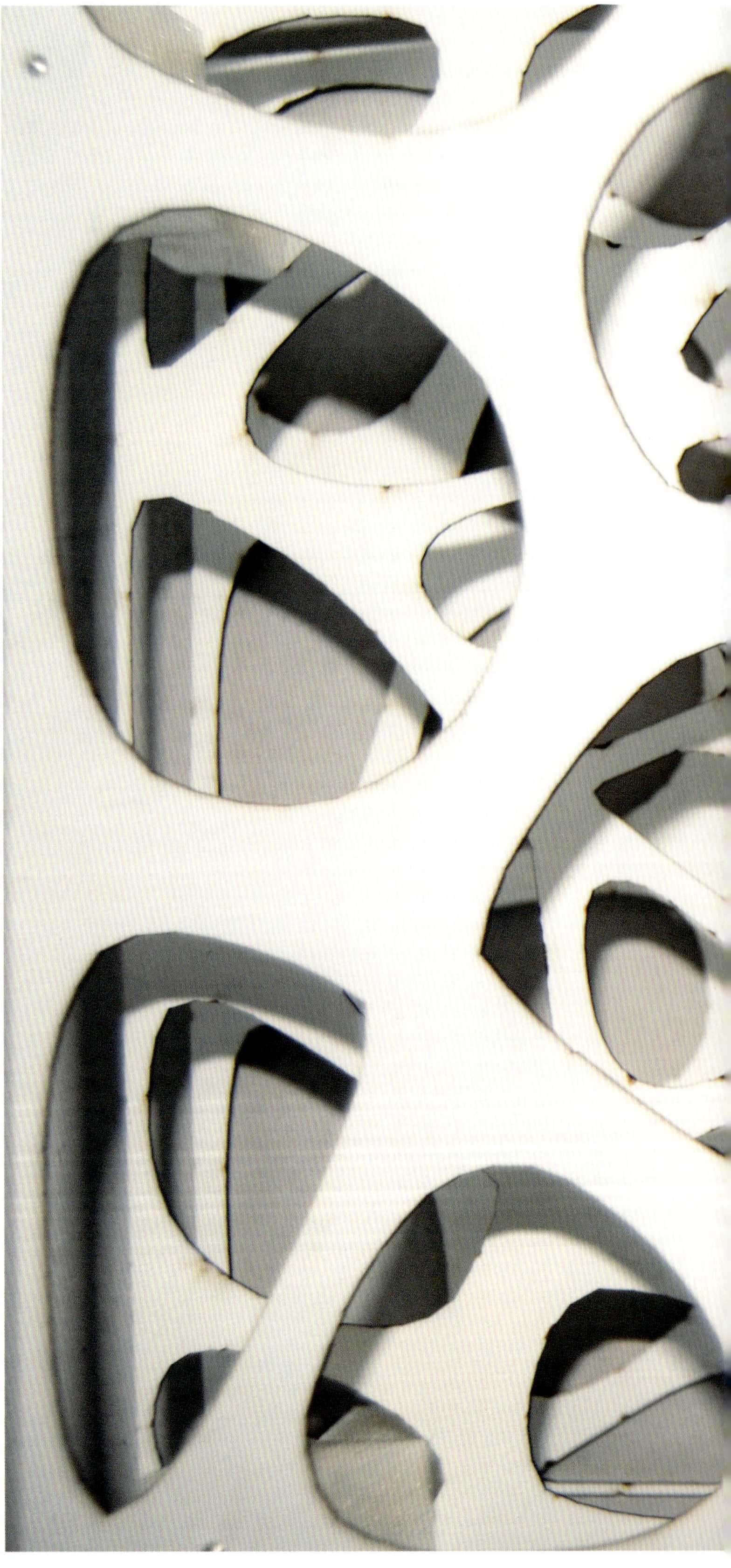

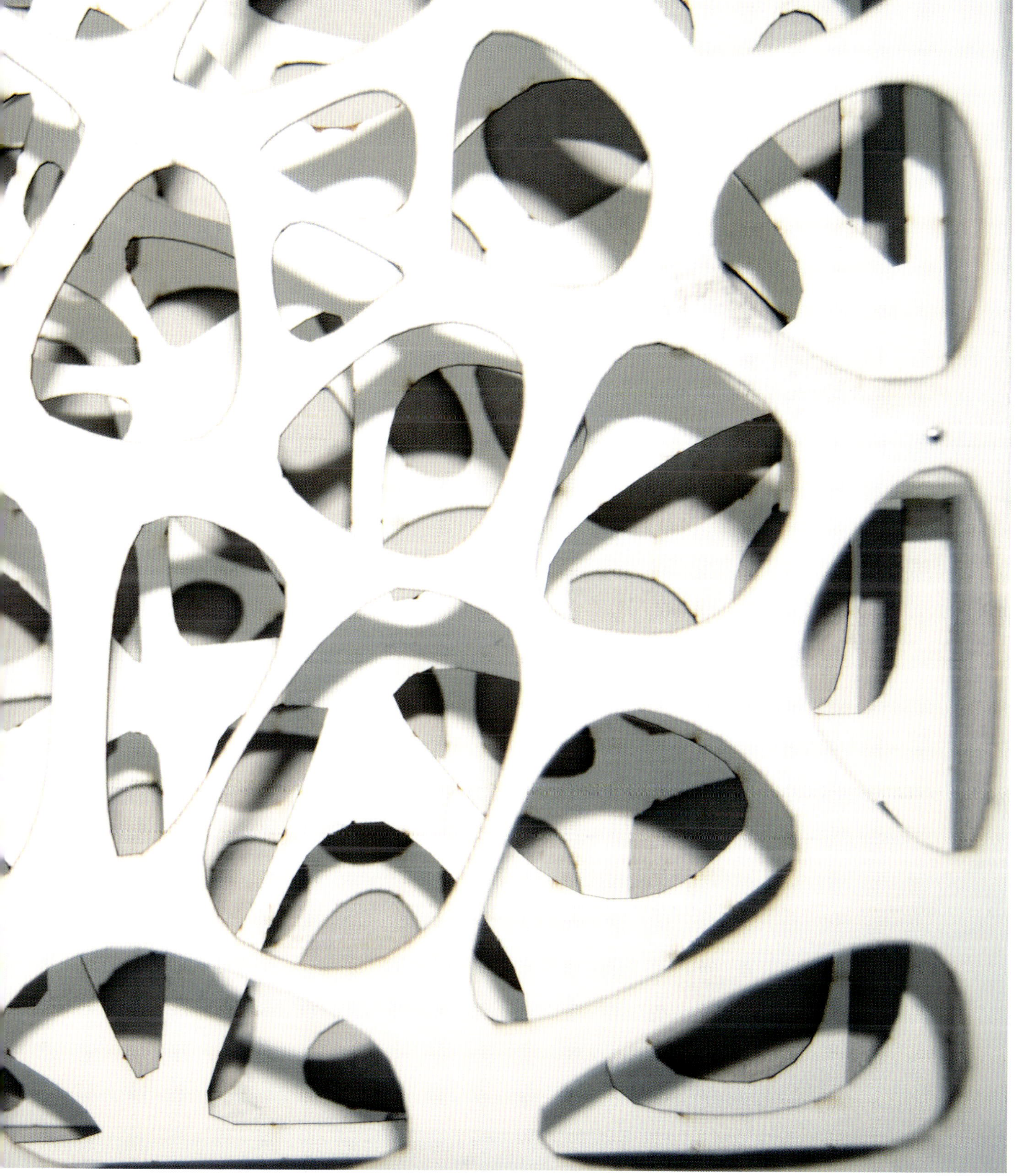

Sarah Schneider
Space Collective (model)
2007

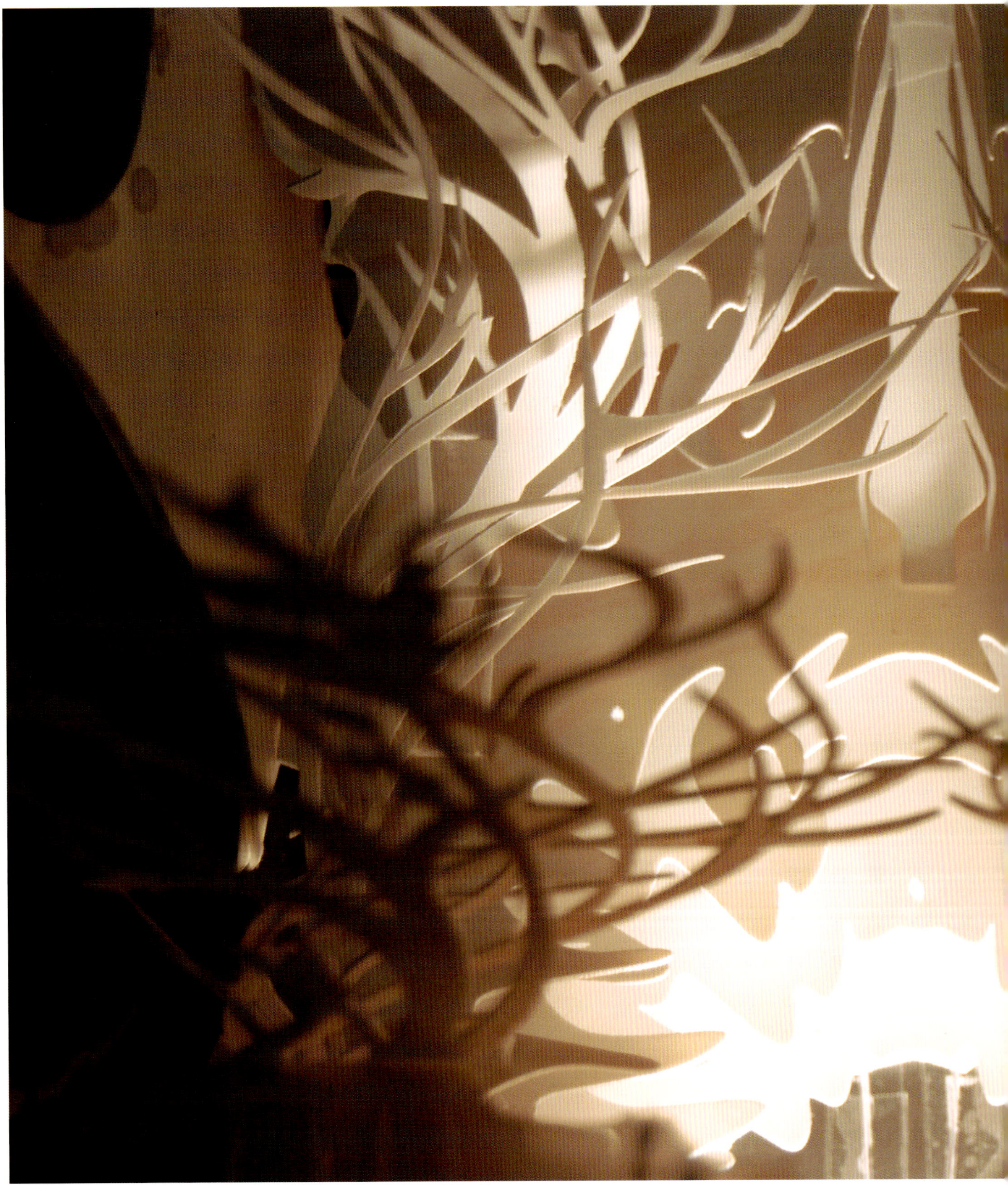

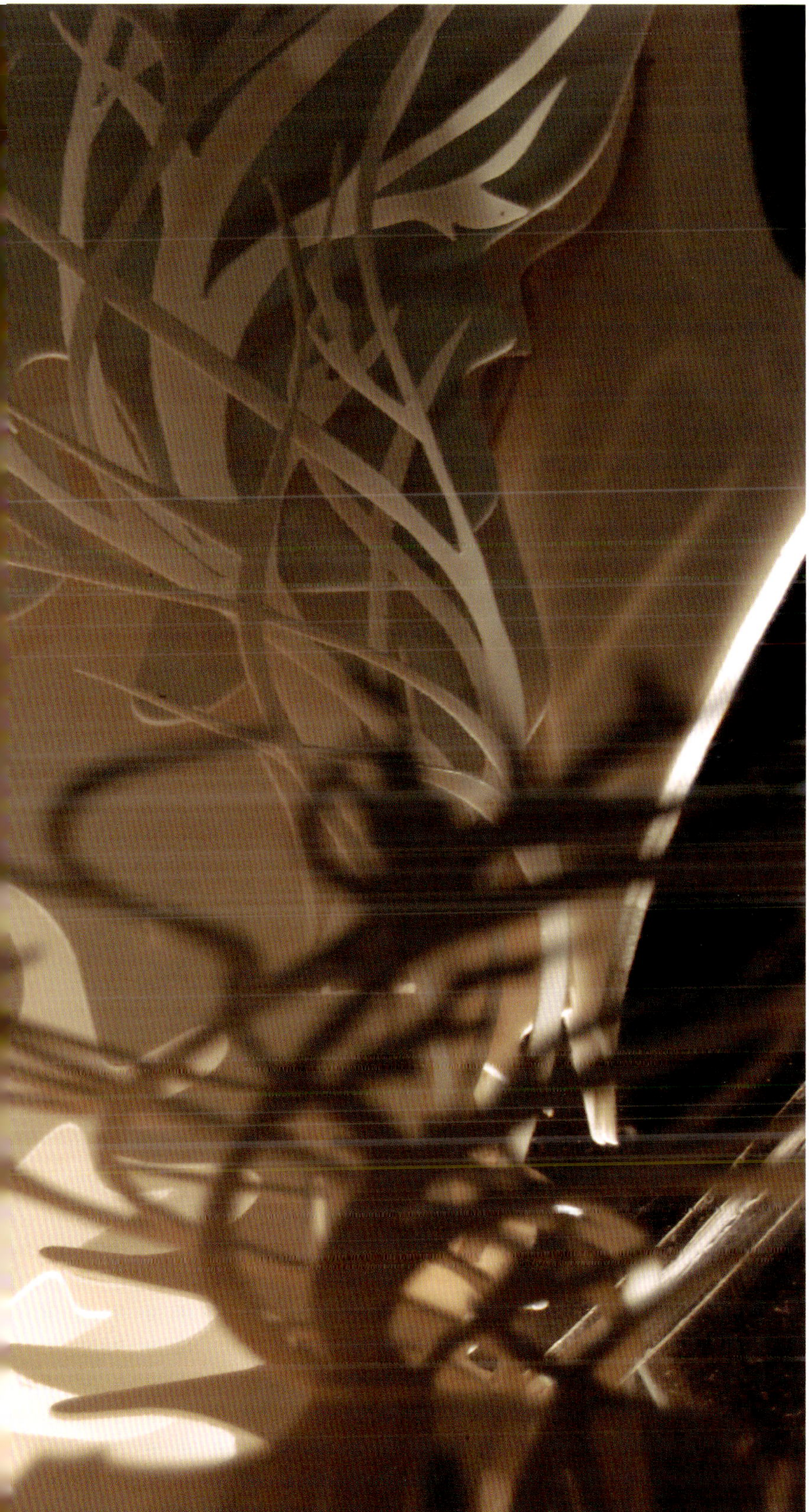

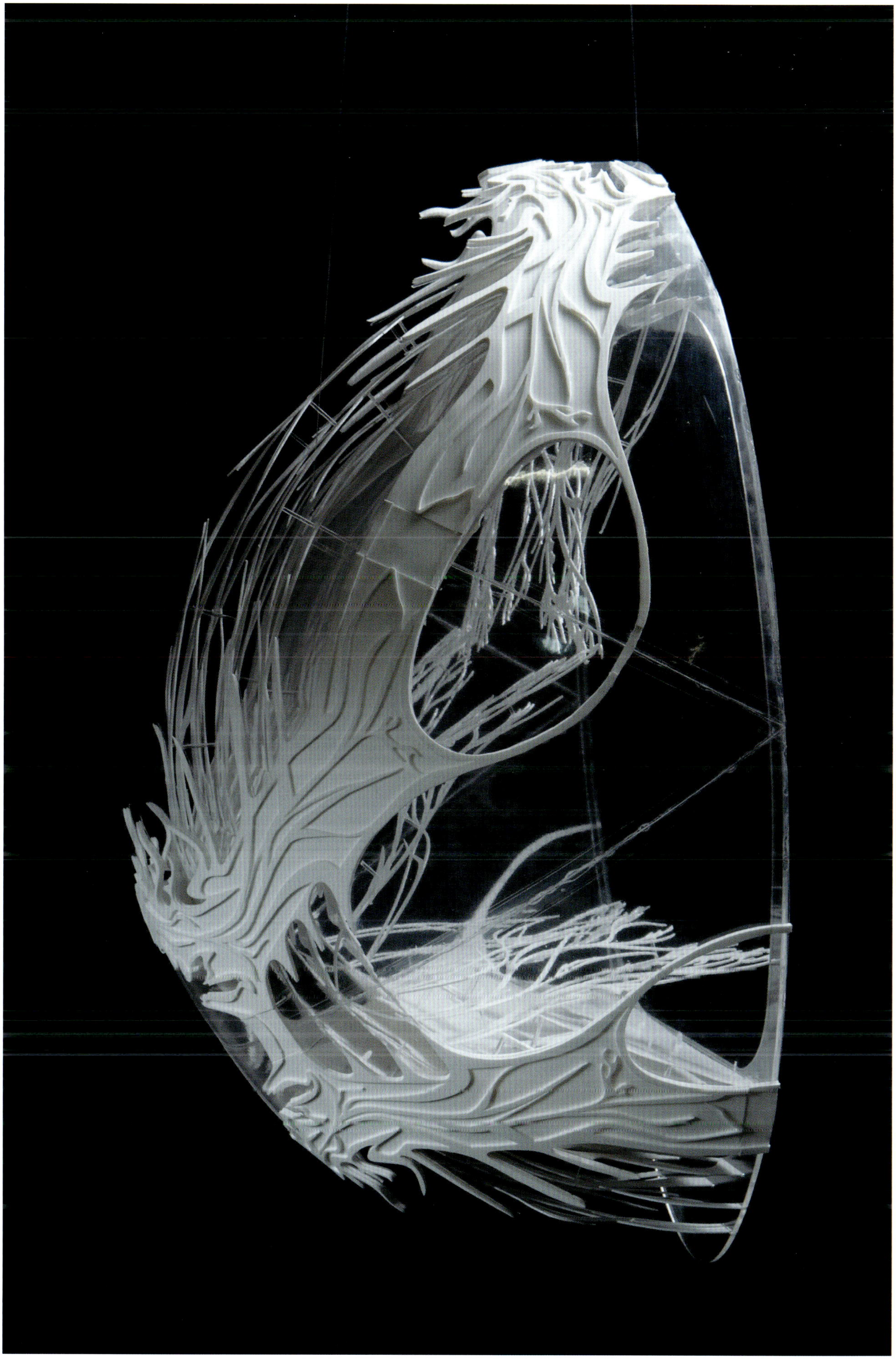

Tim Altenhof
Dominion Center
2005

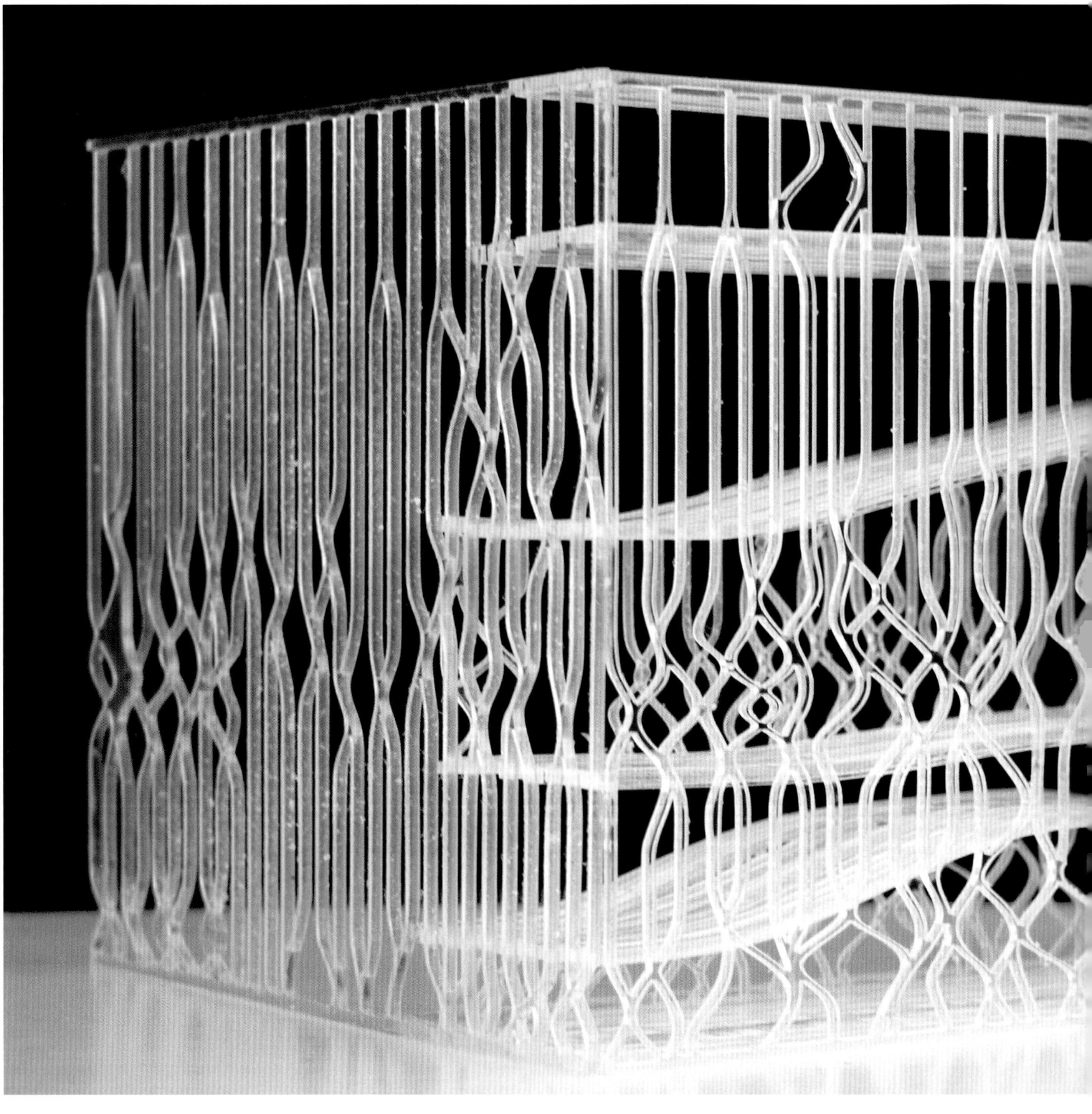

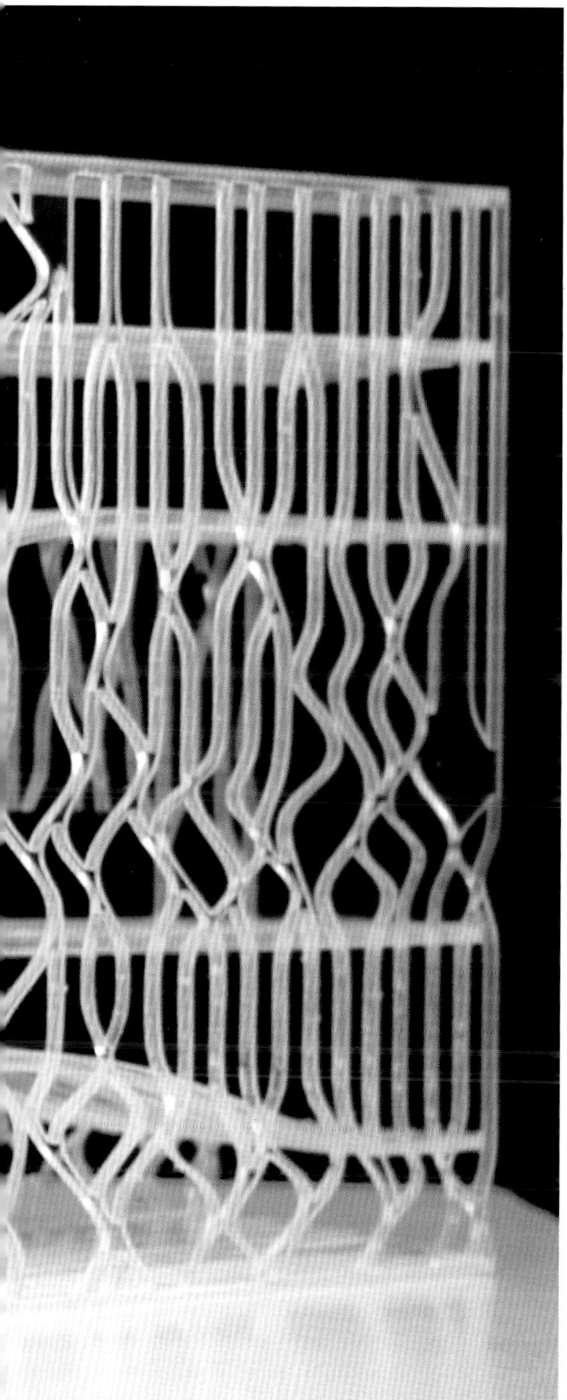

SELECTED EXCERPTS

Perspective as Symbolic Form
Erwin Panofsky
Perspective as Symbolic Form (1927),
trans: Christopher S. Wood
New York: Zone Books, 1991
p.47–49

The art historical mission of the Middle Ages was to blend what was once a multiplicity of individual objects (no matter how ingeniously linked to one another) into a true unity. This new unity—and this is only apparently a paradox—was arrived at only by way of smashing the existing unity: that is, by consolidating and isolating objects which were once bound by corporeal and gestural as well as spatial and perspectival ties. At the close of antiquity, and in conjunction with the increase of Eastern influences (whose appearance here, to be sure, is less a cause than a symptom and instrument of the new development), the freely extended landscape and the closed interior space begin to disintegrate. The apparent succession of forms into depth gives way again to superposition and juxtaposition. The individual pictorial elements, whether figures, buildings or landscape motifs, until now partly the contents, partly the components of a coherent spatial system, are transmuted into forms which, if not yet completely leveled, are at least entirely oriented toward the plane. These forms stand in relief against a gold or neutral ground and are arrayed without respect to any previous compositional logic.

This development can be followed almost step by step between the second and the sixth centuries. A work like the Abraham mosaic from San Vitale in Ravenna is especially noteworthy, for here we can observe quite plainly the disintegration of the perspectives idea: not merely plants, but indeed the formations of the earth, which in the Odyssey landscapes were cut off by the edge of the picture as if by a window frame, must now accommodate themselves to the curve of that edge. It can hardly be expressed more clearly that the principle of a space merely excised by the picture's edge is now beginning to give way to the principle of the surface bounded by the picture's edge, a surface that expects not to be seen through but rather filled. The "foreshortenings" of Greco-Roman art, finally, lose their original representational meaning—that of creating space—and yet retain their fixed linear forms; they thus undergo the most curious, but often uncommonly expressive, reinterpretations: the former vista or "looking through" begins to close up. At the same time it can be seen how precisely here the individual pictorial elements, which had almost completely lost their gestural and corporeal dynamic relationship and their perspectival spatial relationship, could be joined in a new and, in a certain sense, more intimate relationship: in an immaterial but unbroken tissue, as it were, within which the rhythmic exchange of color and gold or, in relief sculpture, of light and dark, restores a kind of unity, even if only a coloristic or luminous unity. The particular form of this unity once again finds its theoretical analogue in the view of space of contemporary philosophy: in the metaphysics of light of pagan and Christian neoplatonism. "Space is nothing other than the finest light" according to Proclus; here, just as in art, the world is conceived for the first time as a continuum. It is also robbed of its solidity and rationality: space has been transformed into a homogeneous and, so to speak, homogenizing fluid, immeasurable and indeed dimensionless.

A Theory of Superflat Japanese Art
Takashi Murakami
Superflat
Tokyo: Madora Shuppan, 2000
Excerpts from p.9 and p.15

The Japanese art historian, Nobuo Tsuji, in his book "The Lineage of Eccentricity," produced the concept of "eccentricity," which was a revolutionary concept in the understanding of post-war Japanese art history. This study of "a lineage of artists with expressionistic tendencies from the Edo period whose shared characteristic was the production of eccentric and fantastic images" looks at six artists: Iwasa Matabei, Kano Sansetsu, Ito Jakuchu, Soga Shohaku, Nagasawa Rosetsu, and Utagawa Kuniyoshi. While praising them as avant-garde of their day, Tsuji implies a similarity to what he calls contemporary "manga and poster art." His work introduces these "eccentric artists" who had not received much critical attention prior to his contextualization of their work. The sequel, "The Categories of Eccentricity," takes up the works of Katsushika Hokusai and Ito Jakuchu, arguing a theory of "decorative culture."

The strange style of timing structure in Japanese television animation, which I had been interested in for some time, matched perfectly with my interest in the six eccentric artists discussed in "The Linage of Eccentricity." In the past I had thought about the logic of that animation by thinking about the movement of the observer's gaze along planes in Japanese art using reproductions of Hokusai and Shohaku's made by the German Manga artist Horst Janssen. I was unsatisfied with the answers I found until I came across the word "eccentricity," which I thought fit perfectly. Having majored in Japanese painting at university, I was surprised to discover that all of the artists I liked fell into this "lineage of eccentricity." At the same time, the book also was a great help in thinking about the formula for composition structure that I am always concerned with as an artist.

I thought that perhaps the way that a picture controls the speed of its observer's gaze, the course of that gaze's scan, and the subsequent control of the information flow might match well with the artists' concepts that Tsuji described in his book. It was from these hypotheses that my theory of "super flat" was born. All of the "eccentric" artists shared a certain structural methodology, in which they created surface images that erased interstices and thus made the observer aware of the images' extreme planarity. [Portions omitted]

That extreme planarity and distribution of power allowed the viewer to assemble an image in their minds from the fragments they gathered scanning the image. This movement of the gaze over an image is a key concept in my theory of the "super flat."

[Remaining portions omitted]

VOLUME: VOID

PROGRAMMED POCHE

Thickened zones traditionally necessary for structure can also perform as an organizational device creating left-over, particularly shaped secondary spaces between or adjacent to primary volumes.

In contrast to the evenness of modernist spatiality, the spatial hierarchy produced by layering volumes from outside to inside allows for varying levels of interiority and a distinct but integral relation between one space and the next. To occupy programmed poche is to feel other volumes pressing in from all sides; to be simultaneously aware not just of the room you are standing in, but also its neighbors. But beyond its phenomenological effects, programmed poche is a logic of integral difference, and thus a strategy for producing mate-

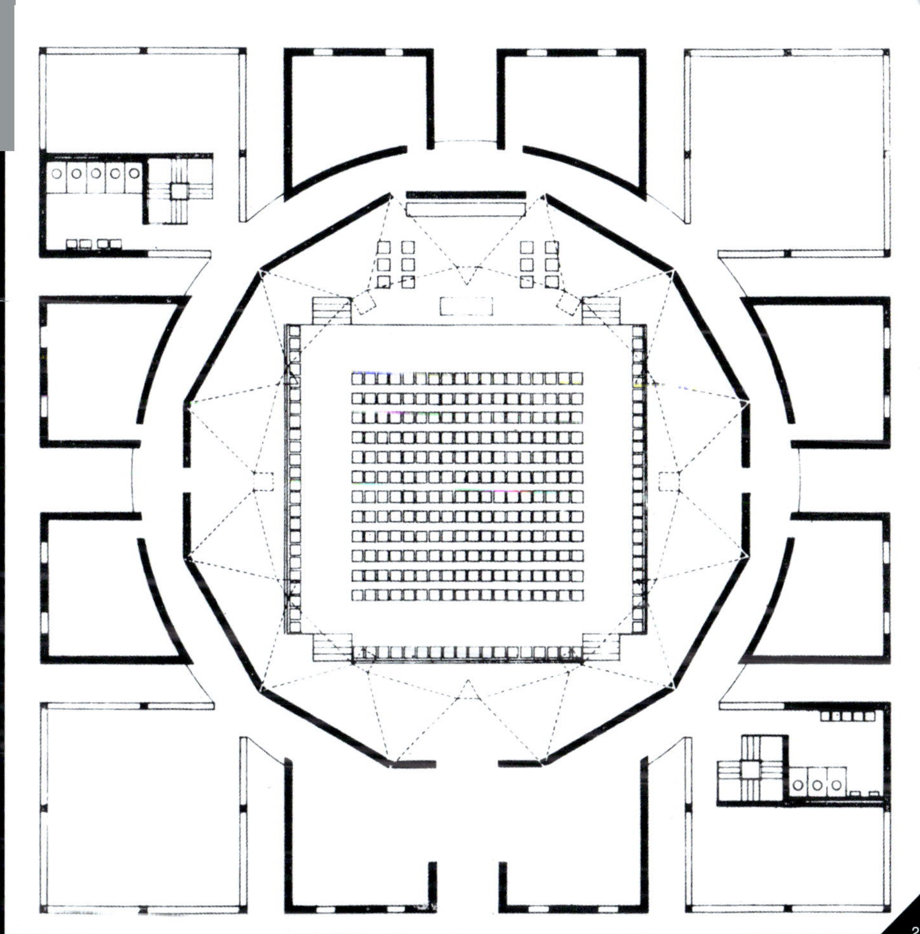

2

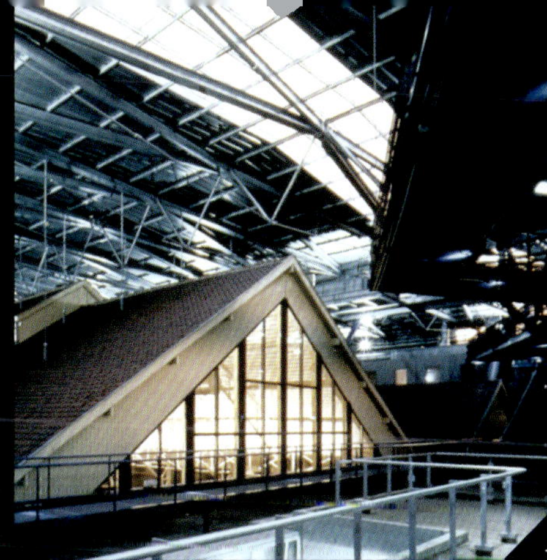

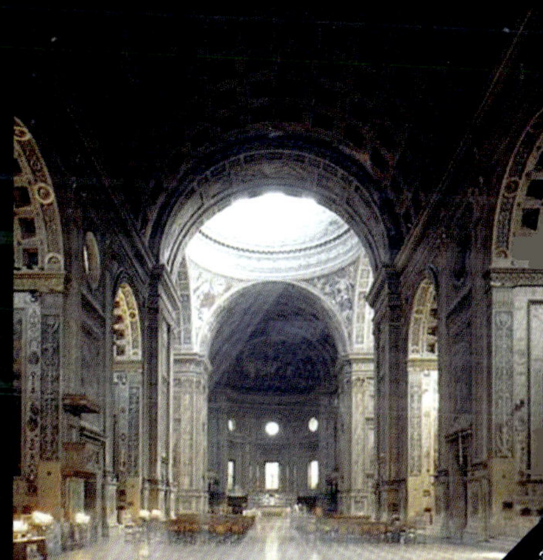

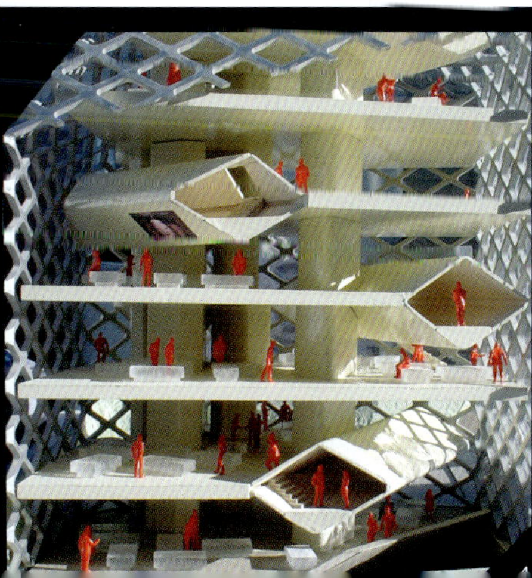

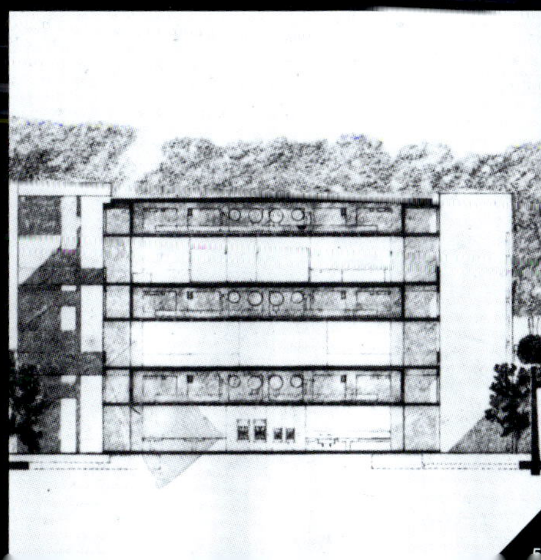

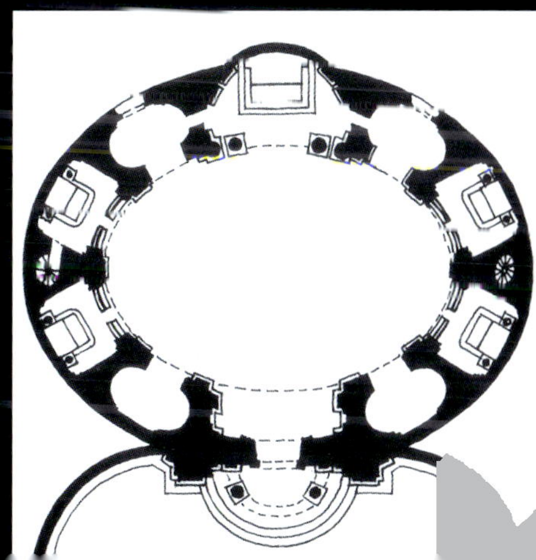

Adam Lind and Jon Anderson
Car Design Center
2006

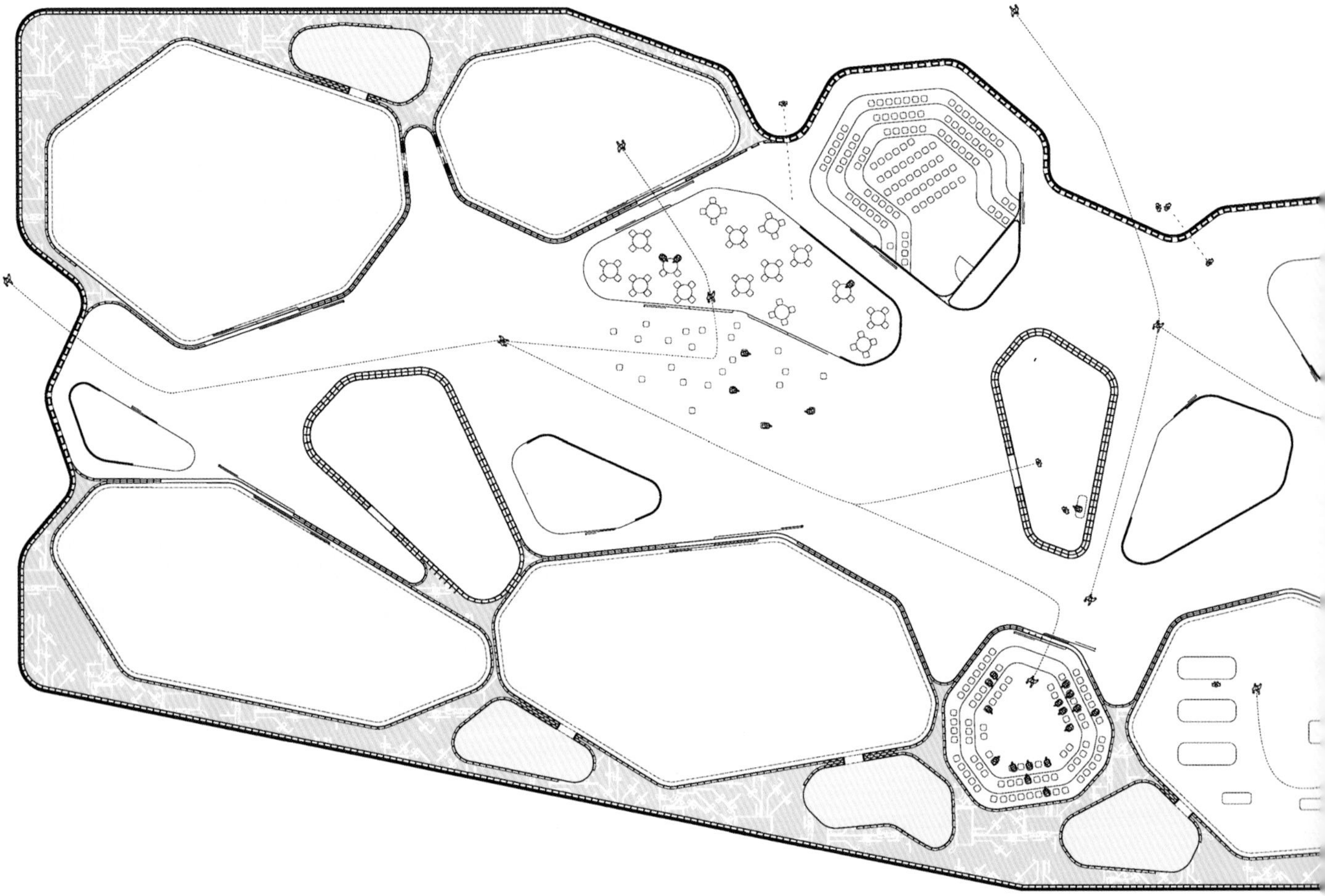

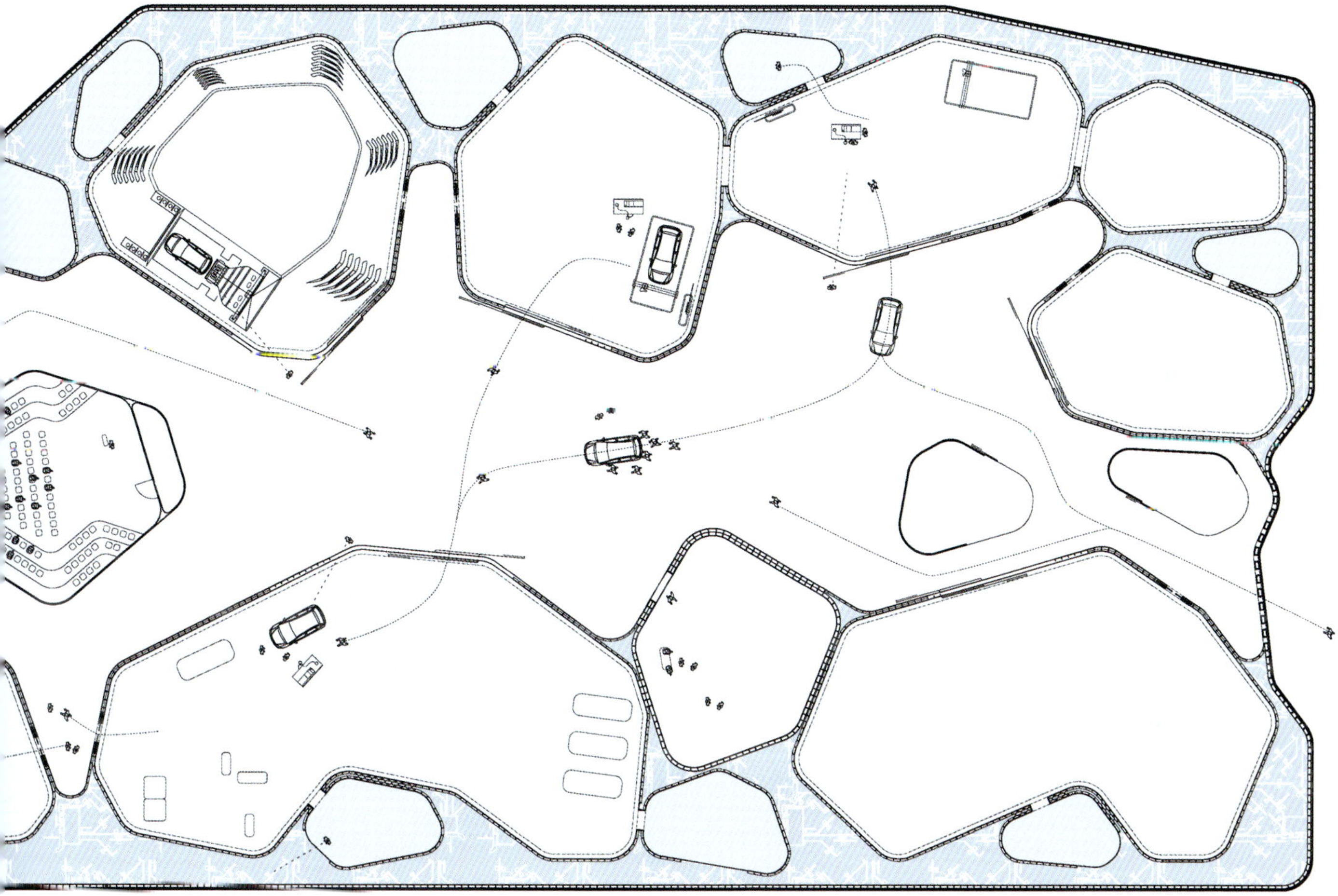

Anna Edthofer and Maja Ozvaldic
Car Design Center
2006

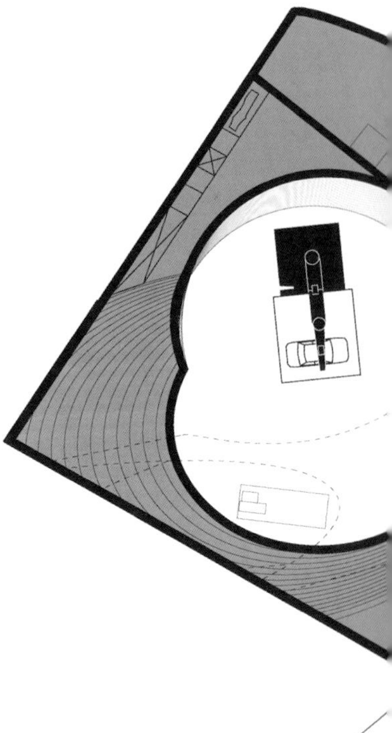

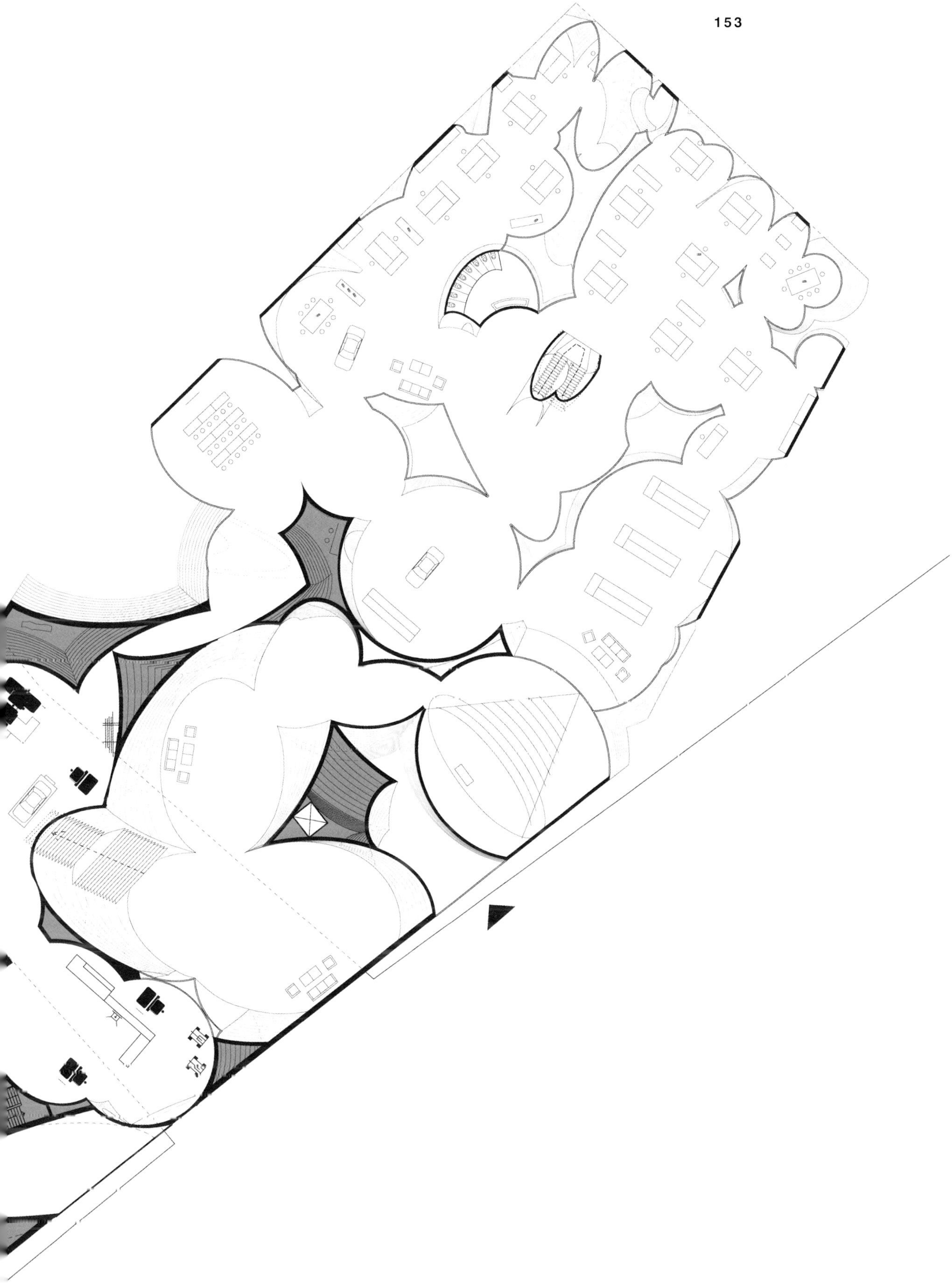

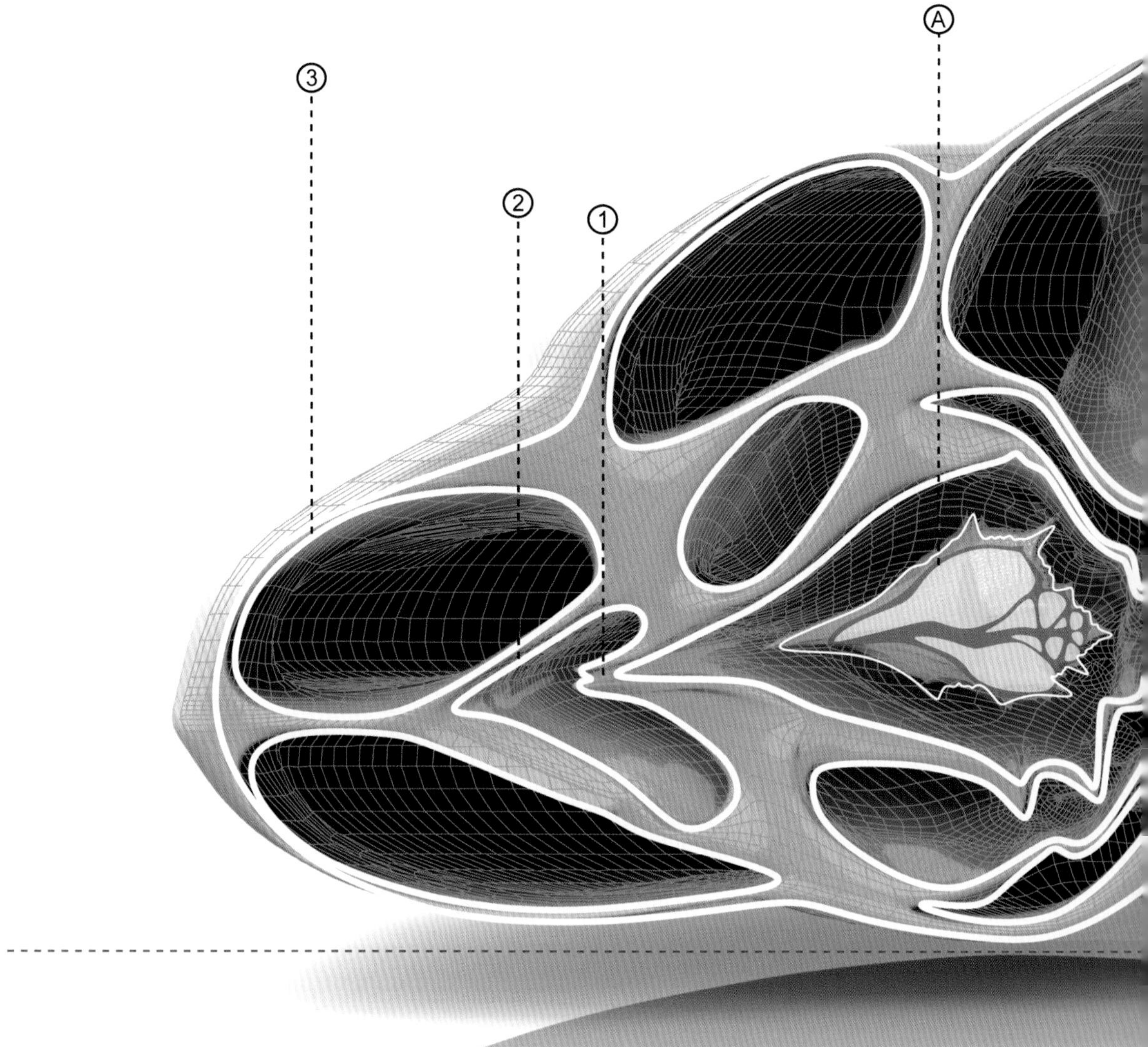
A
3
2
1

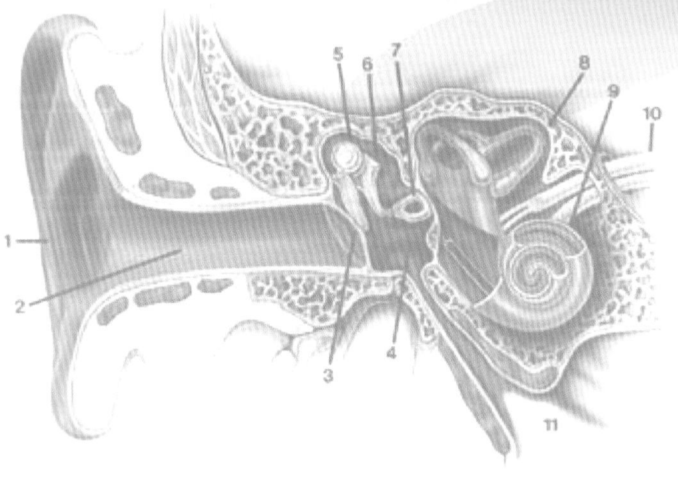
5
6
7
8
9
10
1
2
3
4
11

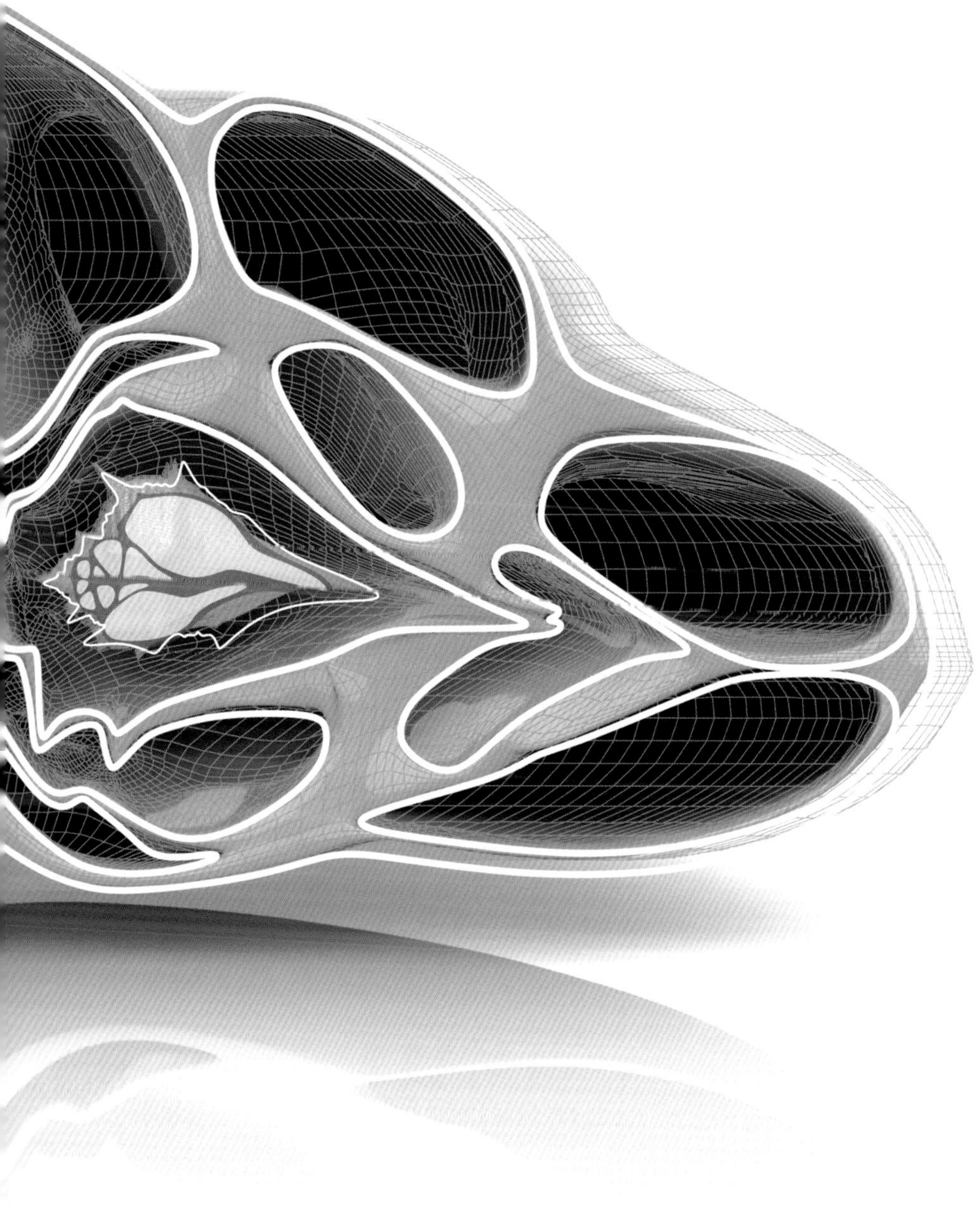

Miljan Radojevic and Joseph Hofmacher

Performance Hall

2007

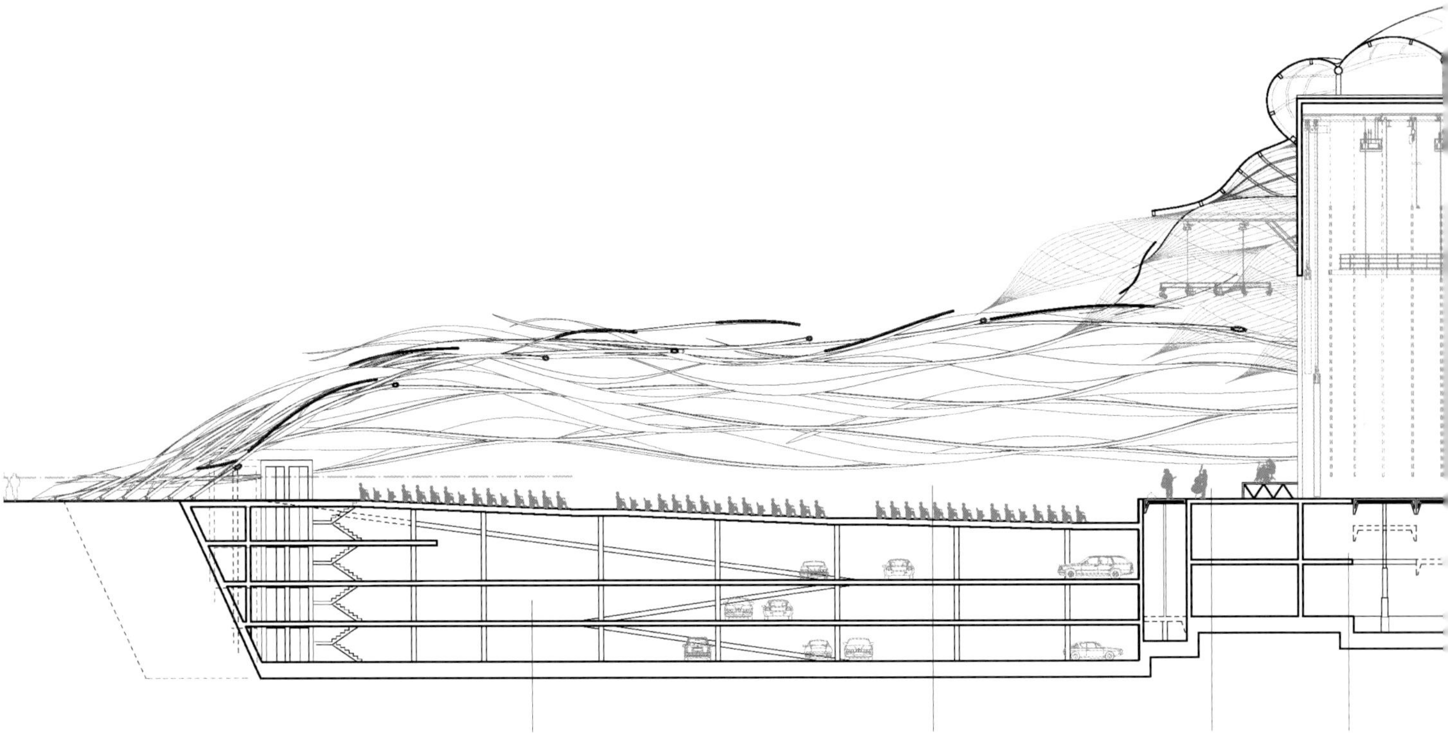

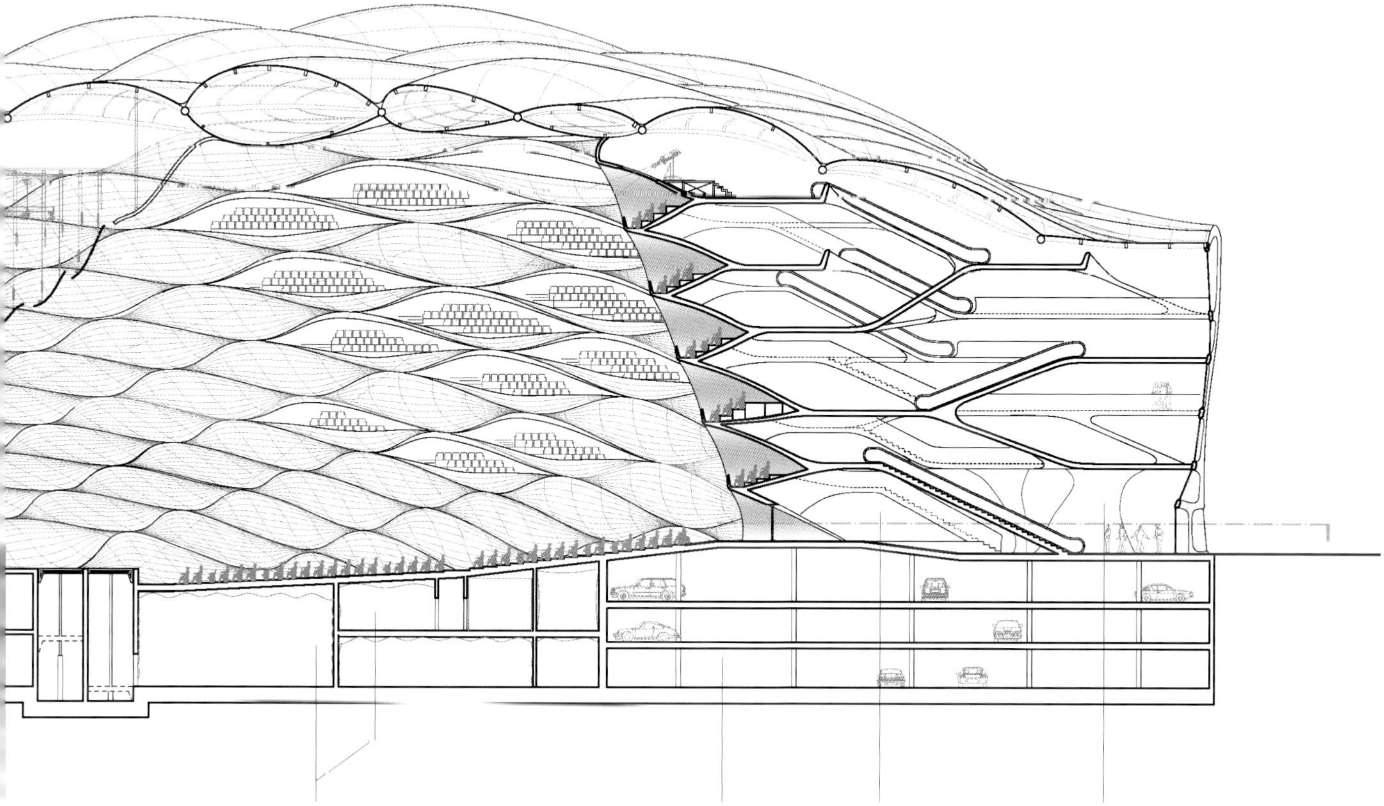

Elisabeth Brauner
Diploma: Center for Phytogenetic Research and Preservation
2007

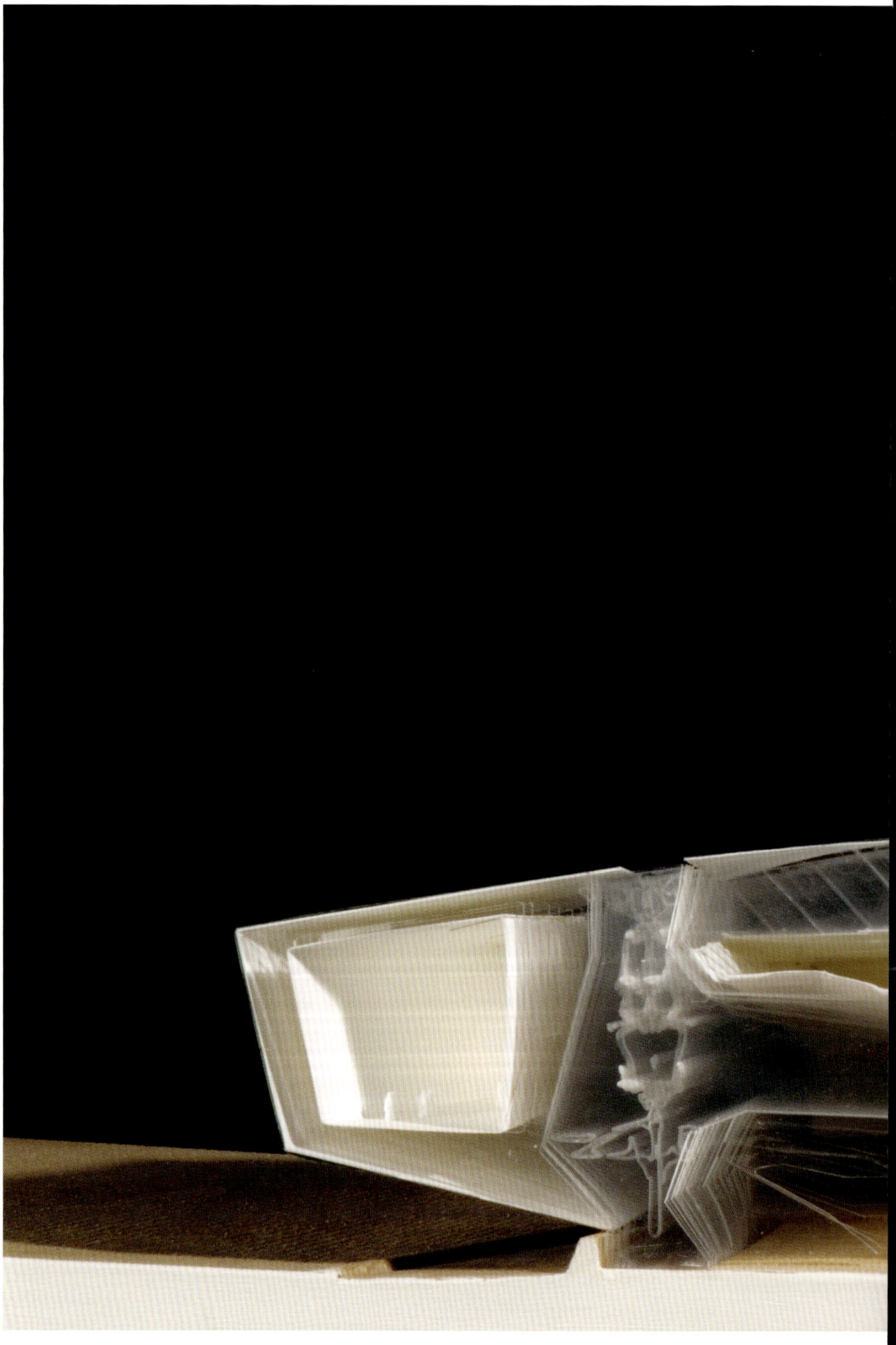

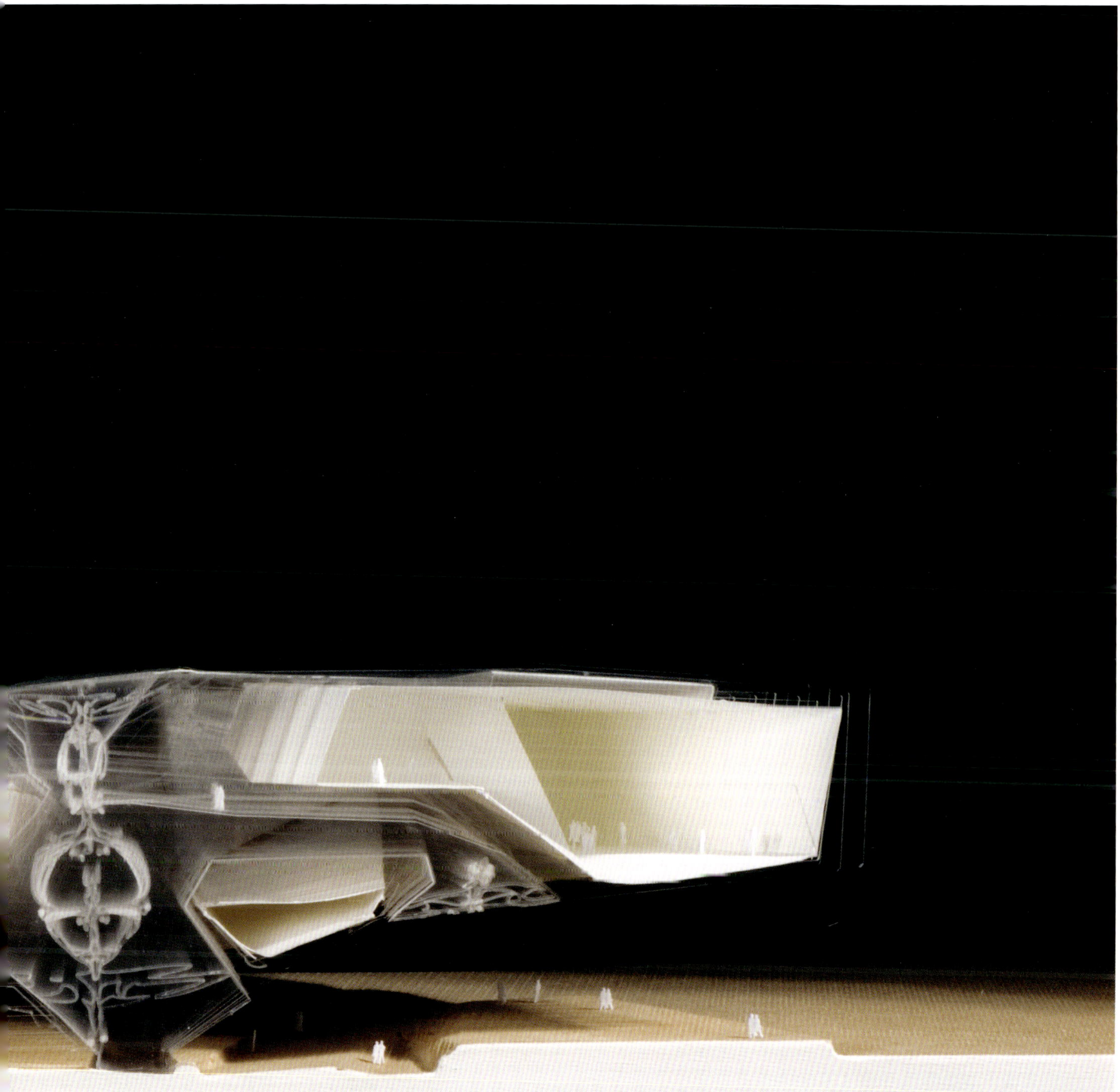

SELECTED EXCERPTS

IntraCenter: The Seduction of the Similar
R.E. Somol
Assemblage n.40
Boston: MIT Press, December 1999
p.69

The project [by Ron Witte and Sarah Whiting of WW] operates most like the onion of Roland Barthes, a proliferation of layers with no real center...

This flayed modulation of interior and exterior produces the effect of loose and sometimes surprising correlations between program and space or room. Often, the enclosed—apparently "interiorized"—zones are those that are actually between programs (for example, the interstitial yet figural art studio/broadcast room zone of the third level) or else support the poche (rest rooms, stairs, structural voids) Thus the figures are programmatically indistinct, while the seemingly "exterior", mat spaces tend to be pure, served spaces. Against the cult of the distinct, the becoming-similar of the IntraCenter produces an organizational mimeticism, a plasticity with regard to figure/field, service/served, and inside/outside. A tank of material and programmatic transitions, the project approximates the body without organs: "the skin as envelop or ring, and the sock as reversible surface." When one enters a figure, one is actually departing a program. More than nested programs, the IntraCenter presents us with ambient program. As Roger Caillois describes the schizophrenic's experience, "I know where I am, but I do not feel as though I'm at the spot where I find myself." The organizational mimeticism of the IntraCenter produces the perpetual effect that, wherever you go, you are sure to be somewhere else. You are not here. Moreover, you are not alone.

The Inside and the Outside
Robert Venturi
Complexity and Contradiction in Architecture
New York: Museum of Modern Art, 1966
pp.82–84

Residual space that is open might be called "open poche." Kahn's "servant space," which sometimes harbors mechanical equipment, and the poche in the walls of Roman and Baroque architecture are alternative means of accommodating an inside different from the outside. Aldo van Eyck has said: "Architecture should be conceived of as a configuration of intermediary places clearly defined." This does not imply continual transition or endless postponement with respect to place and occasion. On the contrary, it implies a break away from the contemporary concept (call it sickness) of spatial continuity and the tendency to erase everyarticulation between spaces, i.e., between outside and inside, between one space and another (between one reality and another). Instead the transition must be articulated by means of defined in-between places which induce simultaneous awareness of what is significant on either side. An in-between space in this sense provides the common ground where conflicting polarities can again become twin phenomena.

Residual space is sometimes awkward. Like structural poche it is seldom economic. It is always leftover, infected toward something more important beyond itself. The qualifications, contrasts, and tensions inherent in these spaces are perhaps cogent to Kahn's statement that "a building should have bad spaces as well as good spaces."

Redundant enclosure, like crowded intricacies, is rare in our architecture. With some significant exceptions in the work of Le Corbusier and Kahn, modern architecture has tended to ignore such complex spatial ideas. The "utility core" of Mies or early Johnson is not relevant because it becomes a passive accent in a dominant open space, rather than an active parallel to another perimeter. Contradictory interior space does not admit modern architecture's requirement of a unity and continuity of all spaces. Nor do layers in depth, especially with contrapuntal juxtapositions, satisfy its requirements of economic and unequivocal relationships of forms and materials. And crowded intricacy within a rigid boundary (which is not a transparent framework) contradicts the modern tenet which says that a building grows from the inside out.

VOLUME: VOID

WOVEN VOLUMES

The interlocking of two or more distinct and differentiated continuous spaces.

Woven volumes attempt to simultaneously differentiate and connect. Maintaining solid enclosure for several continuous sets of spaces relegates them to dichotomous sets—“A” and “B” or “Centralized,” “Intermediate” and “Peripheral”—but folding them together in 3 dimensional space breaks down that stratification. “A” and “B” share a single boundary, locking them in an interdependent negotiation of constraints and priorities. An organizational symmetry, the weave is a global system that allows space “A” to adapt to local constrains and harnesses the generative potential of that manipulation for space “B.” Weaving relies on pure geometry (often minimal surfaces) rather than material properties (transparency and porosity) to reduce spatial boundaries to the most thin and taut of membranes. It unites volumes that are different in material and dimension through a topological sameness.

1 **United Nude**
The United Nude Mobius Shoe, 2009
image courtesy of United Nude
www.unitednude.com

2 **Toyo Ito**
Forum for Music, Dance and Visual Culture, Ghent
image courtesy of Toyo Ito & Associates Architects
www.toyo-ito.com

3 **Ruth Asawa**
Untitled, S.294, looped cooper

4 **Paul Rudolph**
Modulightor Building, New York, 1989
photographed by Donald Luckenbill, image courtesy of Paul Rudolph Foundation
www.paulruldolph.org

5 **Bathsheba Grossmann for Materialise**
Quin
image courtesy of Bathsheba Grossmann
www.materialise.com, www.

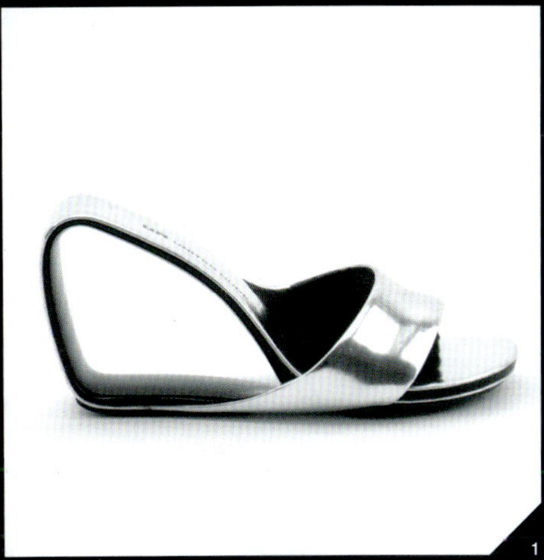

1

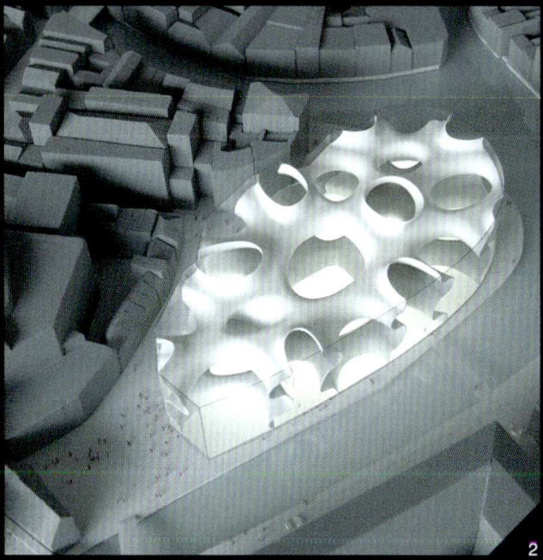

2

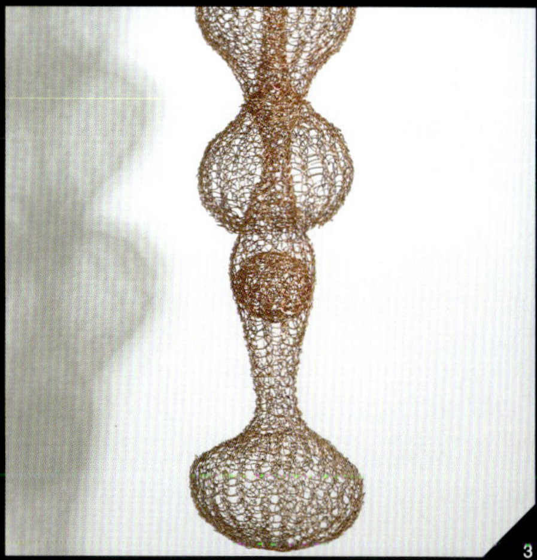

3

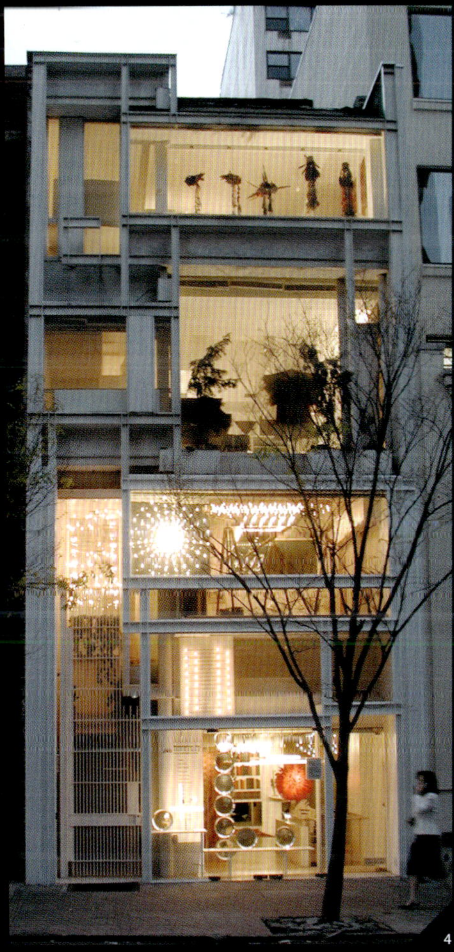

4

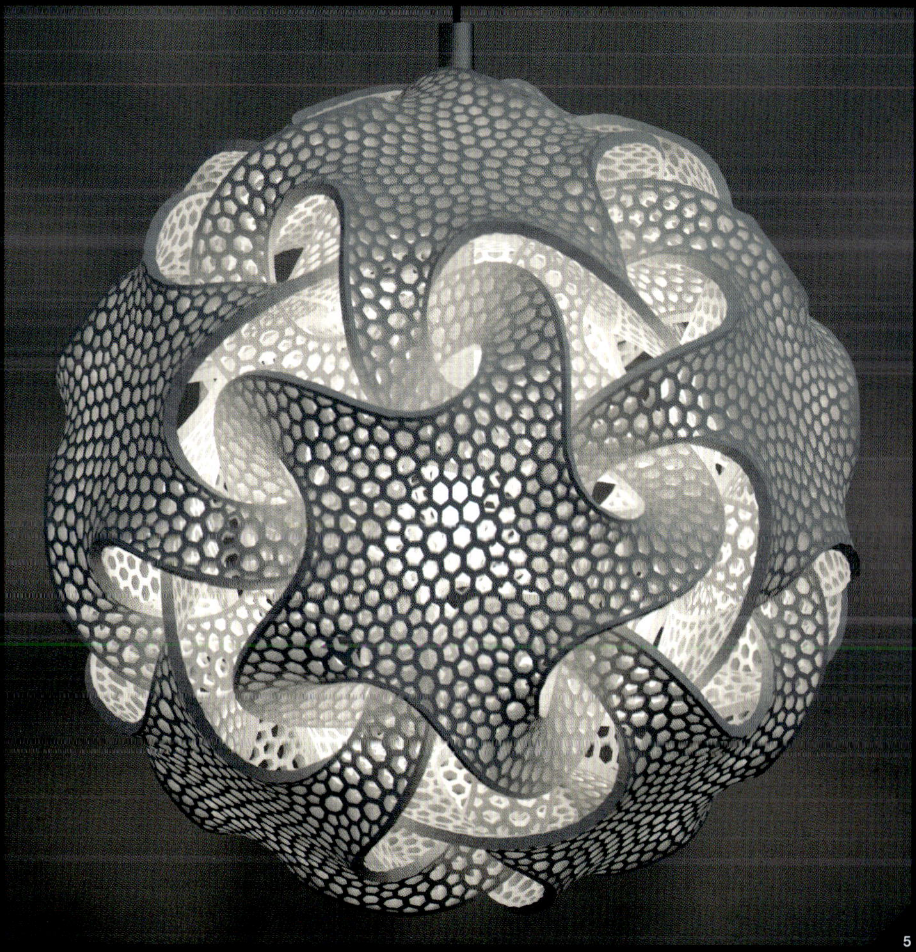

5

Eva Diem
Concert Hall
2005

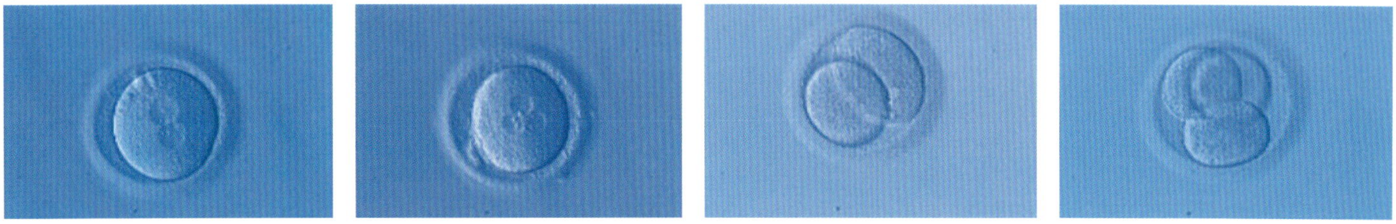

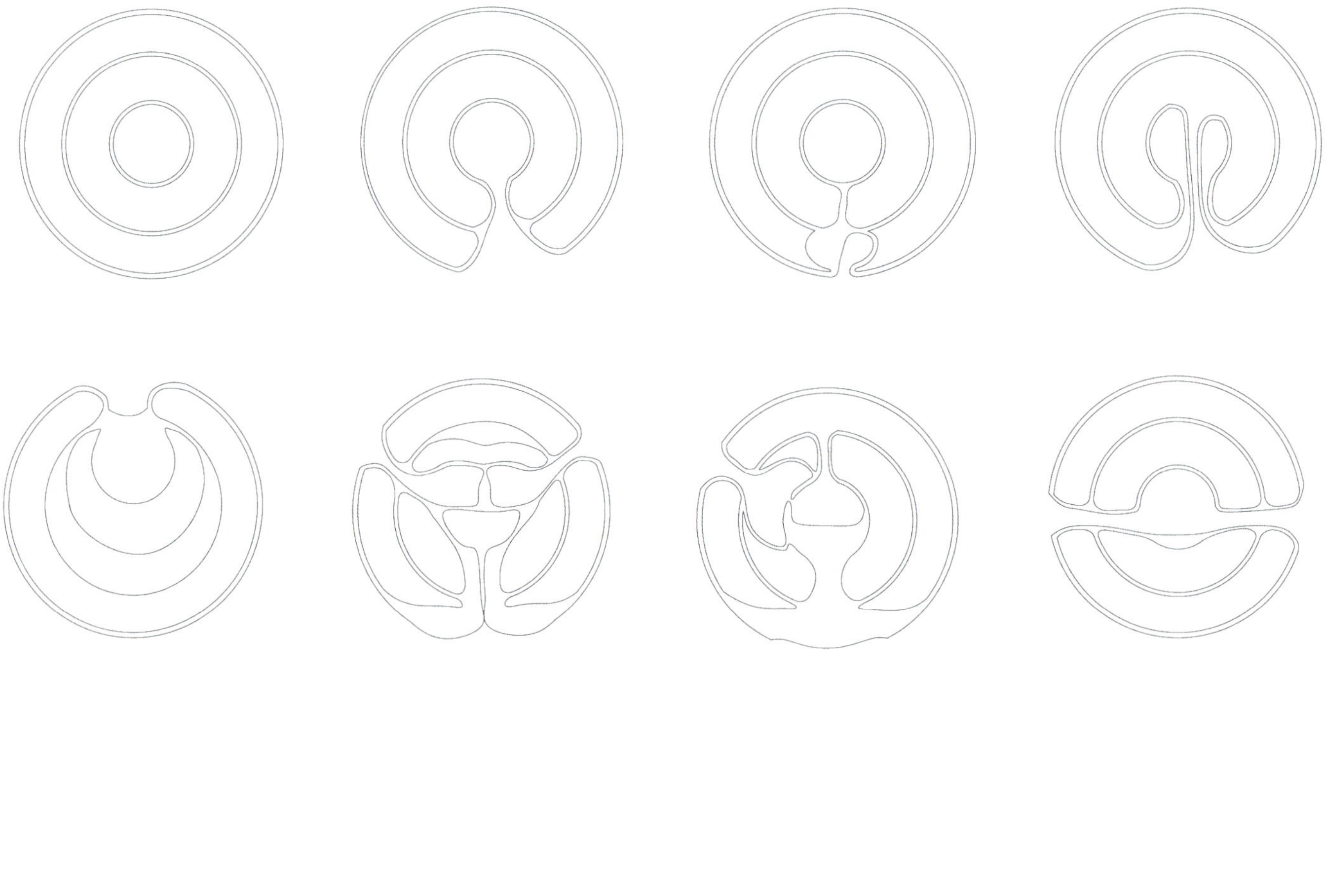

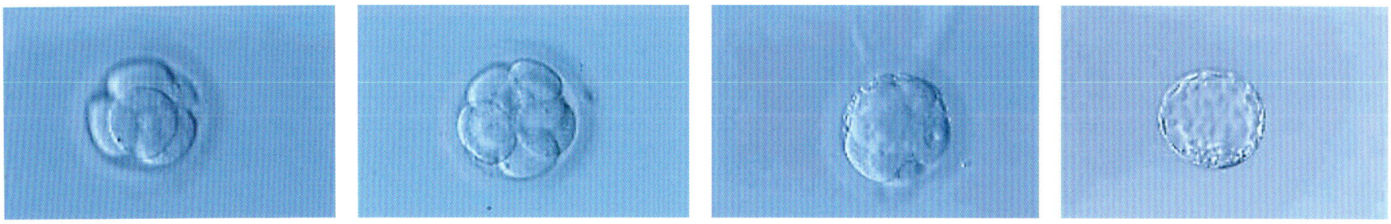

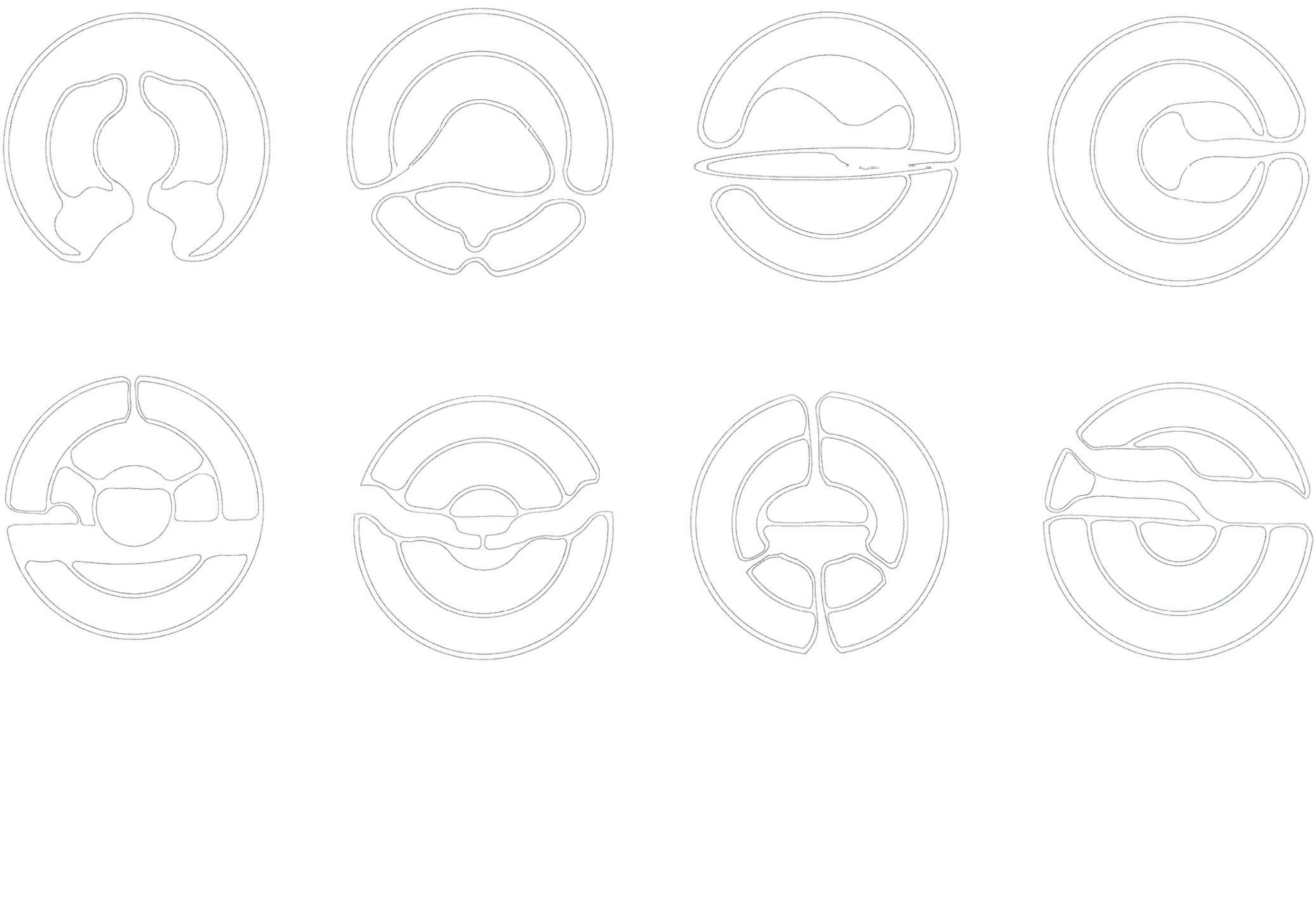

Martin Zangerl
Diploma (wood model)
2006

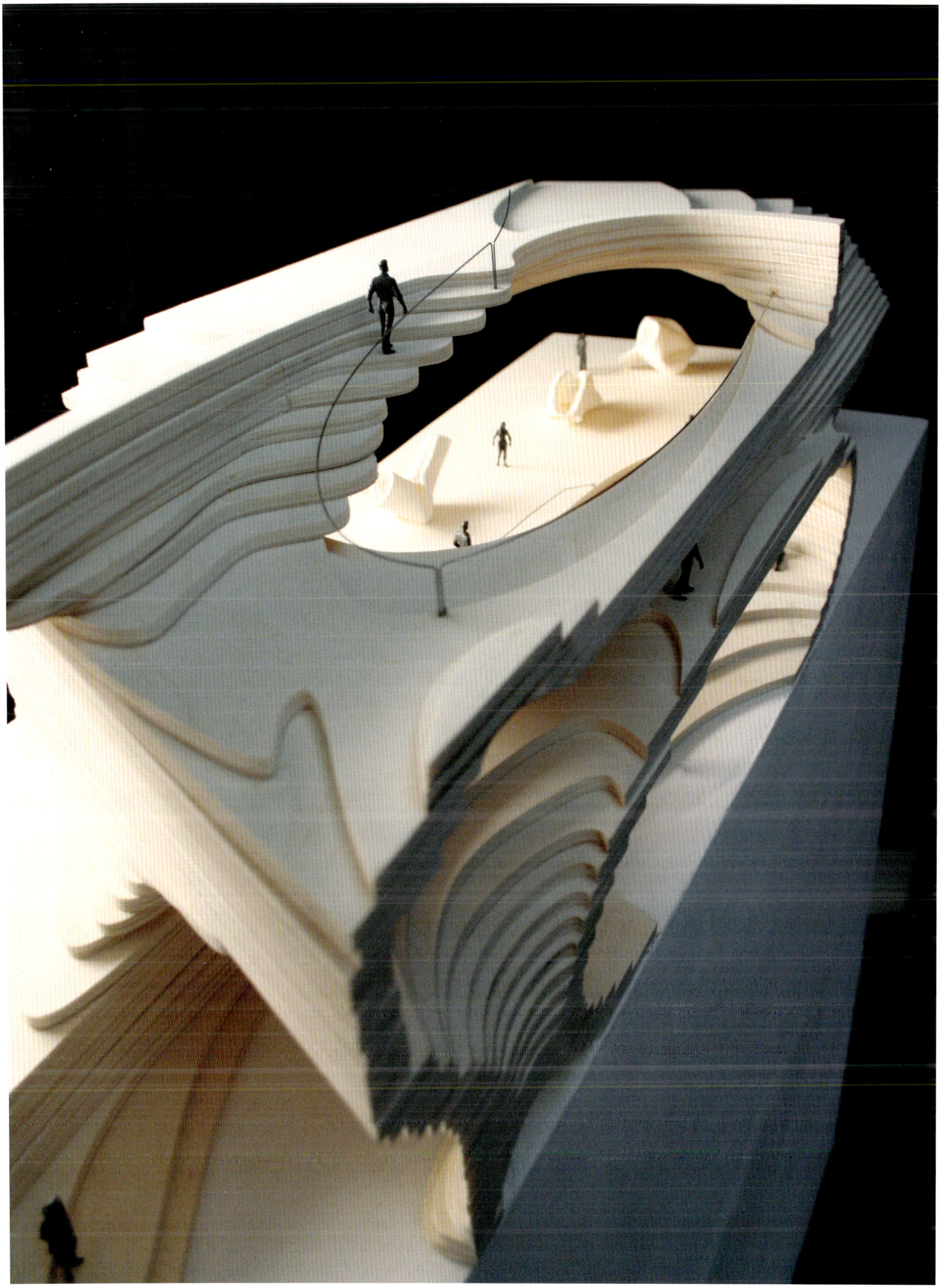

Martin Zangerl
Diploma: Center for Digital Art and Media Technology (print model)
2006

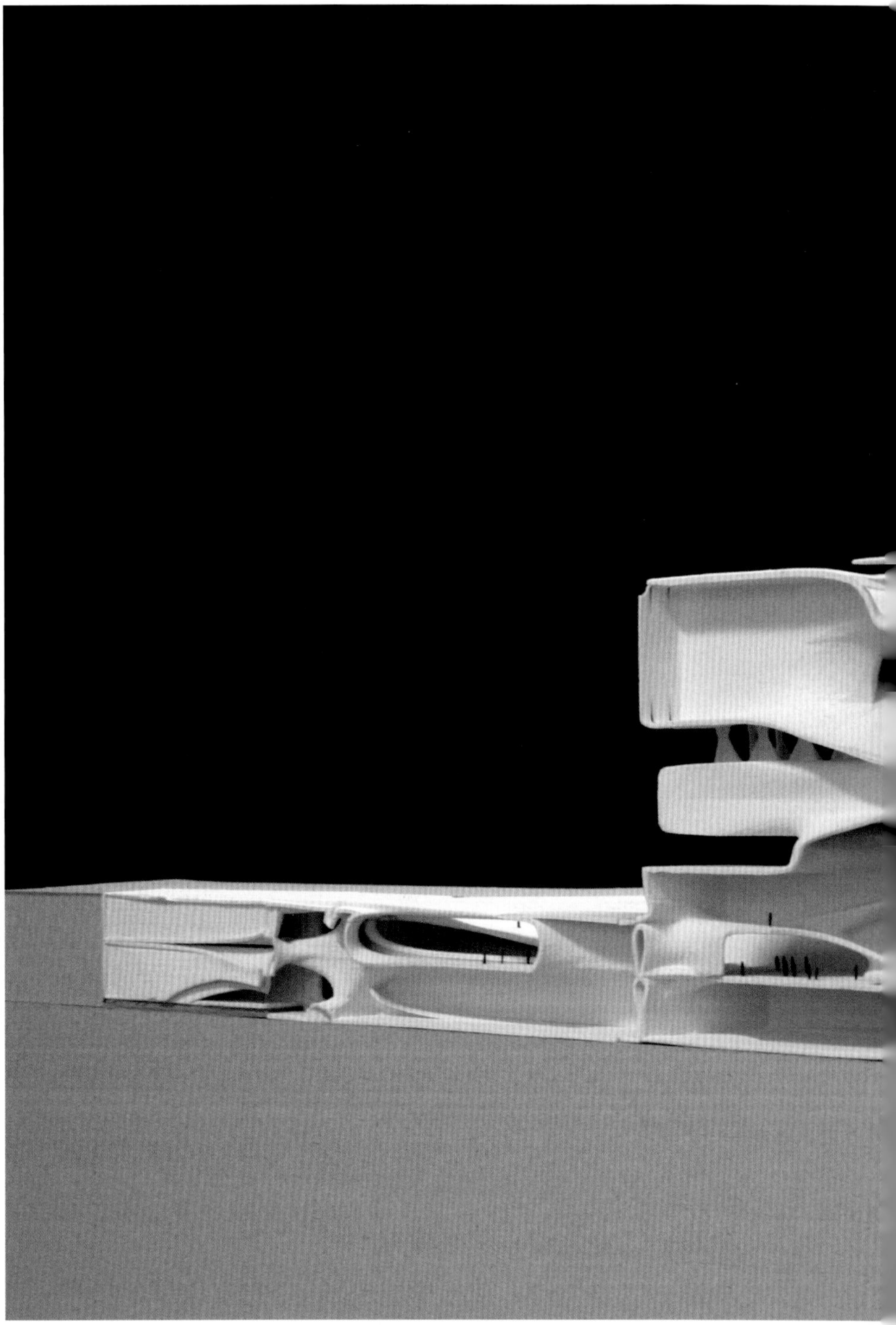

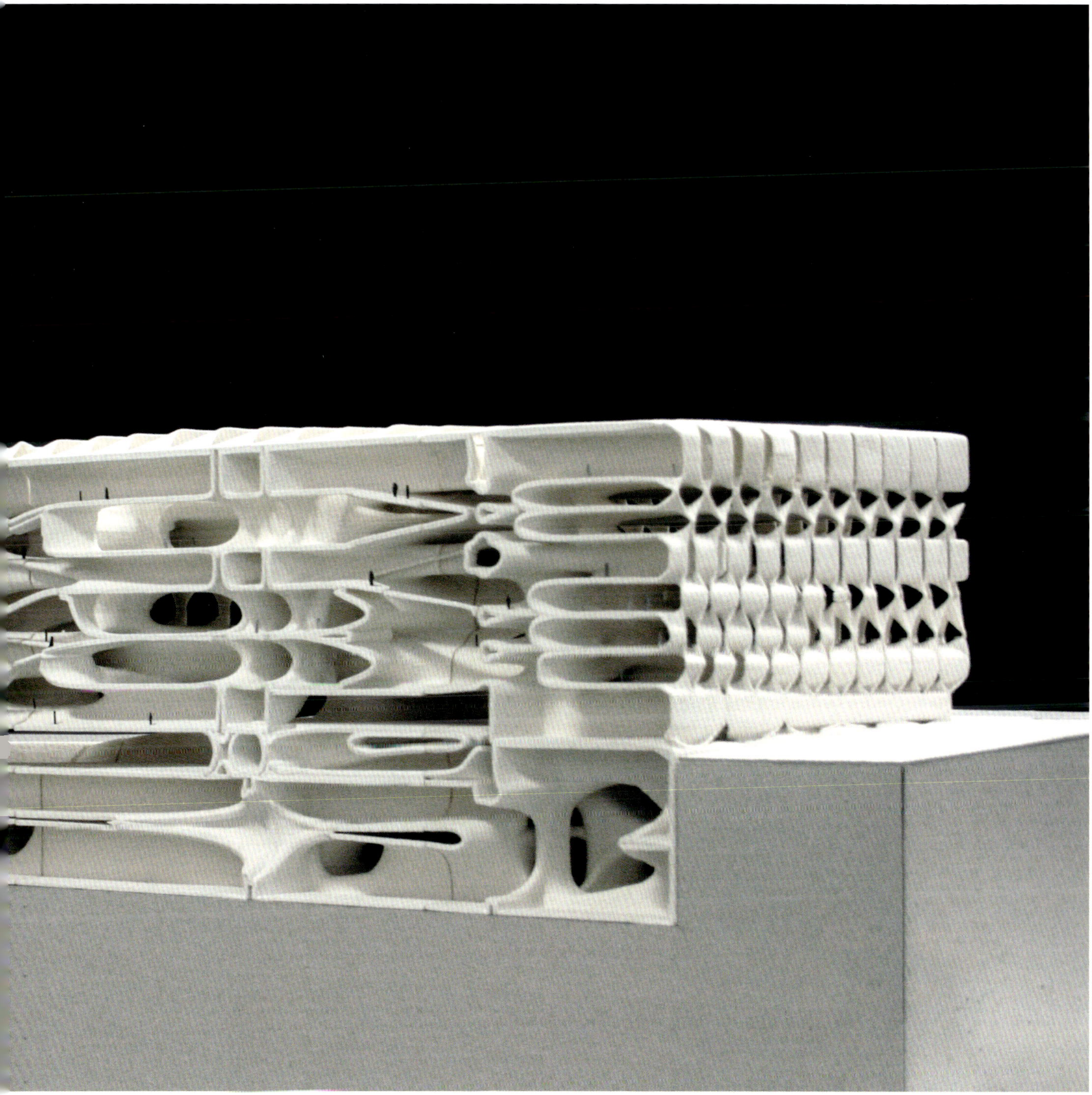

Eva Diem, Maja Ozvaldic and Dumëne Comploi
Interplaying Surfaces
2004

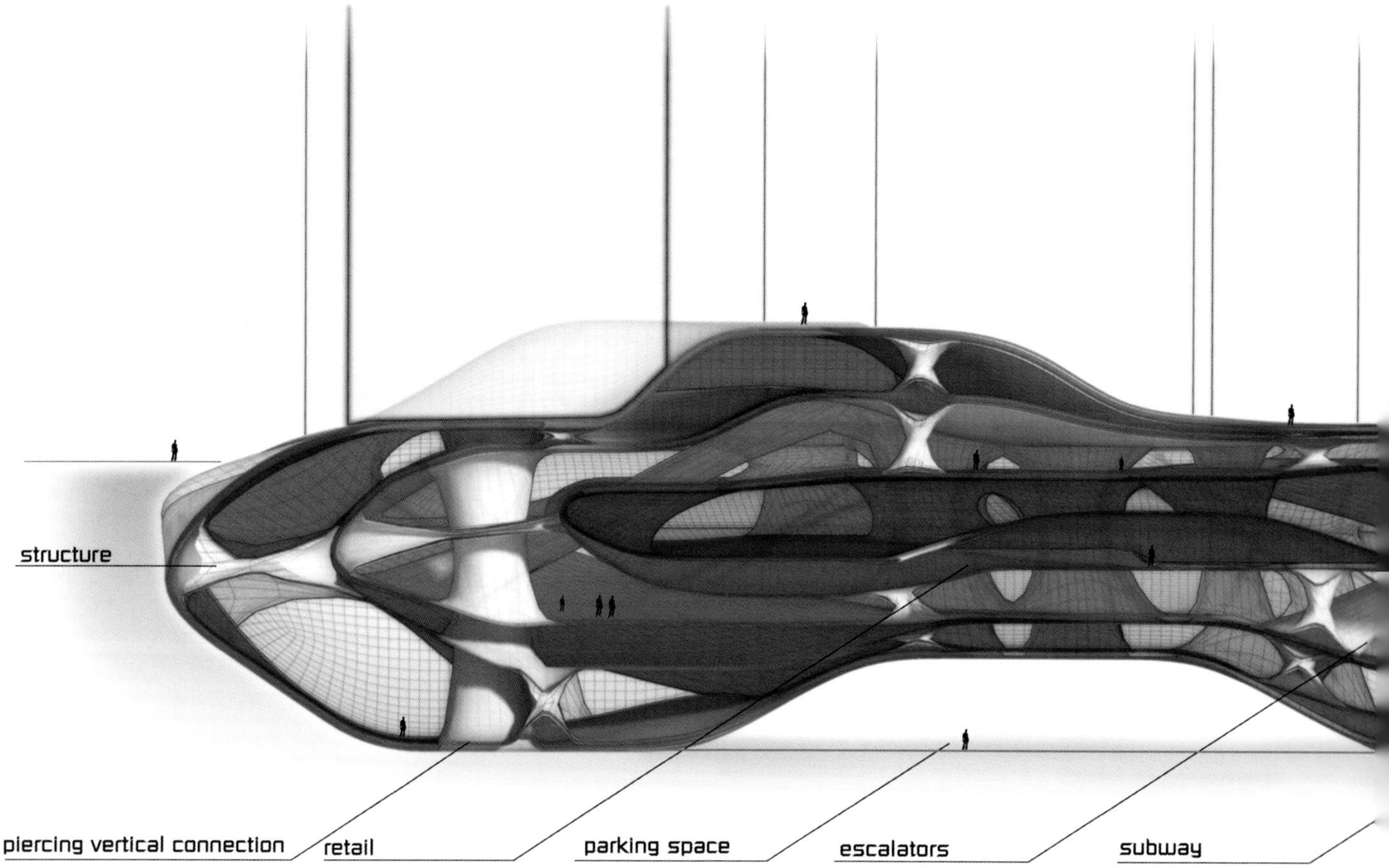

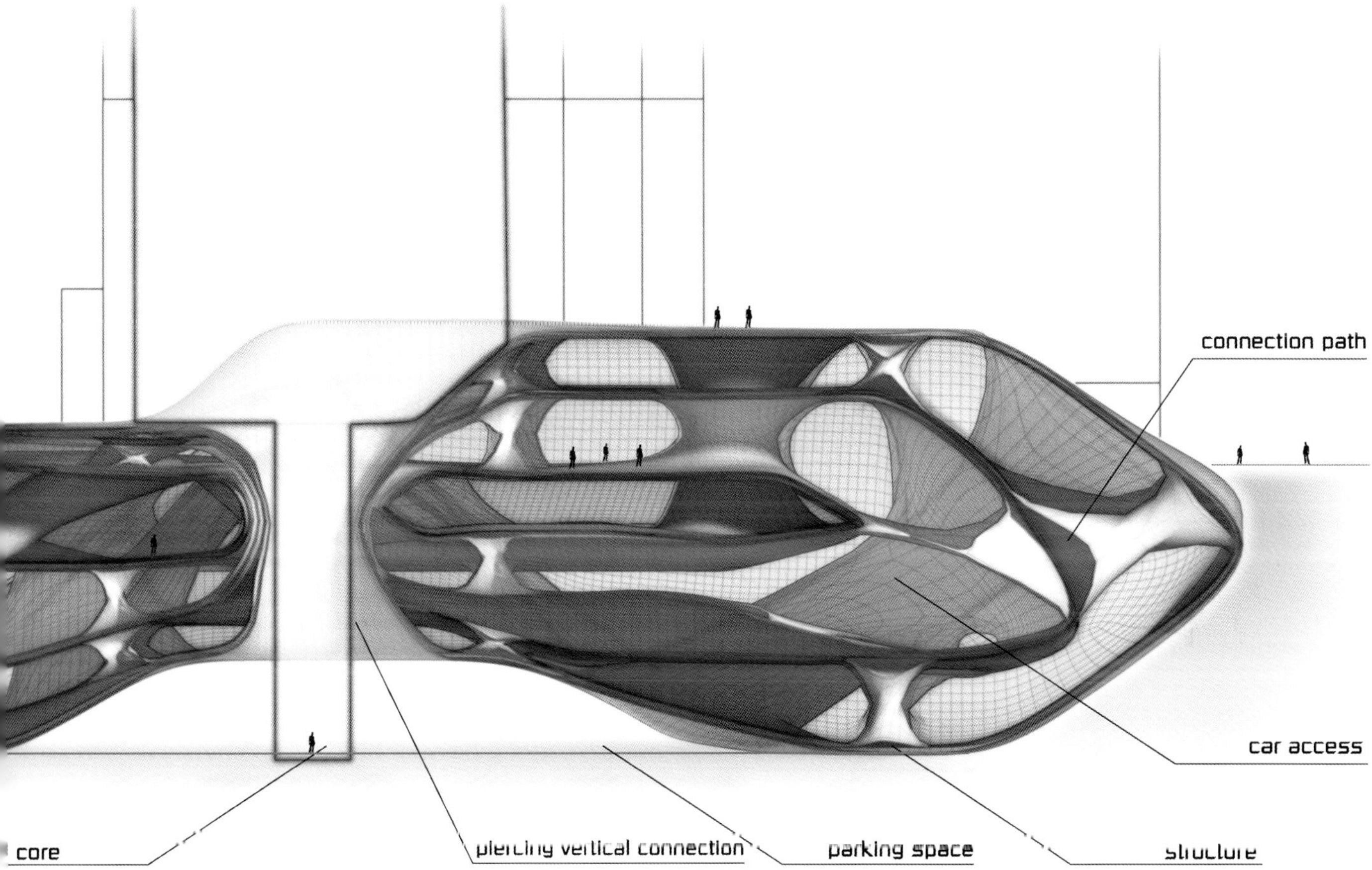
connection path
car access
core
piercing vertical connection
parking space
structure

SELECTED EXCERPTS

Architectural Curvilinearity: The Folded, the Pliant and the Supple
Greg Lynn
Architectural Design: Folding in Architecture
West Sussex: John Wiley & Sons, 1993
p.24

If there is a single effect produced in architecture by folding, it will be the ability to integrate unrelated elements within a new continuous mixture. Culinary theory has developed both a practical and precise definition for at least three types of mixtures. The first involves the manipulation of homogeneous elements; beating, whisking and whipping change the volume but not the nature of a liquid through agitation. The second method of incorporation mixes two or more disparate elements; chopping, dicing, grinding, grating, slicing, shredding and mincing eviscerate elements into fragments. The first method agitates a single uniform ingredient, the second eviscerates disparate ingredients. Folding, creaming and blending mix smoothly multiple ingredients "through repeated gentle overturnings without stirring or beating" in such a way that their individual characteristics are maintained. For instance, an egg and chocolate are folded together so that each is a distinct layer within a continuous mixture.

Folding employs neither agitation nor evisceration but a supple layering. Likewise, folding in geology involves the sedimentation of mineral elements or deposits which become slowly bent and compacted into plateaus of strata. These strata are compressed, by external forces, into more or less continuous layers within which heterogeneous deposits are still intact in varying degrees of intensity.

The Topological Tendency in Architecture
Giuseppa Di Cristina
Architectural Design: Architecture and Science
West Sussex: John Wiley & Sons, 2001
p.7 and p.11

The sensitivity for curved and bent lines is connected, then, to the will to construct fluid spaces by means of continuous, while at the same time differentiated, systems that are capable of embodying the various contextual factors in the development of form dynamically and in a cohesive manner. In fact, these fluid connections through pliant systems describe a viscous space that is capable of complex deformations and has the capacity to change in response to heterogeneous and differentiated contexts.

Topology, also called the "geometry of the rubber sheet," admits all possible transformations of a figure drawn on a rubber sheet when the sheet is manipulated in every possible way without tears or rents. A topological transformation, or *homeomorphism*, of one figure into another is determined by a bi-univocal and bi-continuous correspondence between the points of the respective figures. Topological transformations are the more general continuous transformations that maintain the geometrical properties of the connection and vicinity of the points of the figure (so that near points continue to remain near and far-off points continue to be far away)...

Topology, in so far as it represents a passing from one element to the other with continuity, without any clear limit between them, is thus linked with Perrella's notion of hyperspace. A hyperspace is the topology of an interstitial terrain between binary oppositions that flow transversally in an interweaving of associations. And the topological surfaces that curve and bend above and within themselves in intricate and complex configurations fulfill the condition of hypersurface. The topological transformation of the fold, for example, makes it possible to articulate the surface in such a way that there is no longer any clear distinction between interior and exterior: the space caught between the folds is neither internal nor external, or else it is both, thus corresponding to a field of "spatial indecision."

Non-Organic Life
Manuel DeLanda
Zone 6: Incorporations, ed. Jonathan Crary and Sanford Kwinter
New York: Zone Books, 1992
p. 142–143 and p. 160

Self-organizing processes drive the geological cycle. The tectonic forces behind the burial and folding of sediment are driven by molten rock flowing up from beneath the crust in convection cells, a coherent flow arising after a temperature bifurcation, constituting a kind of self-assembled conveyor belt. The rivers that sort out the pebbles and grains that make up the layers of sediment, can be seen as self-organized "hydraulic computers." The dynamics of a river's flow at different points in its course are governed by different attractors, turbulent flow from strange attractors, and coherent pulses (solitons) from weaker forms of nonlinear stabilization. It is these different "regimes of flow" that give the river its capability of sorting raw materials by grain size, shape and even composition. Finally, the processes of erosion and weathering also act as "filters" or "sieves" sorting out materials by their degree of stability. Mountains are worked over by these processes, removing those components that are not fully stable, and leaving behind those that are strongly locked into their attractors. (For this reason, granite, a highly stable crystalline configuration is typically found on higher ground.)

Thus, adding these historical processes changes our simple picture of the birth of a planet. Instead of a simple sequence of bifurcations taking us from a plasma to crystal, here the formation of hardened structures involves attractors and bifurcations engaged in more complex interactions. The self-organized machinic assemblages they create (conveyor belts, hydraulic computers) provide the labor needed to generate geological constructions in a two-step process. First, the raw materials are selected and sorted (sedimentation), then they are consolidated into permanent structures (cementation or hardening). Because the result of these two operations is geological strata, this process of double articulation has been given the name of "stratification."

According to Deleuze and Guattari, processes of stratification occur not only in the world of geology but in every sphere of reality. Thus the hydrosphere, the biosphere and so on can all be defined in terms of flows of matter and energy and the reservoirs driving those flows...

Because the problems raised by hybrid systems involve both dealing with flows of matter and energy and studying the stratifications that form in those flows, we might do well to learn from the experiences of those who were the first to track the machinic phylum—artisans and metallurgists. Before the advent of modern methods, they did this by instinct and the empirical know-how accumulated through the ages. They had to track everything from stratified ore deposits to a metal's melting and crystallization points, and then to experiment with different ways of crossing those bifurcations through forging techniques; they had to look for their own hybrids, that is, synergistic combinations of metals in which the whole spontaneously becomes more than the sum of its parts (alloys), and to allow the materials to have their own say in the final form produced. All of this involved following a given material's local accidents and imperfections, rather than imposing a rigid, preplanned form on it.

ACKNOWLEDGEMENTS

SPECIAL THANKS TO

Greg Lynn for support and guidance. Alexandra Graupner for support and energy. Roswitha Janowski-Fritsch, Gerald Bast, Wolf D. Prix, the Institute of Architecture and the University of Applied Arts Vienna for their support.

THANKS TO

STUDENT ASSISTANTS

Bernard Baptiste-Jacob
Ernst Susanna
Reigle Matt
Vukmanov Adam

STUDENT COMMITTEE

Diem Eva
Edthofer Anna
Futo Julcsi
Ozvaldic Maja
Psenicka Anna

STAFF

Balliet Kristy 2006–
Buck Brennan 2004–08
Bertram Oliver 2002–
Diles Justin 2008–
Graupner Alexandra 2004–
Lorber Nina 2002–04
Muecke Johannes 2004–08
Murero Martin 2004–
Muhr Christian 2004–05
Rinne Natalie 2002–04
Schoenberger Angus 2002–03

STUDENTS 2003–08

Altenhof Tim Steffen
Anderson Jon Müller
Barunica Katarina
Batliner Curime
Baum David
Baumgartner Siegfried
Benmoussa Hischam
Bernard Baptiste-Jacob
Blaha Reinfried
Brauner Elisabeth
Breinesberger Karl
Busurina Irina
Cavallar Claudia
Comploi Dumene
d'Aram Alexandre
Daneluzzo Mirko
Diem Alexander
Diem Eva
Dite Dagmar
Dreger Günther
Dubreux Gregoire
Dumitru Mihaela
Edthofer Anna
Ernst Susanna
Faisst Cornelia
Fend Florian
Fischbeck Sebastian
Futo Julcsi
Gandon Francois
Gasser Mario
Gehry Sam
Girardi Melina
Graw Nora
Hagmüller Lois
Heinzerling Yngve
Helinurm Joanna-Maria
Hermann Manfred
Hofmarcher Joseph
Hojring Laura
Kaufer Achim
Kaus Sebastian
Kiradjieva Lubov
Kirsch Benedikt
Kissler Bastian
Klausberger Ines
Knebel Dora
Koller Michaela
Körner Julia
Kovacs Barna
Krainer Andreas
Kreuzer Albrecht
Lai Mo (Ching Ying)
Lesjak Martina
Lihl Verena
Lind Adam
Lohwasser Stephan
Ludwig Jan Markus
Matura Jiri
Miklos Deri
Moser Anna
Mücke Johannes
Nagy Krisztina
Nocker Clemens
Ozvaldic Maja
Paller Peter
Pap Bence
Petkova Ioana
Petra-Szöke Attila
Pollhammer Marlene
Pötzelsberger Vera
Psenicka Anna
Radicella Renato
Radojevic Miljan
Rebek Bika Sibila
Rieger Lola
Ritter Stefan
Schindler Gregor
Schneider Sarah
Seraydarian Haig
Simma Thimo
Sobl Stephan
Sommerhuber Lisa
Spacek Mariela
Steirer Cornelia
Stiller Bengt
Stöcklmayr Nicole
Syarova Evgeniya
Szuba Igor
Tornquist Emanuel
Treberspurg Christhoph
Tröster Tina
Vikar Peter
Von Hayek Florian
Vukmanov Adam
Wasshuber Matthäus
Weber Aurelius
Wharton Philip
Zangerl Martin